Lemons for Chamberlain

PRIME MINISTER'S HEALTH.

Mr. Chamberlain is suffering from indigestion after one of Nancy Astor's luncheons. Among visitors to the sick-room was Mander, M.P., bringing a nice basket of lemons.

Lemons for Chamberlain

The Life and Backbench Career of Geoffrey Mander MP

Patricia Pegg

First Published in the UK in 2021 by Mantle Lane Press

ISBN 978-1-9160570-3-6
Mantle Lane Press
Mantle Arts
Springboard Centre
Mantle Lane
Coalville
LE67 3DW
www.mantlelanepress.co.uk

Cover design and interior layout Matthew Pegg
www.mpegg.co.uk

Contents

Geoffrey Mander.

FOREWORD

In 1929 Geoffrey Mander (1882-1962), was elected as the Liberal Member of Parliament for Wolverhampton East. He remained an MP until 1945, his career spanning the depression of the 1930s and the Second World War. He was interested in a wide range of political issues, gained a reputation for asking awkward questions in Parliament, and in particular harried Neville Chamberlain's government over its policy of appeasing Hitler.

In 1957 he began to write *A Back-Bencher Looks Back*, a book about Parliament and his career as an MP. He submitted an outline and specimen chapters to Chatto and Windus. They declined to publish it but encouraged him to submit it to other publishers, saying, "To judge from the material submitted and from the outline of subsequent chapters, the book obviously contains many interesting sidelights on political life and personalities." Despite this encouragement the book was never published. The material was stored in the archives at his home, Wightwick Manor in Wolverhampton, and remained unread for more than forty five years.

After his death, the idea of a biography of Geoffrey Mander was proposed by his youngest daughter Anthea. His sixteen years as a Member of Parliament coincided with one of the most turbulent periods of the 20th century. His close association with important politicians of the time and friendships with a number of Allied leaders meant that his career held considerable historical interest. However his own autobiographical notes were only rediscovered some years after Anthea's death. The 'interesting sidelights' mentioned by the publishers were more lively and entertaining than the lengthy sections on House of Commons procedures. Those elements of Geoffrey's writing form the basis of this book. They are augmented by other material from the archives of Wightwick Manor, for example his youngest son John wrote an autobiography in the 1970s that sometimes casts a critical light on the family. Additional information is from Hansard, The Liberal Magazine, and The Green Can magazine, "published monthly for circulation amongst those associated with the Firm of Mander Brothers Ltd at home and abroad". Material from Geoffrey's book 'We Were not all Wrong' and from newspaper articles has also been used, to provide some background to his political life, including details of his family, the Mander Brothers' business, and the wider history of the period.

Flora Mander with Geoffrey.

INTRODUCTION

For months past a barrel organ has delighted him and he would start up on hearing one and go to the window, at about ten months, creeping there and lifting himself up to look through with his hands on the ledge. He has amused himself with pointing out sheep and cows and birds on his nursery wall-paper, and now he utters a long 'moo' when he sees a cow in the street.

Theodore Mander describing his eldest child, Geoffrey le Mesurier.

The Manders, a Nonconformist family, had founded a paint and varnish business in Wolverhampton at the end of the eighteenth century and they and the company had prospered. At the time of Geoffrey's birth, in 1882, it was still a family firm with sons, cousins and grandsons all working in the business and all profiting from its success.

His father, Theodore, grew up in a family whose strong religious faith influenced everything in life and in particular, in common with some business owners of the time, it affected the way in which the firm was run. An entry from the minute book of Mander Brothers provides an example of 19th century social conscience. It was proposed "that it might be advisable to pay a Medical man a fixed stipend to furnish attendance and medicine to all the workpeople and that his certificate should be required when anyone may be absent through ill health." This was put into practice in 1866.

Geoffrey's concerns seventy years later echoed the 19th century humanitarian attitudes of his grandfather, Samuel Mander. This is part of a letter from Samuel Mander to young Theodore written in 1862. "You know, in America they say the poor black men have no souls, in fact are not men at all, so they treat them the same as they do cattle which is a shocking thing, for they have souls and minds and tender loving hearts like our own." Another letter was written eight years later in which he reported a scheme that had his total support. "After the Irish question, comes that of English Education, one of supreme importance. Two societies have taken up the question, the stand-stills and the progressives. The latter took the field first. They constitute the "National Education League" which seeks to secure the education of every child in the land, using compulsion if necessary, having free schools, supported partly by national grants and partly by local rates."

Many of Samuel's attitudes arose from a strict adherence to Nonconformist beliefs. This doctrine included teetotalism; in practice it meant no drinking of spirits but acceptance of some wine, like claret, thought to have health giving qualities. His letters to his son were full of religious advice:

The way Theodore lived shows how Samuel Mander's constant emphasis on religious and moral questions formed his basic character; Geoffrey would have witnessed evidence of his father's decent liberal principles in action.

In 1878 Theodore married Flora St Clair Paint, a Canadian from Halifax, Nova Scotia. They started married life in a house on the Tettenhall Road, a prosperous area of Wolverhampton, then on the outskirts of the town; Geoffrey and his sister Marjorie were born there. After the family moved to Wightwick their brother Lionel was born in 1888 and Alan, the youngest child, in 1891.

Theodore bought the Wightwick estate in 1886. It included an ancient house and more than 100 acres of land in rural surroundings It was close to The Mount, a house owned by his cousin Charles Mander and next door to another relation, Uncle Harper, both of whom worked in the family business. These houses were all a short carriage drive away from the centre of Wolverhampton and Mander Brothers.

Theodore and Flora commissioned the Liverpool architectural firm of Grayson and Ould to design a new house to be built in the grounds in the Old English style; it was extended in 1893 by the same firm. It is described in the current National Trust guide book as "designed for maximum picturesque effect, with nothing straight or regular… Combining features from different periods is also typical of the Old English approach. The big battlemented tower suggests that Wightwick might have grown up around a medieval pele-tower, the terracotta traceried windows of the garden front are Tudor in style, while the oak casements with leaded lights derive from Elizabethan or Jacobean examples. It was intended to give the impression of a house that had grown gradually over a long period." The house is deliberately shadowy in places, relieved by glowing colours of Morris wallpapers and tiles and with patterned ceilings and elaborately carved panelling. A quotation by Ruskin from "Modern Painters" is carved into the fireplace panelling and other quotations from works by Shakespeare and Robert Herrick circled the exterior of the house on beams below the gables.

Wightwick Manor.

Although no significant collection of paintings was hung in the new house, one of several pictures Theodore did buy was a small watercolour by John Ruskin. Many books by him were collected too. In particular, Ruskin's theories about social welfare, like the ideas of William Morris, interested Theodore and reflected many of his own views. An enlightened attitude towards his employees was one principle that can be seen embodied within the design of Wightwick Manor. Electric light and central heating were installed in the house and put in the servants quarters too. The maids' dormitory had both central heating and an open fire and the servants' spacious bathroom next to it had a very large bath with hot and cold running water. His thoughtful treatment of the Wightwick staff was shared by Flora Mander. When Theodore died in 1900 she left England and travelled in Europe for a few years but she kept in touch and directed the running of the house by exchanging innumerable letters with the housekeeper, Emma Smith. Flora died five years after Theodore when Geoffrey was eighteen. Like his father, Geoffrey was an undergraduate at Cambridge and afterwards, again like his father, he entered the family business and married a Canadian. He was married in Montreal in 1906 to Rosalind Caverhill; they had three children, Mavis, Mervyn and Elizabeth.

His energy, his social conscience, his left wing politics were all evident from the start of his career. When he was twenty four he was appointed as a J.P. for Wolverhampton and he was elected to the town council in 1909. All this was what might be expected of someone of wealth and social standing in the town but he was soon seen by many eminent citizens in Wolverhampton as an alarming radical. In the 1906 election campaign he spoke in support of the Labour candidate who was standing against the sitting Conservative member, Sir Alfred Hickman. He wrote later "my action caused great indignation in Conservative circles in the neighbourhood and I found myself cut in the hunting field by some of them." He shocked the town councillors by proposing a minimum wage for all municipal employees. This was a scheme he adhered to and promoted for many years; like a number of his far sighted ideas it was eventually adopted by government.

When the First War broke out he was prevented by ill health from enlisting, but eventually in 1916, like his brother Lionel, he was able to join the Royal Flying Corps. He began to keep a flying log book in 1917; his notes show that he spent eighteen months learning to fly and then early in 1919 he went to Egypt where on 9th June he "had controls for 3/4 h" and later on the 10th had "bad bump at pyramids". His Egyptian records ended on 4th December 1919 when he returned to England but the log book records a further forty years of journeys by air, usually made with professional pilots.

HANDING ON THE TORCH

VILLIERS—FOWLER—THORNE—MANDER

ELECTORS !

Maintain the LIBERAL SUCCESSION
UNBROKEN SINCE 1832.

Geoffrey Mander's election poster.

1929

In 1929 Geoffrey Mander was elected MP for East Wolverhampton and served until 1945.

A BACK-BENCHER LOOKS BACK

After the First World War I was particularly attracted to the experiment of the League of Nations and I wished to have the opportunity of sitting in the House *[of Commons]* in order to devote myself to forwarding two main causes - Peace through the League and better relations in Industry at home. I attended the meetings of the General Assembly at Geneva, on a number of occasions in the 1920s. I did some part-time work as a journalist there and occasionally when asked what papers I represented I said "The Times and the Observer" This produced astonishment and when pressed further I had to admit that the full title of the journal was "The Walsall Times and The Willenhall Observer" On one occasion I tried this gambit on the Times' representative. He was not amused...

Later I was for many years a Member of the Executive Committee of the League of Nations Union. This was a most powerful body and had the great advantage, during 1932-36, of the co-operation of Sir Austen Chamberlain with all the wealth of his experience as Foreign Secretary behind him. Since the 1939/45 War, I have served on the Executive of the United Nations Association.

On being demobbed in 1919 I immediately took steps to try and find a constituency. I had been very critical of the action of Sir Edward Grey and the Liberal Government in leading the country in 1914 into war, following staff conversations with the French Government quite unknown to the country and to many members of the Cabinet. My first inclination was, therefore, towards joining the Labour party. I was, however, persuaded in the end to stand as a Liberal candidate in a constituency where I should receive Labour support.

In the General Election of 1922 he stood unsuccessfully as a Liberal for the Leominster Parliamentary Division (Hereford) It was at that time, in his election pamphlets, he first set out some of the ideas and principles upon which his future parliamentary career was founded.

GIVE MANDER A MANDATE.
He is in favour of Permanent Peace through the League of Nations, and an end to war.
The League of Nations held its first session in February 1920 and from that date Geoffrey always supported it and its aims.
He is in favour of One Vote and one only for every man and woman of 21, and equal rights for both sexes before the Law.
At this time only women of 30 and over had the vote - the franchise was extended to all women over 21 in 1928.
He supports machinery by which Farmers' and Labourers' Unions can fix a fair living wage compulsory on all, reasonable hours, and the removal of tied cottage hardships, and more and better housing accommodation.
In the 1920s there was a serious agricultural depression - the 1917 Corn Production Act, which kept prices steady and helped farmers to buy their farms and to pay reasonable wages, had been repealed in 1921 - unemployment of labourers followed and many farms had to be sold.
He is a really independent Liberal and will think and speak for himself and vote according to his knowledge of the needs of North Herefordshire and the country as a whole. He believes in a minimum standard of life in health, housing, education and wages, and above that level equal opportunity for all men and women to develop the best that is in them.

Eventually, in May 1929, he was elected member for East Wolverhampton on the retirement of George Thorne, the sitting member. His unique canvassing techniques are remembered by elderly people in Wolverhampton. One or two can still sing the songs he wrote and played on a gramophone as he toured the streets - the chorus of one, sung to the tune of "John Brown's Body" changed "Glory, Glory, Hallelujah" into "Villiers, Fowler, Thorne and Mander" repeated three times and then came the rousing conclusion, "Make Mander your MP!"

East Wolverhampton was a unique constituency. Since the Reform Bill of 1832 it always returned Liberals and yet in ninety eight years it had had only four MPs. This was due largely to Charles Pelham Villiers who represented the seat for sixty three years and who still holds the record for the longest serving MP. He was followed by Henry Fowler (later Lord Wolverhampton), George Thorne and then by the last Liberal to hold the seat, Geoffrey Mander.

After the 1929 election, when the Liberals won fifty eight seats, Labour was back in government for the second time, with Ramsay MacDonald as Prime Minister.

THE GREEN CAN
June 1929.
We offer our heartiest congratulations to Mr Geoffrey Mander on his splendid victory in Wolverhampton East at the recent Parliamentary Election. Mr Geoffrey must indeed feel proud that he will represent his native town at Westminster. Liberal majority - 5,228.

The Green Can was published every month. It printed articles by the firm's directors and employees, there was an active readers' letters section and sports reports - Manders players belonged to Bowls, Football, Hockey and Cricket teams (Geoffrey's batting average for the 1928 season was 7.05).

In 1929 reports included "Accidents in Factories, how to prevent them" and the "Childrens' Annual Party". There were accounts of employees' weddings - one bridesmaid was "attired in a dress of Dubarry georgette and a picture hat of cinnamon brown Bangkok straw, and carried a bouquet of tulips."

Through the years The Green Can published many suggestions from employees. Good ones were rewarded:
January 1929:
That an advertisement board should be erected at Wednesfield and that the sides of the motor lorries should be used for the same purpose.

[Answer] We have contemplated for some time the erection of such a board at Wednesfield visible from the railway, but as our attention has been directed to the matter by the suggestion we will take steps to have it carried out, and an award of £1 is made.

THE GREEN CAN

1929.

At a Board Meeting held on April 12th, Mr Geoffrey Mander was elected Chairman of Mander Brothers Limited in place of the late Sir Charles Tertius Mander *[his cousin]*.

After the General election, the House of Commons met for the first time on 25th June. Geoffrey began his parliamentary career with immense enthusiasm and energy; during his first months as an MP, listed in Hansard, are questions he asked on a range of subjects including: Prohibition of Russian films in Britain, Income Tax, Ultra Violet Rays, the Forth and Clyde canal, Czechoslovakian passports, Wolverhampton Employment exchange, Opium, the status of Swaziland and, of course, the League of Nations.

Very soon he made a reputation with his Parliamentary Questions. "He learnt the technique of putting them in such a way as to get round objections from the Speaker and used them in unique fashion to probe matters that the Government wanted to hush up and to throw a searching light on some vital point whose significance was not generally appreciated." This comes from a booklet issued after Geoffrey's death and it is well illustrated by reports in Hansard, for example on 15th July 1929 he asked four consecutive questions that were given brief replies; he must have bounced up and down vigorously during the session.

HANSARD

18 July 1929

FACTORIES BILL

Mr Mander asked the Home Secretary whether the Government will consider the advisability of including in the Factories Bill powers to set up in factories works councils representing employers and employed?

Mr Clynes: The establishment of works councils in factories for the joint consideration of matters falling within the scope of the Factory Acts, such as the prevention of accidents, organisation of welfare arrangements and the like, is in my opinion a very valuable means of improving conditions of work, and I am in full sympathy with it; but it seems to me, in general, that such councils are likely to do the best work when established by mutual consent. I may add that there is already power, so far as safety matters are concerned, to deal with any exceptional cases. So far as the question is intended to cover other matter not within my jurisdiction, I cannot express any opinion.

Mr Mander: Does the right Hon. Gentleman's answer mean that the Government do not propose to give any statutory powers for the setting up of works councils, but propose to leave the whole thing to voluntary action?

Mr Clynes: The effect of my answer was to indicate that it is not advisable to give statutory powers.

Viscountess Astor: Was it not the setting up of these works councils that drove Italy into Fascism? (Interruption) I think it was: they told me.

Mr Mander asked the Home Secretary whether he is prepared to include a Clause in the Factories Bill giving to workers the right of partnership in the conduct of industry and a share in its profits.

Mr Clynes: No Sir. Such matters would be entirely outside the scope of the Factories Acts.

Mr Mander: Will the right Hon. Gentleman consider the question of extending the scope of the Factories Bill so as to give the workers of this country these elementary rights?

In July, the Chinese Eastern Railway, a joint Russo-Chinese concern was seized by the Manchurian Government. A number of Russian officials were arrested and deported. The Chinese Nationalist government maintained that Russia was using the Eastern Chinese Railway as an instrument for Communist propaganda in China. Diplomatic relations were broken off and warlike demonstrations were held in Russia.

Geoffrey attended the Liberal Summer School held at Cambridge from August 1st to 8th 1929. He addressed the delegates on Security and Disarmament stressing his concern that some practical way of settling international disputes must be agreed.

THE LIBERAL MAGAZINE.

He said it was not enough to outlaw war. "We must provide some alternative way of settling disputes. The temptation which came to us as a big Power to have some cases reserved for the League Council on which we could exert influence was one we must avoid."

The Manchester Guardian reported his suggestions for strengthening the powers of the League of Nations by placing the organisation in the best possible position for carrying out its work in a time of crisis, when communication would be broken. A League wireless station and a League aeroplane service were desirable.

THE GREEN CAN
WORKS COUNCIL AT WIGHTWICK.
The Works Council and their wives, at the kind invitation of Mr Geoffrey, spent a very enjoyable afternoon and evening at Wightwick Manor on Saturday, September 14th. Providence was very kind in favouring us with an ideal day. Tea was provided which everyone thoroughly enjoyed. Mr Geoffrey, in a speech, said some very nice and encouraging things concerning the Works Council, and he believed that it had done some very good work and was capable of doing a great deal in the future that would be of benefit to the firm and the employees. After tea a concert was given, the artistes giving their respective items with great credit, and was thoroughly enjoyed by all. A vote of thanks was passed to Mr Geoffrey for giving the Council the opportunity to visit the Manor and for all the trouble he had gone to to make the visit an enjoyable one. I feel sure the Council with their wives, left Wightwick Manor carrying with them happy memories which will not be forgotten for a long while.

HANSARD
October 1929
Mr Mander asked the Under Secretary for State whether arrangements can be made for Members of this House to participate in passenger flights in the airships R100 and R101?
Mr Montague: My Noble Friend is arranging for Members to be given an opportunity of making a flight in the R101 at an early date. Details will be notified through the usual channels.

THE LIBERAL MAGAZINE
October 1929. HOSTILITIES WITH RUSSIA.
No settlement has been reached of the Russo-Chinese dispute concerning the seizure of the Chinese Eastern Railway. Though there has been no

declaration of war, several attacks by Russian troops on the Manchurian frontier have been reported during September.

Like his grandfather and father, Mervyn began his studies at Cambridge in 1929. He studied economics at Trinity College.

In October 1929, in America, the New York Stock Exchange collapsed and the repercussions were widespread, leading to the depression that affected the world for much of the 1930s. In Britain rising unemployment and the spectre of fascism were major concerns during Geoffrey's first years in Parliament.

A BACK-BENCHER LOOKS BACK

When I first entered the House of Commons in 1929 the Liberal Party was sixty strong. The Labour Government was dependent on Liberal Support from day to day, as it had no independent majority. It was necessary, therefore, for meetings of the Liberal Parliamentary party to be held frequently to decide what action was to be taken on any given subject. They were the centre of considerable political interest as the fate of the Government depended upon them.

The results of our deliberations were invariably very much the same. One third of the party decided to support the Government, one third to oppose it and the other third to abstain, sometimes ostentatiously by remaining in their seats during the Division.

As a matter of fact I had, from the outset, decided to give my support to the Labour Government. They seemed to me to be preferable to the Tories and, as a Radical, my affinities have always been Left. Captain (Viscount) Margesson, the Tory Chief Whip, was naturally active in trying to persuade Liberals to vote with the Conservatives.

After various attempts on me he asked whether there were any circumstances under which I would do so. On receiving a negative reply, he gave up his efforts…

Geoffrey's youngest daughter Elizabeth was at a boarding school in Switzerland and nearly thirteen when he became an MP After his election she took great delight in teasing him.

Sunday

Dear Father,

You are proud being an MP aren't you; will you continue writing me in PLT *[Parliamentary]* paper as I want the shield on it. Don't come out will you, as Mummy has just been. Am getting a little better at swimming but still terribly bad. My hair will be jolly long when you see me but I shall suddenly cut it all off again.

Ma sent me out a sample of "kissproof lipstick"! so Betty, Sos, Elizabeth Glover and I all made ourselves up with rouge, powder and lipstick. We have mumps at school now.

Ha ha.

Love Liz.

10 Kent Terrace,

London.

Darling Pa,

Uncle Alan is having tea with us, he is balder than you, so don't get discouraged...

In 1929, the Parliamentary Liberal Party established a number of committees to deal with various subjects, one of which was Imperial Affairs, headed by Sir Robert Hamilton as Chairman and Geoffrey as Honorary Secretary.

THE GREEN CAN

December 1929

THE AIRSHIP R101 by G. Le M. Mander

I had intended to write an account of a flight in the R101, but as this has now been postponed to the spring, I think it may be that the story of the attempted flight on Saturday, November 23rd, will be of interest to the readers of this journal.

One hundred MPs made the journey in motor coaches to Cardington, the airship station, a few miles from Bedford. On arriving we found that the weather had seriously deteriorated, and wind up to fifty miles an hour was blowing with squalls and rain at times. Rumours began to spread that the flight would not take place. Gradually Members went up in the lift to the head of the steel mast, which stands two hundred feet above the ground, until further progress by this means became impossible, as one of the heavy weights which works the lift collapsed, and fell to the ground with a great clang. We then had to ascend the 314 steps on foot.

In order that the balance of the Airship might be accurately maintained fore and aft, it was necessary for ten members of the crew to come off immediately after ten passengers had embarked, the reverse taking place when we descended.

From the ground the ship appeared to be rolling quite considerably in the strong wind and, not being a good sailor, I looked forward with some anxiety to spending even a couple of hours tethered to the mast where the motion is very much greater than what is obtained when the ship is free. I found, however, that no one felt any effects at all from the motion.

Inside, from the tail where an entry is made, one walks through a long corridor with great spaces behind linen fabric on either side filled with bags of hydrogen gas, and the structure of the machine consists of stainless steel and for smaller metal work duralinum is used. About half way down the ship one comes to the spacious lounge which stretches from side to side of the vessel. It is exactly like the lounge of an ocean liner. An excellent view of the ground over which the ship is passing can be obtained through a window on either side. There is also a dining room where we had an excellent lunch and below this a smoking room. There are a number of cabins in which sleeping berths are placed one above the other just as on a liner.

Everything is made as fireproof as possible, the linen fabric, which came from Belfast, being treated with a preparation which has the effect of making it non-inflammable.

During lunch a heavy squall struck the ship sideways, breaking away one of the metal weights by which it was anchored to the ground. The conditions while we were on board were severe, and the R101 stood them very well indeed.

I anticipate no doubt that in 100 years time airship service will be running as a matter of course regularly round the world.

Almost exactly a year later the R101 crashed killing most of the people on board.

The R101.

1930

THE GREEN CAN

January

We hope the fact that the aeroplane by which Mr Geoffrey was travelling to Switzerland was forced down at Abbeville owing to weather conditions, did not inconvenience him too much but that he arrived at Adelboden in plenty of time to have a Happy Christmas.

Geoffrey must have spent Christmas 1929 with Elizabeth in Switzerland.

In April 1930 The Green Can magazine printed an unusual piece of news taken from a newspaper report:

MPS' COOKING CONTEST

Some day in the near future three Members of Parliament are to take off their coats, descend into the nearest kitchen, and see who can cook the best hot-cross buns. They are Mr Jack Hayes (Soc. Edge Hill) Mr W.J. Womersley (C. Grimsby) and Mr Geoffrey Mander (L. Wolverhampton) The contest arose from a challenge at a recent dinner at the House of Commons. "I can cook," said Mr Hayes to a Daily Mail reporter, "anything from a peanut to an ox." The hot-cross bun cooking contest will be held on the Thursday before Good Friday, the last day of the sitting of the House of Commons, in the kitchens of the House. Each man must bring his own referee and must eat the results of his own cooking. Chefs' hats and aprons will be worn, and nothing but the best British ingredients will be used.

The Green Can editor added: "many of us will be eagerly waiting to see if Mr Geoffrey is looking quite well after Easter.

HANSARD

6 May 1930

BUDGET RESOLUTIONS

Mr Mander: There are hundreds of thousands of people in this country who, through no fault whatsoever of their own, have hardly a penny in the world; and there is a considerable number of people who, really through no merit of their own, have hundreds of thousands and millions of pounds. In the presence of a state of affairs like that, it seems to me to be essentially fair to take as large a proportion as possible from inherited wealth. A man who inherits a million, a quarter of a million, or a hundred thousand pounds, that being what is left after taxation by way of Death Duties is a very lucky man indeed. In the existing situation of the country, when money has to be raised for social and other purposes, I think that the Chancellor of the Exchequer is perfectly entitled to make a levy of this kind.

The next day Geoffrey spoke, again at length, about factory inspections, technical and industrial problems and standards of welfare in the work place.

Our problems today are economic. If we look at things from the point of view of the technical side, we are leaving out the human side, which is one of the most important. We are not going to make any proper progress in the restoration of prosperity until we get labour properly reorganised as an essential factor in industry.

At the end of May he was asking about the general conditions in domestic service, the fact that the International Bank was not subject in any way to public control, whether educational films were still to be duty free and what information was available from factories throughout the country about works councils, pensions, benevolent schemes, works magazines and "the human side of industry generally".

HANSARD
29 May 1930
PUBLIC HEALTH PSYCHO-THERAPEUTIC TREATMENT
Mr Mander asked the Home Secretary whether, in the event of persons being referred by the Juvenile Courts for psycho-therapeutic treatment, any contribution is made from public funds towards the cost?

After two negative replies to his questions he asked:

Whether he is aware that there are only two or three clinics in the whole of the British Isles which are able to give concentrated psycho-therapeutic treatment to persons with functional nervous disorders; that one clinic in London dealing with this kind of patient on these lines has a waiting list of between two and three hundred persons; and what action he proposes to take in the matter?

The Parliamentary Secretary to the Ministry of Health replied and concluded: The Mental Treatment Bill will facilitate further provision on these lines. My right Hon. Friend had not previously been informed of the difficulty indicated in the second part of the question.

Mr Mander: May I convey to the right Hon. Gentleman some information in regard to this matter?

The London clinic mentioned by Geoffrey probably was the Tavistock Clinic founded by Dr Hugh Crichton-Miller. The clinic was set up to provide mental health treatment; it achieved considerable success with its treatment of shell shocked soldiers after the First War.

Geoffrey was always very grateful to Dr Crichton-Miller who treated him after a period of ill health and enabled him eventually to join the Royal Flying Corps in 1916.

The exact nature of Geoffrey's illness is not recorded anywhere but the death of his father in 1900 when Geoffrey was eighteen, his mother's death in 1905, his need to cope with his bereaved young brothers, his marriage and the birth of his first two children, gave him heavy responsibilities at a relatively early age. These duties together with his work at Mander Brothers and the maintenance of the Wightwick estate may have contributed to his illness.

HANSARD

4th June

Mr Mander asked the Minister of Health the number of beds that are available in this country for cases receiving psycho-therapeutic treatment?

Mr Greenwood: Psycho-therapeutic treatment is available in the normal course at many institutes under the jurisdiction of the Board of Control, for such patients as are likely in the opinion of the medical staff to benefit from it. But beds are not specially set aside for such cases in these institutions.

THE GREEN CAN

QUESTIONS IN PARLIAMENT.

It was lunch time on Monday, June 16th, but those who assembled in the Mess Room, John Street, thirsted more for information than they hungered for lunch! The occasion was an address by Mr Geoffrey Le M. Mander, MP, on parliamentary procedure given by special request and with particular reference to questions in the House.

At the outset, we learned that, in order to make certain of a seat at question time, a Member should be present at prayers. (Possibly some of us mentally recalled the libel that the Chaplain looks at the Members and then prays for the country!)

Some questions, said Mr Mander, are by request answered orally; to others, printed replies are given. It was the oral answers that created most interest, especially when supplementary enquiries followed. A Member must give two days notice. When the Speaker calls him by name, he does not put his actual question but merely indicates that he asks "Question N*[umber]*". Always the answer is ready, unless the Minister to be interrogated feels that in the interests of the country the enquiry should not be publicly put. The House is always fair, said Mr Mander, and an intimation privately given that a question is undesirable usually receives patriotic acquiescence. Mr Mander drew attention to the great importance of questions. There are three Members, we are told, who are outstanding seekers for information Mr Day, Mr Hore-Belisha and Mr Mander himself.

July 23rd

The heat here is unbearable, the only things to do are to swim and eat which are both quite fun. We slept out on the balcony last night. The moon was a wonderful orange colour, it looked much bigger than usual and you could scarcely believe it was the moon. Why did it look orange like that? Do you know? Have you heard about Mother's operation which she is to have to cure her tiredness? *Evidently this was not as serious as it sounds, she lived a further 27 years.* She has just come and bought a wonderful kind of watch as a present which you never have to wind up, as every time you move your wrist it winds.

Love

Liz Mander

THE LIBERAL MAGAZINE
MR MANDER ON FOREIGN AFFAIRS

In the House of Commons on August 1st. Referring to the coming meeting of the League Assembly, Mr Mander said, "One of the most important questions that will arise this year, as it has arisen every year, is undoubtedly international disarmament. The position is most serious. The League has so far failed to carry out its obligations, and the various States of the world, particularly the ex-Allies, have failed to carry out their four-fold pledge to reduce armaments to a proper level, and unless something is soon done in a practicable basis, it will be impossible to prevent Germany and the other ex-enemy States from arming themselves. If the pledges made to them, that their disarmament was a preliminary to general disarmament, are not carried out, what right have we to say they shall disarm? There is a great danger if steps are not taken to deal with disarmament on a proper basis."

Geoffrey and his first wife Rosalind Caverhill had separated in 1926 and were divorced in 1930. It was while he was canvassing during the 1929 election campaign that Geoffrey met another Liberal candidate, Rosalie Glynn Grylls.

The Reform Club
25 Oct. 1930
Dear Mr Mander,
I saw my niece Hilda Grylls and my great niece Rosalie Glynn Grylls today.
What they told me of your engagement to Rosalie pleased me very much. Your intentions in regard to settlement on Rosalie I consider most generous. I should like to see you personally and hope you will give me an opportunity of seeing you when you come here. I shall help in any way I can.
I wish you both health and happiness and assure you I have confidence that you will find in Rosalie qualities of temper and mind that have endeared her to many especially
Yours very faithfully,
Alfred Back.
Will you lunch or dine here with me one day at your convenience?

Lord Great Chamberlain's Office,

House of Lords.

October 25th 1930

Dear Sir,

The Lord Great Chamberlain desires me to inform you that it gives him pleasure to accede to your request for your marriage to take place in the Crypt Chapel.

You are probably aware that you will require a special licence.

Will you be good enough to inform this office of the time and date when your marriage will take place.

Yours faithfully,

G. J. Townsend.

Grand Hotel,

Eastbourne.

10th November 1930

Dear Sir,

I am in receipt of your letter of yesterday's date, and have much pleasure in reserving you a double room with bathroom, facing sea from November 18th, next, at 32/6 per day, according to the terms of my previous letter. Thanking you for your patronage, and assuring you of our very best attention at all times,

Yours faithfully,

S. Eeley Managing Director.

HANSARD

15 November 1930

Geoffrey spoke at length at the end of a debate on holidays with pay.

I support the Bill because it seems to me that its principle is absolutely sound. The directors have their holidays on full pay, the managers have their holidays on full pay, and the clerical staff likewise have their holidays on full pay. Why should not the worker have his holiday in the same way, and so raise his human status while giving him the holiday to which he is entitled? There is one industry, with which many of my constituents as well as myself are associated, in which some interesting and valuable work has been done in connection with holidays. I refer to the work of the Joint Industrial Council of the National Paint, Colour and Varnish Industry. In October 1920, after discussion by both sides together in their council, they arrived at a scheme for giving a fortnight's holiday with full pay. That has been in operation throughout the whole country ever since, and there has been no difficulty whatsoever in carrying it out.

Soon after, the House divided: there were one hundred and eighty four for the Bill and only sixty three against.

GREAT CHAMBERLAIN'S OFFICE, HOUSE OF LORDS
Certified that a Religious Service was held in the Crypt Chapel of St Mary Volta, following the Marriage of Geoffrey Mander MP and Mary Rosalie Glynn Grylls at the Henrietta Street Register Office, on the Eighteenth day of November, Nineteen hundred and thirty.
Esmé Gordon-Lennox.
Secretary.

This report on the 11th Assembly of the League of Nations, from November 1930, is from an unidentified newspaper
HARD HITTING AT GENEVA.
WHAT EUROPE CAN LEARN FROM BRITAIN
From Geoffrey Mander MP. Geneva, Tuesday
Brighter Council meetings are likely in the near future, as the breezy, plain spoken M. Hambro is to represent Norway, who have just been elected.
The Council of the League could do with a little stirring up, as its members are inclined to be a shade too portentously polite and reserved towards each other. This tendency is increased by the attendance of too many ambassadors, gentlemen whose profession it is to smooth things over with fine phrases.
However, the debates on minorities in Sixth Committee have lacked nothing in hard hitting. M. Zaleski (Poland) was tauntingly aggressive. M. Curtius (Germany) showed dignity and discretion in effective response. M. Marinkovith (Jugo-Slavia) was abusive and harsh, while M. Briand (France) remained eloquent and unconvincing.
If the European nations would only follow the example of the British

Geoffrey's wedding to Rosalie Glynn Grylls.

Empire and give liberty to minorities instead of trying to force them into a rigid national mould, revision of treaties and boundaries would become quite unnecessary and peace would be more firmly established.

Geoffrey also wrote a report for The Liberal Magazine that ended:

On the whole it may be said that though some progress was made and there was no retrogression, the feeling was for transitory international reasons less satisfactory than for some years past, but nothing would provoke more discouragement than the return to Geneva next year of Sir Austen Chamberlain and his school of thought. The situation was admirably summed up by the very successful President, M. Titulescu, in the words "not satisfied, not discouraged".

December 14

Dear Father,

Miss Bamforth has started a branch of the League of Nations Union, of which I am a member and have to represent Holland, so you'll have to tell me about it. By the way, darn her, she said she would be pleased if you would come and speak sometime; I said in a meaning tone, you certainly wouldn't mind, but -!

We are going to a carol service this afternoon. I love carol services where you can sing your favourite hymns and carols at the top of your voice.

I'd like a camera for Xmas please, like mother gave me, the lens were Nagel; if you can't get the same, would you please give me money so that I can get it here.

Love Liz

Geoffrey's fascination with parliamentary business meant that he wrote far too much about the arcane, complex, inner workings of the House of Commons in his autobiography, but it was this great knowledge of procedures that enabled him to become such an effective back-bencher.

There are various types of Committees on which Members can serve. Select Committees (started somewhere about 1571) are, in fact, the House itself in miniature. They are appointed to deal with certain specific problems. There are also joint Select Committees, that is an equal number from the Lords and Commons.

As an example, one on which I served was to deal with the organisation of the Palace of Westminster and pay particular regard to the feeding arrangements for the large staff, seven hundred in all. It was found that many of them took their mid-day meals in twenty six mess-rooms in the House where they worked and we thought it would be a good plan to have a cafeteria available to all. It was found, however, that long established habits had such a grip on them that they preferred to remain as they were though the arrangements were far from satisfactory.

The Ecclesiastical Committee receives the measures passed on by the Church Assembly, and when it has considered them, sends on those which are not rejected, to Parliament for approval. I was put on to the Committee and served for about a dozen years. It consisted of a certain number of ecclesiastically-minded laymen. Many measures went through without any difficulty. When we were not quite satisfied and required further information, a gathering of Archbishops, Bishops and other clergy would assemble and we would cross examine them.

The usual practice was that when it appeared that a measure was likely to receive substantial opposition in the House, it was dropped. As an example the measure which would have made it possible for a clergyman to be deprived of his office if he married his deceased wife's sister. This was too much for a body of laymen to tolerate, for, after all, according to the law of England, a man may secure such a wife. The measure was dropped and nothing more was heard of it.

The Society of British Printing Ink Makers.
Dacre House, 5 Arundel Street, Strand, W.C.2
19th December 1930
To the Rt. Hon. W. Graham MP President, Board of Trade, Whitehall S.W.1.
Dear Sir,
Re: Dyestuffs (Import Regulation) Act 1920
We feel it our duty to bring to your notice the following fact. Mr G. Le M. Mander, MP in the House last Wednesday night voted in support of the Government on the above named matter. In doing so Mr Mander, who is a member of the Council of this Society, acted against the considered

judgement of its members, and as Council we desire to make this known to you, and thus put on record our disapproval of his action.

I have the honour to be,

Yours faithfully,

(Sgd) Chas. J. Richardson

Chairman of the Council.

22nd December 1930

Dear Sir,

I have to acknowledge the receipt of your letter of 19th December, informing me that your Council disapproves of the action of Mr Mander in voting against the amendment to the Expiring Laws Continuance Act introduced to continue the Dyestuffs (Import Regulation) Act.

In reply, I can only say that I have no doubt Mr Mander in this question, as in every other, voted as a member of Parliament and not as a member of your Council; and I am sending him a copy of this correspondence.

Yours faithfully,

William Graham

22nd December 1930

My dear Mander,

I am enclosing a copy of a letter I received from the Council of the Society of British Printing Ink Makers, and a copy of my reply. I felt so indignant at the last phrase of the letter in particular that I considered publishing the correspondence as illustrating the kind of pressure interested parties try to exert in matters of this kind. In fact I am still prepared to publish the correspondence if you wish it.

Yours sincerely,

William Graham

THE GREEN CAN
A WOMAN'S WORKS COUNCIL
By G. Le M. M.

My wife and I had the pleasure of attending a meeting of the Women's Work Council of Messrs. Cadbury Brothers at Bournville on January 16th and thereby had an opportunity of seeing this most interesting piece of human mechanism in full operation.

The Council is confined entirely to women, there being another one for men. This is found to be a most effective arrangement, and the women appear to make the fullest use of the opportunities thus given to them for initiative and self government. Two men attend as representatives of the Men's Council.

The meetings take place fortnightly at 9 a.m. and last for about an hour to an hour and a half. The chair is taken alternately by the Chairman of the Council, Mr Edward Cadbury, and the Vice-Chairman, a working girl. The latter was presiding on this occasion, and carried out her duties with great ability.

I have suggested that perhaps they might care to send over a representative to attend some meeting of our Joint Works Committee, though our operations are on a much less elaborate scale in view of our smaller numbers.

Geoffrey enjoyed chess and often played games by post with Elizabeth in Switzerland; he received letters from her like this one:

January
You can't move your Queen to Qb3 as I take you with my pawn or Queen, or knight.
But as we aren't allowed to change, my 5th move is that my [unreadable] pawn takes your Queen.

Feb 9

Dear Father,

Sorry for being such a stupid ass about the chess. Tell Miss Woodhouse that I hadn't any stamps so I couldn't write her. That man at Les Avants preaches rather good sermons. A girl here has had an accident lugeing and injured some organ in her side so we aren't allowed to go head-first any more. The first time the preacher came here he mistook four of us for boys, and we had to go and be introduced to him as girls. He said he knew there was something wrong, because everyone laughed in the service when he talked about boys.

My move is Q-Qb3 also.

The snow is disappearing rapidly but it is still frightfully cold. We have been skating the last few days. We have a new Matron here and she is very nice. You probably won't get this letter as I haven't any stamps left.

Love

Liz

THE GREEN CAN

Mr Mervyn Mander, after spending a year at Trinity College, Cambridge, has recently gone to the University of Pennsylvania at Philadelphia, USA. where he will be taking a special course of business training.

On February 5th Mr Geoffrey Mander addressed a luncheon meeting of the Industrial Co-partnership Association at the Holborn Restaurant, London, on "The Case for Works Councils," with Viscount Mersey presiding. Mr Mander gave his own experience based on the working of our Works Committee here, and explained the provisions of the Bill on the subject which he has introduced into the House of Commons.

HANSARD

30th April 1931

Mr Mander asked the Prime Minister if, in view of the recommendation of the unemployment committee of the International Labour Office with regard to carrying out of joint public works through the League of Nations, he will reconsider the question of removing the Government veto on the construction of a Channel Tunnel?

The Prime Minister: The recommendation to which the Hon. Member refers must be read as applying to cases in which obstacles to practical action can be removed by international action. This is not the case with the Channel Tunnel. I would also refer to the very full discussion in regard to the Channel Tunnel which took place on the 30th of June last in which I drew attention to the fact that the proposed scheme would only provide employment for a very small number of men[?]. As regards the last part of the question, I would remind the Hon. Member that the discussion on this matter was left to a free vote of the House.

May 26th

Dear Father,

Our form mistress, Miss Bamforth, is very anxious to know exactly what happens to a bill when it has passed its second reading and goes into committee. As she has to teach VI a. and b. about it and she is not quite sure, she has asked me to ask you, so please answer at once.

I'm sorry but I've thought a lot and I can't think of anything more to say.

Love

Liz

June 8th

Dear Father,

Thanks for explanations on bill. We've been swimming. Am going to be braver and dive higher this year. Nothing to say.

Love

Liz.

THE GREEN CAN

DINNER-TIME TALK AT HEATH TOWN

On Monday, June 8th, Mrs Geoffrey Mander gave a talk on the life of a woman undergraduate at Oxford. Mrs Mander dealt with an average day in the life of a woman undergraduate, or Undergraduette, as they are more often, flippantly called. At the conclusion. Mrs Mander was asked the college fee for one term, the answer was £50. The women's colleges were able to make it less than the total charge for a man, as they were run on more of a school system.

Geoffrey had joined the Wolverhampton Archeological Society in 1904 and during the 1930s he was one of its Vice Presidents The group encountered some difficulties over the years - "They visited Mr Bowen who had written flatly forbidding any kind of digging on his land. Further correspondence met with no reply." The group later took part in 1937 in an excavation of a Roman site near Watling Street in Staffordshire on land leased to them from a more sympathetic owner. Boys from Wolverhampton Grammar School took part in the dig and finds included Roman brooches, coins, Samian ware and roofing tiles.

HANSARD
July 1931
ROMAN BATHS, WALL, SOUTH STAFFORDSHIRE.
Mr Mander asked the First Commissioner of Works if he is aware of the work being carried out at Wall, in South Staffordshire, in the protection of the Roman baths by roofing; and whether he is prepared to consider the adoption of similar methods elsewhere so that Roman cities may be made available in a permanent condition for the inspection of the public? The First Commissioner of Works (Mr Lansbury): My department is aware of the work at Wall, and of the method of protection adopted. This method would be used where it was suitable.
Mr Mander: Will the right Hon. gentleman consider the possibility of making a tour during the Recess, and possibly pay a visit to these baths himself?
Mr Lansbury: Life is too short.

A report on Manders' Gala Day appeared in The Green Can in August and began:
Moisture in many of its forms is good and even desirable. One notable connoisseur on this subject asserted that after much research he had come to consider that the variety usually found inside a glass was the only kind to be looked upon with an appreciative eye.
Be that as it may, I think it was unanimously agreed that when it applied to meteorological conditions generally, and our own Gala Day in particular,

it should come under the general rationalization scheme.

Promptly to schedule, operations commenced with the aid of about fifty helpers, three and a half visitors and their dog, and small quantities of gentle rain.

The afternoon's events were reported, the rain continued to fall and at the end: Prizes were distributed by Mrs G. le M. Mander. Things quietened down afterwards with the exception of the Dancing, and with a chorus of quite cheery "good-nights" we wended our way homewards.

On 18th September 1931 Geoffrey received a letter from the Ministry of Works.

I have enquired into the case of Moseley Old Hall, about which you wrote to me on 12th September. The house is a fine example of the period, although not, perhaps, of outstanding national interest. My department could not, of course, contemplate buying it under the Ancient Monuments Acts, and inhabited dwelling houses are excluded from other provisions of these Acts. If you are convinced that there is real danger that the house will fall into decay, the local Archaeological society might be able to help, or the National Trust, although I imagine neither body is in a position to do much financially.

Moseley Old Hall, Wolverhampton, "not of outstanding national interest", is a house in which Charles 1st hid after the Battle of Worcester and where he first met the Catholic priest, Father Huddleston, who attended him, more than thirty years later, on his death bed in London in 1685. It was from Moseley that Charles travelled to Bentley and then to Boscobel where he hid in the famous oak tree.

Eventually in 1962, the year of Geoffrey's death, the National Trust took over the management of Moseley and opened it to the public in 1963.

A BACK-BENCHER LOOKS BACK
QUESTIONS

The value of parliamentary questions *[is that they offer]* opportunities to private members by which they can raise any subject that they consider to be of public importance. For several years I held the record for the number of questions asked by a back-bencher. My total was about 14,000. At the time each one was put with a deliberate object in view to further what I considered was either the public interest or for the benefit

Moseley Old Hall.

of my constituents and ranged from asking the Minister of Health to allow the Cosy Corner Cafe, Heath Town, in my constituency, to supply foodstuffs, to asking the Secretary of State for Air to intervene to prevent a constituent's son in the RAF in Egypt from marrying.

For some time Geoffrey and his first wife had owned a house in London at 53 Seymour Street, off Edgware Road. As this was some distance from the Houses of Parliament, when he became an MP and after his second marriage, he bought 4 Barton Street, a house within walking distance of Parliament.

In September 1931 the Japanese army invaded Mukden in Manchuria. Japan was a member of the League of Nations and so the Tokyo government accepted a League resolution calling on the army to withdraw but the army ignored both its own government and the League. It then went on eventually to control the whole of Manchuria and part of Mongolia. The government was totally dominated by the army and when the League of Nations again called on the army to withdraw, Japan simply left the League.

FROM 'WE WERE NOT ALL WRONG'
By Geoffrey Mander (published 1942)
The League had never yet had to meet a conflict between a great power and one less able to defend itself. The militarists in Japan thought they would just give a push to the door to see if it was open.
Now let us have the story of the period in the actual words of the League of Nations Union itself, in extracts from resolutions passed either by the Executive Committee, General Council, or in other ways.
"The Executive Committee desires to lay before HM Government its conviction that if the Council of the League in this crisis fails to maintain the authority of the Covenant, the result must be an irreparable injury to the moral position of the League and to the sanctity of treaties, and will imply a formal acceptance of force as the arbiter of international life." As an example of clairvoyance this is not bad.
"If the League goes, the civilised world will again lie exposed to the forces which brought it to the verge of destruction in 1914." Remember this was eight years before the war actually broke out.

A widespread feeling of unrest was spreading across Britain at this time with demonstrations against pay cuts in London and by Naval ratings in Scotland.

A BACK-BENCHER LOOKS BACK

In the crisis period of 1931, a departmental committee appointed by the Minister of Mines, Mr Shinwell, was asked to deal with the Miners' Welfare Fund. This fund was raised by a levy of one penny per ton on all coal raised and was used for the setting up of pit-head baths, clubs, bowling greens, and similar activities. It was a period when economies were being looked for in every direction and it was hoped that this committee would produce some such recommendation. In the end the position was this: [Lords] Chelmsford and Erskine were in favour of the abolition of the levy entirely, [Lord] Macdonald and I were quite as much in favour of its maintenance indefinitely. As it was obvious that unless we could get agreement probably the levy would be abolished altogether, we agreed on a figure of [half a penny] per ton as a temporary measure. I had some miner constituents who I knew would not like this but it was really the best that could be done in the circumstances, in their interests.

The compromise made by the committee to settle the question of the Miners' Welfare Fund is one example of the many attempts by Ramsay MacDonald's government to resolve the financial problems caused by high unemployment. Eventually, unable to reach an agreement on whether to cut benefits or to increase taxes, the government split and fell. Instead of tendering his resignation to the King, MacDonald offered to form a National Government - a coalition with Conservatives and Liberals.

In the election of November 1931 Geoffrey retained his seat and Ramsay MacDonald's National Government was returned with a large majority. Before the election Geoffrey had received a letter of encouragement from Elizabeth.

Dear Father,
Go it about the election. One of the staff has a wireless here so I may be asked to listen in while the results are given out. Is Mavis there dutifully helping you to kiss babies and give an extra big tip to the working man?
Love
Liz

One of the members of the new government was the former Conservative Prime Minister, Stanley Baldwin.

A BACK BENCHER LOOKS BACK

During my years in the House of Commons, Mr Baldwin always showed me great kindness and I had a deep admiration and affection for him as a man. His supporters in the House used to say that he talked more with members of the Opposition than he did with them. He had to be roused to give his best in debate for by nature he was indolent, at any rate very easy going. When he was roused, his powers were most effective.

In the Wightwick Manor archives there is a collection of letters written to Geoffrey Mander in response to his involvement with an immense range of local and international questions and they only hint at the vast number of letters he must have written. There are replies to his letters of commiseration after candidates and friends lost seats at the 1931 election, including one from Philip Noel Baker who later was re-elected, and during the war served as Parliamentary Secretary to the Ministry of War Transport:

"How very good of you to write to me as you did. On many grounds I was of course very sad at being beaten, on others much less so. I have been longing for years for a chance to go away to the country and live a quiet life for a few months on end!

May I say that your election was almost the only one that gave me genuine unmixed pleasure."

From Arthur Henderson:

"I very much appreciate all you write about my work as Foreign Secretary and the pleasant way in which you express the hope that I shall retain my position as chairman of the World Disarmament Conference."

THE GREEN CAN

At the annual meeting of the Research Association of British Paint, Colour and Varnish Manufacturers, Mr Geoffrey Mander was elected President in place of Mr S.K. Thornley of Messrs. Thornley & Knight.

Stanley Baldwin.

In 1932 a letter was sent to the Secretary-General of the League of Nations proposing the formation of a Peace Army as a means of preventing world war. A copy of a letter sent to the Press at the same time is held in the Wightwick archives.

The 2nd Sino-Japanese war had begun the previous year; it lasted until 1945.

In March the I.R.A. announced that violence would continue until Ireland was a republic.

> 24 Rosslyn Hill,
> Hampstead,
> N.W.3.
> April 1st 1932
> Dear Mr Mander,
>
> Thank you very much indeed for all your kindness. I think that, as Sir John Simon has replied to me that the situation which evoked our offer of a Peace Army has changed, there is nothing more to be done. We are going ahead with our plans and hoping to organise a Peace Army in every country in the world. We have however decided that we ought not to bind ourselves to the League of Nations, as we should in that case always be acting under the directions of our own Government; and this might not always suit us!
>
> Our idea therefore is to have this organisation in existence and, when it seems advisable, to offer it to the League of Nations for a definite occasion. We should not therefore be justified in pressing it upon them now.
>
> I am more than grateful - we all are - for your kindness and interest in the matter. May I ask now whether you are sufficiently interested to care to help us in our organisation?
>
> I don't know how far you go with us but I needn't say how rejoiced we should be if we could count on your help.
>
> Yours sincerely,
> A. Herbert Gray, A. Maude Royden, H.R.L. Sheppard.

Maude Royden (1876-1956) was an active supporter of women's suffrage from the early 1900s giving hundreds of speeches a year. After the first war, she was mainly concerned with the role of women in the Church. For over twenty years she was an ardent pacifist but in 1939 stated that the rise of the Nazi regime posed a greater threat than any war.

When the BBC started the first religious service, Dick Sheppard was famous as the "radio parson". He became a Canon of St. Paul's Cathedral in 1934.

Herbert Gray was a Congregational Minister.

THE LIBERAL MAGAZINE

April

BILLS OF THE SESSIONS

National Industrial Council Bill - This Bill introduced by Mr Mander and other Liberal Members, provides for the immediate establishment of a National Industrial Council, for the following purposes: to examine Parliamentary Bills affecting industry; to discuss reports from the Ministry of Labour on the industrial situation; to promote industrial conciliation and the settlement of disputes.

Works Councils Bill - This Bill, introduced by Mr Mander, supported by other Liberal Members, provides for the establishment of a Works Council in every factory or workshop in which fifty or more persons are normally employed.

A BACK-BENCHER LOOKS BACK

There was a Bill which I introduced called Works Councils Bill, and arose out of my own experience of industry where I had found the immense value of joint consultation between employers and employed of all ranks. I put forward precise proposals to be secured by legislation. This placed on the Minister of Labour the responsibility of preparing draft schemes which, after careful consideration by all involved, could be put into operation if there were refusal to act voluntarily.

Some of the subjects to be included in the Works rules, which were to be jointly agreed between both sides, were as follows: hours of work - period of notice of dismissal to be given on either side - arrangements for paying wages - dismissal for moral or disciplinary offences - arrangements enabling an aggrieved individual to state his case to some responsible person or body and similar arrangements to discuss dismissals on the groun d of shortage of work.

I cannot pretend that I received a great deal of support for this measure outside the ranks of the Liberal party.

I feel it was worthwhile because the general subject is of overwhelming importance in the sphere of industrial democracy and efficient management.

RADIO TIMES
April 30 1932
Wolverhampton
A great industrial town shows the world what it can do in the way of music. First, Mr Geoffrey Mander, MP, will sing the praises of Wolverhampton, and for two hours afterwards Wolverhampton will sing for itself. (Midland Region 6.30 - 8.40)

Geoffrey and Rosalie Mander's first child, John, was born in 1932 on 28th May. He was Geoffrey's fourth child and his second son.

At this time Mavis was in Australia, where she had married her first husband, Roger Partridge. In August she gave birth to Carl, Geoffrey's first grandchild.

FROM JOHN MANDER'S UNPUBLISHED AUTOBIOGRAPHY
The three children from my father's first marriage all popped up at one time and another at Wightwick. Mervyn, my half-brother, I scarcely saw, Mavis I only knew from hearsay to be a beautiful, headstrong, untameable creature, a character out of an early Waugh novel, the incarnation of a Bright Young Thing. Younger, and therefore a little closer to me came red-haired Elizabeth who was a quiet, gentle soul, much like my father in many ways. That then was "the family" which ever way one looks at it, her *[his mother's]* first years at Wightwick cannot have been easy. *She was only four years older than Mavis.*

John noted that his own birth upset Mervyn..

He was certainly deeply wounded - he was no longer the only son. My father's treatment of Mervyn and myself could not have been more different. Is it that my father as a young man was solemn, strict, a

Rosalie Mander with John.

Victorian? Such a man would no doubt have pressed any son of his - but especially the eldest - into a pre-formed mould, and it is certain that Mervyn must have suffered, for his lifelong stammer certainly had very early origins. Was my father then, a different man at twenty-five than he was at fifty? Had his early puritan harshness given way in middle age to an indulgent kindness? It is difficult to think of any other explanation. His elder children all complained that he was 'unapproachable,' very withdrawn. Yet he was certainly fond of children. My half-sister Elizabeth, remembers as a little girl sitting on the terrace at Wightwick being lectured on the political situation in the Middle East.

The attitudes of Mervyn and Elizabeth towards the new baby were quite different. This is Elizabeth's letter to her step-mother written early in May, a few weeks before John was born, when names for the new baby were being considered. She gave them marks out of ten.

Dear Rosalie,

I have thought of some more: Rex, Gay, Isabel, Jack, Virginia???

Now for your list: John 2 (too common), Richard 6, Christopher 9, Eve 4.

The long list continued and at last ended:

Also how do you like Marylee?

I am afraid Father does not like any of my suggestions much. Thanks so much for the chocolates last Thursday, by Father.

Love

Elizabeth

THE GREEN CAN

June 1932

We offer our congratulations to Mr Geoffrey Mander, MP and Mrs Mander on the birth of a son on Saturday, May 28th.

HANSARD

7 June 1932

LEAGUE OF NATIONS (SECRETARY GENERAL).

Mr Mander asked the Secretary of State for Foreign Affairs whether he will consider the advisability of proposing, with a view to securing as the next

Secretary-General of the League of Nations a citizen of a nation wholly detached from European controversies, that an American should be appointed?
Mr Eden: No, Sir.

THE GREEN CAN
August 1932
HIKING - BY MOTOR.
By G. Le M. Mander

During the past and present summers my wife and I have made a practice whenever we had a half -day to spare, of motoring to various places of interest in the neighbourhood, and it is remarkable to find the large number of spots well worth visiting within 20 or 30 miles of Wolverhampton.

From the top of Clent Hills (highest point 1,000 feet) a magnificent panorama of the country round can be obtained, in which one is greatly assisted by the thoughtful act of the Stourbridge and Kidderminster Rotary Clubs in erecting a toposcope indicating what's what.

At Uriconium Mr Jackson is always delighted to explain to visitors all that is known of this Roman settlement on the Severn, founded before A.D. 60 and finally destroyed by fire early in the fourth century. A most interesting place, as is also another Roman city, Letocetum or Wall, near Walsall [Lichfield is nearer] founded about A.D. 50, and one of the rest stations on the Watling Street, also used for keeping watch on the fierce and savage Celts of Cannock Chase and South Staffs. Only the baths are uncovered, but there is an excellent museum here as at Uriconium. Sedgeley Beacon, the highest cultivated tableland in England, and Dudley Castle with its history of ancient and modern struggles, were taken by us on the way to Kinver Edge, where 200 acres of delightful hillside and wood under control of the National Trust are available to the public for ever as a memorial. How infinitely more inspiring than a statue... Wyre Forest, through Bewdley, and back by Arley, is a pleasant run, but there is no bridge at Arley, a beautiful little village on the Severn, and cars have to cross on a ferry; the passage was not recommended even by the ferryman. It may be that these few notes will be of value to some who like to make short motoring trips (though many places mentioned can be reached by bus, bike etc.) with a definite object in view, and if I can stimulate others to give of their own experiences and discoveries on the same lines I think many of your readers would benefit.

THE GREEN CAN
BOWLS REPORT.
"September 1st, at Wightwick Manor, Mr Geoffrey's team won their 'Annual Friendly' against 'The Mermaid' by 25 points. Mr Geoffrey won his encounter against F. Robinson 15-13, and it would be a good idea to invite him to become a leader of the League Team, seeing there is so much difficulty in getting our men to play. Mrs Geoffrey Mander put up quite a good game for "The Mermaid" by scoring 9, and Miss Elizabeth bowled well to reach a score of 6 for the same team. As in previous years Mrs Woodhouse *[the housekeeper]* presided over the refreshments in the Billiard Room, Mrs Mander also seeing to it that no one went away without having sandwich and beer or cakes and minerals and cigarettes."

This article, written by Geoffrey, also appeared in the September edition of The Green Can.
SKYWRITING.
Among the duties that fall to Members of Parliament is service on select committees appointed to report on some particular subject of public interest, and in that way I have recently been sitting on the Select Committee on Skywriting.
Though not a subject of world shaking importance it was very interesting. We had to recommend what action, if any, should be taken by legislation, or otherwise, to check or control sky-shouting, smoke-writing, signs attached to aircraft and cloud-writing. The evidence was given in public, and our report has been published, so I am betraying no confidences in what I now say.
Sky-shouting is the broadcasting from an aeroplane of appeals by voice to a whole town to use, for example, somebody's tooth powder or lipstick. It has been tried in America, Sweden, and over Milan. There would be no escaping the voice. Its adoption in this country is so improbable as to make any action unnecessary as things are. All the same, the idea rather

appeals to me from an electioneering point of view. It would save a lot of trundling of loud speakers on motorcars if I could address all my constituents at one inescapable meeting.

Smoke-writing we are familiar with - the emission of smoke by aeroplane by day in the form of letters advertising generally some popular newspaper, though not as yet The Green Can. This seems to have become so boring that few people trouble to look up at it, and can well be left alone.

The main subject of our investigation and, indeed, the cause of it, was cloud-writing. This consists in projecting at night into the clouds, at an average height of 4,000ft, powerful beams of light. Major Savage the patent holder carried out a number of experiments in industrial centres to test the feeling, and threw onto the sky the name of a well known beverage. No dissatisfaction appeared to be caused, but a powerful press agitation was raised by various societies interested in the protection of amenities. Evidence against skywriting from this angle was given by a number of well known people. The members of the committee severely cross-examined these distinguished persons, and it seemed a weakness in the objectors' case that most of them had never seen what they condemned. Many said it made no difference whether they saw it or not, and the Dean [of Westminster] capped all by saying he would look the other way if he ever had the chance of seeing it. We saw a demonstration at Hendon, and it struck one as distinctly beautiful and pleasing, calculated to add to the amenities of large industrial areas when brooded over by dull, heavy clouds. It all depends really on the way this powerful invention is exploited. For instance, to project onto the clouds on a Sunday evening over a cathedral an appeal to take somebody's pills would be an outrage.

Even if legislation is passed imposing restriction as in rural areas etc. there is bound to be a period of voluntary control, and this may show to what extent the fears of abuse are justified. An advertisement can only be seen for about a mile from the point of projection. On the average about one hour per night per year is suitable for cloud writing. The charge is at present about £50 an hour.

The legal position is interesting. Ownership of the air space extends without limit above a portion of land, but how difficult to bring an action of trespass or prove damage by a ray of light.

Provided it is conducted on reasonable lines there seems to be a place for this new discovery without interfering with any legitimate interests.

THE LIBERAL MAGAZINE

During the first week of October the Liberals of Wolverhampton, led by Mr Geoffrey Mander and Mr George Thorne, the present Member and the late Member for East Wolverhampton, celebrated the unbroken Liberal representation of the Borough since 1832. "For a hundred years," Mr Geoffrey Mander wrote in the Manchester Guardian, "East Wolverhampton has had a Liberal representative in Parliament. On no single occasion has the constituency returned any candidate but a Liberal. This is a record unique in the political history of this, and probably any other country. It is interesting to note that in 1832 there were only 1,700 electors with a population of about 67.000. In 1932, with a similar population, there are 43,000 electors."

During the early 1930s several of Geoffrey's holidays were spent rowing down the Severn; the nearest access to the river is about 12 miles from Wightwick at Bridgnorth, in Shropshire.

From a report in the Wolverhampton Express and Star. October 1932.

W'TON MPs RIVER TRIP DOWN THE SEVERN BY EASY STAGES.

"The Severn is beautiful. Our trip was easy going from start to finish owing to the big rise in the river, which carried us safely over the fords," said Mr Geoffrey Mander, MP for East Wolverhampton, when asked today about the trip he made from Bridgnorth to Worcester in a rowing boat on the Severn yesterday. Mr Mander was accompanied by Mrs Mander and Mr Richard Acland, son of Sir Richard Acland.

This is a mistake - Richard Acland's father was the Liberal MP Sir Francis Acland.

Mr Mander's idea is to cover the whole of this beautiful river from the source to the mouth (as far as is navigable) in distances of about 30 miles. Last year the party rowed from Bridgnorth to Shrewsbury.

THE LIBERAL MAGAZINE

Mr Geoffrey Mander said on November 1st:

Russia is a new country, certain of tremendous commercial development in future, whether we like the way they are running their affairs or not. If we pursue our present policy, adopted from political prejudice, we shall be continuing the same fatal policy as we have followed for the last 10 years. At one time 2,000 American engineers were in Russia, while practically no British representatives were there, on account of political prejudice and not only political, but commercial prejudice. Orders for machinery and other things worth many millions of pounds have gone to America which might just as well come to this country. They *[the Government]* are pursuing a policy now which is affecting the employment of a considerable number of people in this country, and which in the distant future will affect the employment of hundreds of thousands of our workers.

In November the new baby was christened John Geoffrey Grylls in the crypt of the House of Commons.

The Green Can magazine heralded in the new year with a gloomy editorial.

The year 1932 has not bought any alleviation in the industrial situation. The situation is gradually getting worse, both in world trade and in the trade of this country, and no change for the better can be expected until certain definite steps are taken in world politics. It can only be hoped that what instructed opinion everywhere feels to be the right course, will be taken, and the long agony of unemployment and depression brought to an end.

The report on Mander Brothers was more cheerful.

The chief event of the past year for us has been the introduction of a system unique in industry whereby hours have been reduced to 40 per week without a reduction in earnings. The history of this matter is well known to our readers and will, we believe, in years to come be looked back upon as a notable landmark in industry.

11 Downing Street,
Whitehall. S.W.
13th January 1933
My dear Mander,
I am ashamed to find that a very kind letter you wrote to me at the end of last session has remained unanswered. I am declining all invitations to speak at lunches and dinners so far as I decently can. Such functions are always tiring and often the engagement has to be kept to one's real inconvenience when the time comes.
I find that with the multifarious work that falls to my lot I must confine myself as far as possible to the daily grind.
With all good wishes for the New Year, I am,
Sincerely yours,
Stanley Baldwin.

An obituary was printed in the Green Can in February, for Arthur King, who had worked at Mander Brothers for fifty years. He was associated with the firm's export business and obviously had an interesting career:

> His first venture in the Firm's behalf had to be undertaken without time for adequate preparation. A situation had arisen in Bucharest which required the immediate transfer of stock from the possession of an Agent in financial difficulties to some new Agent who had to be found. The young Mr King promptly accepted the task and left for Romania the next morning, without waiting for a passport. On arrival of the train at the frontier station, the youthful commissioner was startled to hear stentorian calls for "Passeports," up and down the platform but, without a moments hesitation, he descended from the carriage and hid himself, swiftly rejoining the train as it was again on the move. It became necessary, however, in order to effect the necessary transfer, to go through a legal process and, being found to have unlawfully to have entered the country without a passport, he was detained in the charge of two stern myrmidons of the law, armed with drawn swords, while investigations were made. Fortunately, British prestige stood high in Romania and Mander Brothers' special representative was rescued by the British Consul.

He eventually became the Foreign Manager and Geoffrey wrote in his obituary: "To him, the Foreign Office was everything - indeed, it was a little difficult at times to persuade him to admit that the Home Department existed at all." On his retirement the Directors decided to send Mr King on a tour round the world so that he could visit as many Mander branches as possible to enable him to say goodbye to their Agents.

THE GREEN CAN
March 1933
In the first round of the Parliamentary Squash Rackets Handicap Tournament, Mr Geoffrey Mander, MP (plus 4) beat Sir Adrian Baillie, Bt, MP (plus 2) 9-7, 10-8, 9-7.

In Spring 1933 Geoffrey started to make arrangements for another rowing holiday travelling down the Severn from Welshpool to Shrewsbury. He received numerous letters of information about the river from Mr T. Golling whose chief business was set out on his letter heading -"Hatter, Hosier and Outfitter, 16 High Street, Shrewsbury."

Shrewsbury April 4th

The river is very shallow between Welshpool and Pool Quay and the boat will have to be towed in many places. I would advise you to obtain permission to use the Canal. I have marked the most important landmarks as a guide. You will not see more than eight houses the whole trip.

April 11th

In giving advice on River trips which I frequently do, I always make a strong point on the danger of having a hole knocked in the boat at certain places in the River which so often happens through carelessness. Here are two cases out of many - the Captain of the Pengwern Boat Club with a party left Crew Green for a trip downstream, 120 yards below they ran on a pile under the Bridge, the boat sank in 15 feet of water, the captain's wife nearly lost her life.

The Mayor of Shrewsbury with several Town Councillors and the Chief Constable came down river from Montford Bridge, at Fitz Weir they ran on a stake, the boat sank and in less that half a minute the whole party were up to their necks in water which was 12 to 15 feet deep, luckily the boat did not sink to the bottom, not one of them could swim, they were rescued by ropes thrown from the bank. Most of the accidents would have been avoided if care had been taken. Any further information you may require I will do my best to supply.

Yours faithfully,

Golling.

POST CARD

The North Dean Club and Guest House, Hughenden Valley,

High Wycombe.

15th April 1933

It's so funny to be on a holiday in England! and very interesting. Peaceful as W*[ightwick]* without its gloom.

Love Liz

THE GREEN CAN

May 1933

A FURTHER SEVERN TRIP by Geoffrey Mander

In accordance with our plans for endeavouring to row down the Severn from source to sea so far as this is possible my wife and I and Mr Richard Acland on Saturday, May 6th, left the Kepax ferry, above Worcester at 9.30a.m. with the object of rowing 30 miles to Gloucester. In rowing the stretch from the ferry to the lock just below Worcester we received a warning of the conditions that awaited us, as we found a strong wind blowing up the river, making the water very choppy and the going slow. We struggled on, all three taking turns at the oars, until we reached the lock just below Tewkesbury at 3.30. when we decided to hold a council of war and review the whole situation. The lock-keeper and his wife very kindly provided us with a much appreciated cup of tea.

The storm continued unabated, and the wind showed no sign of falling so we decided with great reluctance to postpone this section to another occasion.

We have now accomplished the journey in stages from Shrewsbury to Tewkesbury and shall hope later in the season to deal with the portion between Welshpool and Shrewsbury.

HANSARD

19th July

SEX EQUALITY

Mr Mander asked the Home Secretary whether the Government propose to introduce a measure giving equal rights to men and women, with a view to facilitating the drawing up of a general treaty on the subject through the League of Nations?

Sir J. Gilmour: His Majesty's Government has no such proposal under consideration and as at present advised they do not think it practicable or desirable to attempt any extension of the general affirmation of the Sex Disqualification Removal Act of 1919.

Mr Mander: Am I to understand from the reply that the Government are not disposed to give equal rights to men and women?

Viscountess Astor: Do not the Government really think that it is about time that England took the lead in this question of equality among the sexes?

Sir J. Gilmour: I have nothing to add to the answer which I have given.

Viscountess Astor: The answer was not very satisfactory.

A BACK-BENCHER LOOKS BACK

On the occasion of the Dinner of the Harrow Association, held prior to the Eton and Harrow match on July 14th, 1933 Mr Baldwin did not appear on the Toast list but he yielded to vociferous requests for a speech. He said that India, during the next twenty five years would need the services of first rate men and that any young man of ability could not find a better field for his ambitions. He emphasised that the old methods of direct rule by the British in India were now passing away and that it would be their more difficult and nobler task in the future to help to train the Indians to rule their own country. This was said with great passion and sincerity and it happened at a time when Mr Churchill and ninety Conservatives were opposing the India Bill night after night. Fortunately the wide vision and statesmanship of "S.B." as he was always called, prevailed in the end.

The Green Can published an account of the opening of new Mander Brother's offices on Monday 24th July.

Mr Geoffrey Mander said that it had been intended in 1929 to build new offices at Heath Town *[Mander's factory on the outskirts of the town]* but owing to the world depression they had contented themselves with fitting up the old paint and ink works in St. John's Street *[in the centre of Wolverhampton]* into new offices as they saw them today. No doubt ultimately the offices and the Varnish works would go to Heath Town, but it seemed likely they would remain in the present offices for a considerable time to come.

The only part of the buildings that had any historic or romantic associations was the old chapel, which had been originally erected towards the end of the 17th century. It was known for certain that a chapel was erected there in 1701, and in 1715 a mob led by Jonathan Wild, a notorious highwayman, attacked the chapel and broke it up. In 1791, the time of the "Church and King" riots, Mr Benjamin Mander, the great-great-grandfather of the present directors had to defend his hearth, home and business with drawn sword. The echoes of these controversies had now passed away, but one echo still remained. Mr Smyth *[Geoffrey's cousin]* informed him that a parrot which had lived for many years in the Seven Stars Hotel *[next door]* had succeeded in reproducing the sound of the creaking machinery used in the manufacture of paint and ink, and this voice at times broke through into the new offices.

Sir Charles *[Mander, another cousin]* in a characteristic speech which was presumably intended to be humorous, commented on the fact that it was only in a brave endeavour to keep abreast of the times, that he reluctantly agreed to the concentration of all the administrative offices under one roof. In particular he felt that the transfer of his own office had inflicted upon him considerable disturbance and even hardship. A blue pencil had been lost and his unique filing system had been put out of order by the disappearance of his waste paper basket.

In July the Green Can published a list of some of the suggestions that had been submitted in 1920 as possible titles for the new magazine, They included: Monthly Manderisms, Mander's United, Mandanoos and The Mandertory.

Two archive press cuttings from 18th and 20th September 1933 record a visit by several MPs "and other notabilities under the leadership of Mr G. le Mesurier Mander MP" to Budapest to study economic and political conditions in Central Europe.

The Green Can published some information on this visit.

During his recent visit to Budapest, Mr Geoffrey Mander received a visit from Mr E.S. Kalmar, who previously to the War was one of the Firm's travellers for Austria and Hungary for the branch which had its headquarters in Vienna. Mr Kalmar has a vivid recollection of the months he spent in 1910 at Wolverhampton, and still carries the steel knife given him at that time with the Firm's name upon it.

Mr Geoffrey Mander was able to collect and spend some blocked pengoes owing to the Firm, during his visit. These amounts had for some time been standing to the credit of the Firm, but owing to currency restrictions were not allowed to be exported outside the frontiers.

Geoffrey's daughter Mavis gave birth to his second grandson Anthony on 21st September 1933 in Kenya

THE LIBERAL MAGAZINE

On December 13th, Mr Geoffrey Mander moved the following resolution: "That this house would welcome a declaration by his Majesty's Government of their willingness to consider the formation of an international police force under the control of the League of Nations with a view to increased security and better maintenance of world order."

This was not intended to be a police force to combat international crime for which Interpol had been established in the 1920s, but a peace keeping force.

Speaking in support of the resolution, Mr Mander said, "It may surprise some that those who are passionately devoted to the preservation of peace should be prepared to consider in any circumstances the use of force. I want to say at once that there is nothing illogical in that. I claim to be a realist in this matter, and what one has to recognise is that we cannot maintain peace and order in the world merely by passing pious resolutions and trusting in the good will of the people to carry them out. It is merely the right use of force. It is clear that for many generations, for hundreds, and possibly thousands, of years to come, force will rule in the world to some extent. Is it not better, therefore, that that force should be at the disposal of the judge, or some independent authority, rather than at the disposal of parties to the dispute as has been the case in the past?"

I believe that the increasing gravity of the international situation - and I do not think it is possible to exaggerate the gravity of the crisis in which we find ourselves - is forcing us to consider any method, any way out that we can see, however contrary it may be to our past habits and conditions. I believe that people are being compelled now to give consideration to the question of whether the League ought not to be supplied in some way with the necessary teeth in order to see that its decisions are carried out.

There was a great deal of sympathy expressed for the Police Force idea. In spite of the cynical view towards it taken by some people, the vision has become a reality. *[1957]*

A BACK- BENCHER LOOKS BACK

The Privy Council wrote to Lady Joan's father Lord Dartmouth, informing him that his daughter had been nominated High Sheriff *[for Staffordshire]* and asking if she were qualified, which meant possessing property in the county. He wrote back at once, without consulting her, stating that she owned no property. She was immediately struck off the list.

On reading this account I wrote to the Clerk to the Privy Council, commenting on what had occurred and expressing the view that it seemed to me that some sex prejudice had entered into the way the matter had been handled. The reply was that this was not so and that the normal course had been followed as in the case of any male nominee. I then asked whether I was to understand that it was the custom of the Privy Council when a male was nominated to serve in the office of High Sheriff, to write to his father, unknown to him, and ask whether he was qualified. The Privy Council could think of no effective answer to this.

HANSARD

19 December 1933

WOMEN JUSTICES

Mr Mander asked the Attorney-General what fresh appointments are contemplated in the 164 county divisions and 31 boroughs where there is no woman magistrate, and therefore no woman eligible to serve on the new juvenile courts?

Sir Victor Warrender (Vice-Chamberlain of the Household): I have been asked to reply. The figures given in the question refer to the position on the 1st November last. Since then 72 new women justices have been appointed, and the question of the further appointment of more women as justices specially for the work in juvenile courts has been and is receiving the careful consideration of my Noble Friend, the Lord Chancellor.

Mr Mander: Do I understand that it is intended gradually to appoint women on every bench, so that the Children Act can be fully carried out, and will the Hon. Gentleman represent that to the Attorney-General?

Viscountess Astor: Will the Hon. Gentleman bear in mind that there are over 20,000 men magistrates and under 2,000 women magistrates?

Geoffrey was not the only member of the family to write articles for The Green Can. His wife reviewed a play produced by Mander's Dramatic Section:

Miss Sharratt should be particularly congratulated on her performance as it involved rather a lot of 'doing nothing in particular and doing it very well.' The audience especially enjoyed the pair of entrancing pyjamas she held up to view during her leisurely packing for the elopement.

His cousin Charles spent some time in America and accounts of his progress were printed each month in the magazine:

While the American has kept some of the Shakespearian words which we have discarded, such as 'gotten', they have invented a gold mine of expressive phrases.

On one occasion in California, wanting to buy a reel of cotton, I asked in a store if they kept such an article and was told - 'we doan' hardly sell nothin else but!' The meaning was perfectly clear.

Charles' sister Daisy travelled in the Baltic with a group of guides and scouts and her reports appeared in instalments in The Green Can; Peter Neville (Geoffrey's nephew) wrote an article "Why I Went to America." - he took a course on business administration at Harvard.

1934

In April 1934 Mussolini won dictatorial powers from the Italian parliament.

It was also in 1934 that Hitler became dictator of Germany and took the title 'Fuhrer'. The previous October Nazi Germany left the League of Nations; now Hitler announced that Germany would not pay any more war reparations - these were the payments due to the Allies for damage done during World War One. By cancelling this debt he was able to afford to put in motion an ambitious programme of public works, this included building a new network of roads extending to Germany's borders and a stealthy start to rearmament. It was becoming clear that Hitler was pursuing increasingly aggressive policies that rejected a number of settlements agreed when the Treaty of Versailles was signed after the First War.

WE WERE NOT ALL WRONG

It is essential to keep clearly in mind the fundamental difference that existed all along between the National Government and their opponents before the war; it went to the root of the whole controversy of national defence, and showed itself in every debate; there was no sort of agreement as to the right method to be adopted - the Opposition regarded collective defence as the only practical way, and any refusal to take it seriously as a fatal step. In theory, and for election purposes, all parties were at one in accepting the collective system of the League *[of Nations]* but in fact, ever since 1931 the National Government's Foreign Secretaries sabotaged it. The League was an instrument, a piece of machinery, and depended for its effectiveness on the men in charge. The real point is that the Opposition believed both with passion, and in the cold light of reason, that the Covenant could be made to work - the Government never did.

Mr Churchill was certainly the first, the most vehement and the best informed of those who pressed for increased air armaments, and for a time it must be admitted that he had little parliamentary support from any quarter. When it became clear, however, that all the hopes of collective action had finally been abandoned by the Government, and that we were going forward alone, the position changed. Mr Churchill had access to sources of information which proved to be very reliable as to what was going on in Germany and he realised too, much sooner than those outside it, that the Government had no use whatever for the League of Nations as an instrument of practical policy, and that reliance, therefore, would have to be placed mainly on purely national armaments.

A debate on Foreign Affairs, held on 18th May, was reported in The Liberal Magazine.

Mr Mander said: "We are at the parting of the waves in the world today. I was talking only a few days ago to a man who recently made a tour of nearly every capital in Europe, and he discussed with all the leading statesmen and others in different walks of life the one question, 'When is war coming?' They all gave him their view, and they all ended up with this one remark: 'In the long run and in the main it all depends upon what England is going to do.' I hope that this country will make it clear that where ever in the world an aggressor raises a hand the British Government will be there, not alone, but with others, to play their part in striking that hand down."

Geoffrey's travels down the Severn, by boat, with his wife and Richard Acland continued on 26th May, and once again he wrote about it in The Green Can.

A four-oared sculler was transported by lorry from Shrewsbury to a spot on the right bank a few yards above where the waters of the Vyrnwy enter the Severn on the left. The spot is about half-way between Welshpool and Shrewsbury, and is a very suitable distance for a day's row.

The day was beautiful with brilliant sunshine, not too hot, a little wind, and the rise of two or three feet in the river above summer level was sufficient to take us safely over the various places which are otherwise dangerous in the sense that boats are liable to strike stones or stakes and go to the bottom. We reached the most difficult part of the trip at Montford. Here there are three possible ways of passing an island which has a gap in the middle. To keep to the left would involve almost certainly running against a stake from a disused eel weir. To take the middle passage would involve a more or less right-angled turn through a gap in a hedge with a rapid flow of water. The correct course is to keep to the right through the boat pass. This needs careful looking out for. The entrance is marked off by stakes, and involves making a way without much difficulty through two willows that have grown close together across the stream.

During the upper part of the journey the Hereford cattle took an extraordinary interest in our passage and galloped in great excitement along the banks accompanying us as far as they could. The whole journey under the conditions of water we had was really a very agreeable and easy one, and can be strongly recommended.

A letter from three Conservative MPs to The Times, on 7th June 1934, conveys something of the heated political atmosphere existing in parts of London at the time.

We were present at Sir Oswald Mosley's meeting tonight. We make no comment on the policy of the Blackshirt movement, but we think a protest is worth recording at once against the method by which it was sought to maintain order. We were involuntary witnesses of wholly unnecessary violence inflicted by uniformed Blackshirts on interrupters. Men and women were knocked down, and after they had been knocked down, were still assaulted and kicked on the floor. It will be a matter of surprise to us if there were no fatal injuries. These methods of securing freedom of speech may have been effective, but they are happily unusual in England and constitute in our opinion a deplorable outrage on public order.

HANSARD
4th July
ROYAL NAVY.
BRITISH AND FOREIGN SHIPS (INFORMAL VISITS)
Mr Mander asked the First Lord of the Admiralty what visits have been exchanged between the British and foreign navies during the last five years similar to those now in progress with the German Navy?
The First Lord of the Admiralty (Sir Bolton Eyres Monsell): Informal visits are not arranged on any reciprocal basis and there is therefore no exchange of visits in the strict sense of the term. British ships are continually paying

visits to foreign ports, and foreign ships to British Ports, but the number of such visits is so large that I regret it is not possible to supply particulars without causing a disproportionate amount of labour.

Mr Mander: Does not the First Lord feel that it might be desirable, in view of the outbreak of savagery in the last few days in Germany, to postpone this visit for the time being?

Questions on the subject continued and no reply was given to Geoffrey's inquiry.

THE GREEN CAN
Thursday August 16th
BOWLS REPORT
The Annual Friendly Match Between Manders and the Mermaid Bowling Club *[was]* played on the lawn at Wightwick Manor, at the invitation of Mr Geoffrey and Mrs Mander. The weather brightened up considerably by the time Mr Geoffrey and Mr Fox commenced the first of twenty games. In this game Mr Mander had the assistance of his youngest son *[John was two]* and whether this had any bearing on the ultimate result, I can't say, but Mr Fox eventually got the measure of his opponent, and won 15-9. Mrs Mander on the other hand, threw in her lot with "The Mermaid" and opposed to H. Hitchen, lost her game 15-8, without any outside help.

Cutting from THE DAILY SKETCH
21 September 1934
Mr Geoffrey Mander, MP, left London yesterday to attend a meeting of the inter-Parliamentary Union at Istanbul. With him is Mrs Mander.

THE GREEN CAN
November
GREEN CANS ABROAD
By G. Le M. Mander
In the recent tour which my wife and I made across Europe, as far as Constantinople, or as it is now known, Istanbul, we naturally formed all contacts that were possible with firms' representatives, customers and products. We had the pleasure, while the train stopped at Milan for ten minutes, of an agreeable conversation with Mr Sagona, the manager of

our branch there, who very kindly came to the station to see us, and looked in his usual excellent form.

Continuing the journey we at once on arriving in Istanbul got in touch with Messrs. Tucker, who have been our agents there for fifty years, and Mr Thomas Tucker was exceedingly kind in placing himself at our disposal. He was good enough to charter a motor boat and take us out for a trip to Princes Island in the Sea of Marmora, an island inhabited now mainly by Greeks, with a very interesting historic past.

The same morning, I had paid, with Mr Tucker Jr. a visit to several of our customers. All were very pleasant, and as the custom is, offered me cups of Turkish coffee. These, fortunately, are in very small cups and well sweetened, but the coffee is very strong, and after that morning's work I vowed I would never touch coffee again.

The great difficulty about doing business in Turkey now is that the Turkish Government under the dictatorship of that most remarkable personality, Mustafa Kemal Pasha, who has revolutionised the whole country, are insisting on agreements with all countries involving an exact balance of trade, and this is to be obtained by clearing arrangements which involve payment of money into a central bank. England has not got one, though negotiations are taking place at the present time. Other countries that have made such agreements are regretting having done so, because they find that they are supplying goods for which they cannot obtain payment. The choice in a sense seems to be between doing no business at all, and supplying goods for which no payment is received. However some time or other presumably a scheme not quite so idiotic will be evolved.

The next contact was with our agent in Prague, Mr Janour, who also is handicapped by trade restrictions, in this case taking the form of quotas. I took certain steps which may enable us to get some goods through, and the position generally seems to be somewhat easier. Mr Janour is in the cycle trade. He sells bicycles sent in from France and other countries. Some of them he puts together himself and varnishes. He also sells toy motor-cars for children. Cellulose is everywhere used for ordinary motor-cars abroad, and the best outlook for our products seems to be industrially-scientific instruments, cinemas, cycles, etc.

It is lamentable to note the tremendous obstacles still being placed throughout Europe by all countries against doing trade with each other, and the sooner this tendency is reversed the better it will be for all.

HANSARD

13 December

GERMANY

Mr Mander asked the President of the Board of Trade what steps he proposes to help traders in this country in view of the recent practice of the German Government in consenting to transactions between this country and Germany on the basis of exchange of goods and then withdrawing the consent to receive the British goods after the German goods have been dispatched and insisting on cash for goods bought from Germany while payment for goods sold to Germany is held in the State bank?

Mr Runciman: I have no information as to the practice described by the Hon. Member, but if he will let me have particulars of the transactions to which he refers I shall be glad to have the matter looked into.

GERMAN NAVY (NEW CONSTRUCTION)

Mr Mander asked the First Lord of the Admiralty when he first received information with regard to the launch at Kiel on 8th December of the German cruiser Nurnberg, which was not listed as building or projected in the official return of fleets as on 1st February 1934; and if he has any information with regard to the two German warships "Saar" and "Tsingtau," recently completed at Kiel and Hamburg, whether they are seaplane carriers or in what category of ships allowed to Germany in the Treaty of Versailles they are included?

The First Lord of the Admiralty (Sir Bolton Eyres Monsell): Official information that the "Nurnberg" was included in the construction to be put in hand this year was received on the 9th April last, and information that she would be launched in December was received on the 2nd October. According to the information available, the "Saar" and "Tsingtau" are auxiliary vessels used as depot ships for minesweepers and patrol vessels and are unarmed. There is no information that they are designed as seaplane carriers.

HANSARD

18 December

This debate, on the draft Unemployment Assistance Act, lasted over seven hours.

Mr Mander: The Hon. Member for Stirling and Falkirk (Mr. J. Reid) referred to the question of the relation of wage rates to the assistance that is to be given. He asked whether we were going to subsidise wages, but that does not seem to me to be the alternative. The real alternative is not to subsidise wages, but to take such State action as you can in the lower-paid trades to raise wages to a very much higher level.

I have seen some references to the special allowances that are to be made for clothing for those who have to keep up a smart appearance - teachers, shop assistants and clerks. No doubt that is a very sound principle, but there is an even stronger point to be made from the point of view of the working man. Because of the heavy work that he has to do, his clothes wear out very much more quickly than the clothes of the other classes to which I have referred, and I hope that if the extra allowances for clothing are going to be made, full allowances will be made with regard to the clothes of working men. For instance, moulders require very strong boots, overalls and things of that kind. In the long run, the clothing of working men costs more than the clothing of the teacher or the clerk. I hope that the regulations will be rejected. At any rate, I shall vote against them.

The following day the debate continued and late in the evening it was approved by a majority that did not include Geoffrey.

At the end of 1934 there were skirmishes between Italy and Abyssinia along the Abyssinian border and in January 1935 Emperor Haile Selassie appealed to the League of Nations for help against Italian aggression in North Africa.

THE LIBERAL MAGAZINE reported a debate on the Supplementary Estimate for the Unemployment Assistance Board, following the one held on 18th December on the draft Unemployment Assistant Act. This time the debate lasted two days and members from all parties again criticised the Assistance Regulations as being full of anomalies and likely to cause considerable hardships.

> Mr Mander: Many people who were bitter critics of the public assistance scale are now obliged to say that it was a model of generosity compared with the treatment that is being received today. Making all allowances possible, it seems incredible that the Minister could have intended reductions on that scale to take place when the previous scale was already low enough.
>
> Sir Percy Harris: Yesterday I came across a case of an old age pensioner, a widower, living with his son who was also a widower. He had from the public assistance committee an addition of 5s. 3d. to enable him to make his contribution to the home. Under the new Regulations that 5s. 3d. has had to go. The son, who is aged fifty seven, finds his income reduced because the old age pensioner is living with him. The old man said he had no alternative but to go to the workhouse and no longer be an embarrassment to his son.

There was a discussion in Parliament on 19th February on Air Defence Measures. Geoffrey wanted to know whether the War Office supported various schemes put forward by the Red Cross and other organisations to provide help to the public in case of enemy gas attacks. He asked also if results on experiments in the East End to make houses proof against aerial gas attack could be announced. The Prime Minister, Ramsay Macdonald, said that discussions were being held on the subject of help for the public but no experiments had been carried out to make houses proof against gas attack.

Between 18th February and 8th March 1935 Hansard records seven occasions on which Geoffrey harried the Government about what he saw as their reluctance to support international inspection of armament factories and on 5th March, after an ambiguous answer to his latest question, he stated, "In view of the unsatisfactory nature of the reply, I beg to give notice that I shall raise this matter on adjournment at the earliest possible moment".

That evening he returned again to the same question.

> I desire to call attention to the situation at the meeting of the Commission of the Disarmament Convention at Geneva which is dealing with the American draft proposals on the manufacture and trade in arms, and the information disclosed as to the attitude of the representative of the British Government. When the Debates took place in this House in December last, the Government gave us every reason to believe that the representatives of the British Government were going out to Geneva full of enthusiasm and determination to play a leading part in supporting the American Government in order to make a real success of their proposals. It is, therefore, very disappointing to find that quite a different situation has actually developed during the past two weeks.
>
> Lord Stanhope put forward certain proposals that are a definite improvement on the present draft but apart from that, his whole effort seems to have been to weaken and remove useful points and to whittle away the main advantages of the scheme.
>
> The seriousness of the position lies in the fact that the United States Government, not always co-operating in the most useful way, have on this occasion taken an admirable initiative at Geneva and are doing their best to put an agreement through.

After Geoffrey had spoken for about nine minutes, the Lord Privy Seal (Anthony Eden) replied with a speech that was just as long. The Liberals were not impressed by his answer and the last word came from their leader Sir Herbert Samuel who stated:

> The fact that His Majesty's Government are only supported by Italy and Poland among the nations and that we are taking a directly opposite

attitude from that of the United States and many other Powers, is in itself rather significant that His Majesty's Government are not necessarily in the right in this matter.

Letters to Geoffrey in the Wightwick archives at this time include one of thanks from Antony Eden for a letter of appreciation, another from Geneva about a League of Nations flag and several communications from Sir John Simon when he was deputy leader of the House of Commons in the Conservative government. Before this he was the Foreign Secretary in the coalition government.

WE WERE NOT ALL WRONG

It is widely held that Lord Simon, although possessing one of the acutest legal minds in Europe and consummate gifts of advocacy, was, in fact, the worst Foreign Secretary since Ethelred the Unready - though this, I have always considered, is hardly fair to Ethelred.

Ernest Bevin had spoken about Lord Simon, before this, in 1933:

"A petulant Foreign Secretary is a very dangerous person for the country to possess, for it must be remembered that the Foreign Secretary wields powers probably greater than that of any Minister in the country."

THE LIBERAL MAGAZINE reported Geoffrey's views on Collective Security:

Suggestions from time to time by the Foreign Secretary have created the impression abroad that England could not be relied upon to play her part in bringing about collective security. I can conceive that if more than a year ago, at the beginning of the Nazi regime, firm language, followed if necessary by strong action, had been used in co-operation with other countries it might have been a wise thing to do. There are, however, times and occasions for all things, and to bring forward a critical and, up to a point, offensive, though true, document at the very moment when the Foreign Secretary was going to Berlin to try by conciliation and good will to get agreement is surely the worst possible tactics, for it was bound to hit Germany on the raw.

THE GREEN CAN

On April 1st Mr Mervyn Caverhill Mander became a Director of the Firm, and so becomes the first of the 6th generation to be associated with the conduct of the business. During the last two and a half years he has been working in different departments of the business, and is well known to most of the employees of the Company. We wish him every success in his new responsibilities.

A dinner was held at Wightwick at the end of May to celebrate Mervyn's election to Mander Brothers' board.

HANSARD

19th June 1935

GERMANY: HERR HITLER'S SPEECH

Mr Mander asked the Secretary of State for Foreign Affairs whether a reply has been received to the seven questions recently put to the German Government through diplomatic channels, with a view to getting some precise information on some of the points raised in Herr Hitler's speech of 21st May; and whether the questions and answers can now be published?

Sir S. Hoare: His Majesty's Government have in fact asked for elucidations of a number of points raised in the speech in question, but the replies which they have received have not yet brought matters to a point where they could suitably be made public.

On 21st May Hitler brought in general conscription; this followed his announcement in March that Germany would be expanding the German army to six times the number stipulated in the Treaty of Versailles. He proposed to introduce an air force and to increase the size of the navy. Assaults and boycotts against Jews in Germany also increased in the spring of 1935.

HANSARD

19th June

LEAGUE OF NATIONS (BRITISH DELEGATION)

Mr Mander asked the Prime Minister [Stanley Baldwin] who will compose the British delegation to the meeting of the Assembly of the League of Nations this year; and whether he will consider the advisability, in view of the seriousness of the international situation, of himself heading it for a period?

The Prime Minister: I hope to be in a position to make an announcement shortly.

Mr Mander: May I ask whether the suggestion made in the question will be considered?

The Prime Minister: Any suggestion made by the Hon. Member will be considered.

This extract comes from a debate on foreign policy held in Committee and full of long speeches, it started at 3.41 pm and ended with the last speech at 10.13 pm.

Mr Mander: In the very grave situation in which we find ourselves today I think that many people are being driven more and more to the conclusion that we shall have to adopt something in the nature of an international police force under the League of Nations. If the present Abyssinian dispute were to pass without this country or the League of Nations making any attempt to make the Covenant work there would be a tremendous revulsion of feeling against the Government. At the same time, I know that we cannot possibly act alone, we have merely to carry out our obligations as a member of the League.

A report in THE GREEN CAN by Geoffrey.

NAVAL REVIEW AT SPITHEAD

I have never attended a naval review before, but this unique occasion seemed too good a one to be missed, as there was an opportunity of seeing at one time something like eighty per cent of the whole British fleet.

On arrival from London, my wife and I went on board the "Southsea," a paddle steamer which had been retained, together with the much larger hospital ship, the "Maine," for Members of Parliament, Ambassadors, Delegates from the Dominions and others. The members of the cabinet itself went on the Admiralty yacht "Enchantress."

We left at 1.50 to take up our station, and shortly afterwards the royal yacht "Victoria and Albert" arrived with the King and Queen on board. Some time was now occupied by visits from the various admirals in their barges to the King's yacht. The weather was delightful throughout, with sunshine and just sufficient breeze to make the heat bearable. Most of us being known to each other, we had little difficulty in filling up the time, some few, including a lady and a member of the Government, taking advantage of the wait to dive in either from the ship's side of from the boats higher up to enjoy a swim. The King then proceeded between two lines of battleships from one end to the other and back between other lines, and we followed about a mile in the rear. The ships looked magnificent, the Home Fleet being painted light grey and the Mediterranean Fleet dark grey, and no doubt Mander Brothers' products played their part in producing a most attractive result.

Towards 7 o'clock we steamed back to the main line, and in accordance with instructions went on board "Maine" for dinner. We had time before returning to the "Southsea" to pay a visit to Nelson's ship, the "Victory"which was lying quite close.

The illuminations began at 10pm with a simultaneous illumination by electric lights in outline of the whole fleet. At intervals there were brilliant firework displays, and one very attractive effect was obtained when every man throughout the fleet appeared to be holding a red light, all being extinguished at the same moment.

We reached port again shortly before midnight, and arrived in London, after a wonderful day, at 2am.

Some of my friends asked me why I was interested to see the Fleet, in view of my well known interest in peace. My reply was that I looked upon the Fleet as potentially a most effective contingent of an International Police Force under the League of Nations for the maintenance of world order.

In 1935 the Flying Log Book records seventeen days of travel in Europe for Geoffrey and his wife, starting from Croydon in August and including Malmo, Stockholm, Riga, Berlin and Bremen. Geoffrey wrote, yet again, an account of his travels for The Green Can.

> From Malmo to Stockholm the journey was made by a night train. Stockholm on Sunday in the rain is not an exciting place, but we paid a visit to one of the wonders of the world, the new Town Hall, and met Canon Carnegie, the Speaker's Chaplain, who was paying a visit to these parts.

They travelled by seaplane to Estonia and after a few days carried on to Riga, where:

The most interesting event in which we took part here was a picnic organised by the Prime Minister, Mr Ulmanis, at which the Ministers and Diplomatic Corps were present. It took place at the opening of a new factory for curing lampreys (none of us could remember which English king died of a surfeit of these) and the tables were loaded, in addition to lampreys in every conceivable form - hot, cold, soup, etc. with every known luxury both to eat and drink. After this we proceeded in small motor fishing boats through the lakes around, and landed on an island, where bonfires were burning, and many tables again groaning with the aforesaid luxuries.

A few days later they had lunch, arranged by the British Consul, with Mander Brothers' local agent and after an odd conversation about business, during which neither man understood the other, eventually it was discovered that Geoffrey was talking to the wrong man who had the same, common, name.

They travelled to Kaunas, the capital of Lithuania, and they were driven round by the American born head of the Press Bureau in the Foreign Office there.

She was good enough to take us the next day for a long motor run along the strip of silver sand about a mile wide by forty miles long which runs in front of the port of Memel towards Konigsberg. There are huge sand dunes used for skiing in the winter, but most of them are covered with fir trees. On this strip also is one of the few places where elks abound and we saw ten on the journey.

They spent some time in Berlin and then arrived in Bremen to catch their ship home.

The sailing time turned out to be 12.00 instead of 2.00 as we had been told, and the boat train had gone, so the only thing to do was to taxi thirty five miles, and we caught the boat with quarter of an hour to spare.

Mervyn's engagement to Elizabeth Mettlich, a translator from Cologne, was announced in August.

Mussolini stated in August that he would settle the Abyssinian dispute by force not negotiation. A few weeks later Ramsay Macdonald, Lord President of the Council stated: "Britain and Italy are friends and have no jealousies and no rivalries."

In September both Mussolini and the Abyssinian Emperor Haile Selassie rejected a League of Nations peace plan and on 3rd September the Italian army invaded Abyssinia, forcing Haile Selassie into hiding then, months later, into exile.

In October 1935 Geoffrey spoke in a parliamentary debate on the International Situation.

> I hope that we shall not come to the position in which the only sanctions to be applied are those which are satisfactory to and are agreed to by Signor Mussolini. From the quotation given by the Secretary of State it seemed to me that he almost envisaged that situation. Surely the sanctions that we ought to have in operation are those which Signor Mussolini does not like. That is the only kind that will be effective. It has been made quite clear that France is unwilling to cooperate with us in any circumstances in the application of a sanction of that kind. The duty is incumbent upon us to put France up against it, to make her choose every time whether she is going to rely on Italy or on Great Britain and the League of Nations. If that is done she is bound to come down every time on the side of the League.

A long article about Geoffrey was printed in the Wolverhampton Express and Star on October 15 1935 as part of a series, "Midland Portraits." It covered his family background and education

> Eldest son of the late Mr. S. Theodore Mander, he was born on March 6th 1882 and educated at Harrow and Trinity College, Cambridge. He is a barrister-at-law of the Inner Temple and has filled many important posts in Staffordshire, having been the High Sheriff of the county in 1921.

It listed his political interests:

> He has achieved national fame for the pertinent questions he asks in the House of Commons. As he has made a close study for many years of foreign affairs and is one of the ablest and most knowledgeable MPs on this aspect of politics, it is only natural that many of his questions should be devoted to the problems of the League of Nations, peace and disarmament. He takes great interest in any movement calculated to foster peace in industry and good relations between employer and employed. He is also deeply concerned in anything that affects the lives of his constituents, regardless of party, whether it be pigeon-flying, bowls, billiards, allotments, the

British Legion, football or cricket, or the more serious affairs of life. Mr Mander has an original turn of mind, which has expressed itself in his political activities and in his recreation. He once made a tour of the canals in his constituency in an ordinary horse-drawn barge in order to study the possibilities of national development.

After mentioning that his favourite poet was Browning and that he enjoyed the cinema - particularly "The Mystery of the Wax Museum" - the article ended with a paragraph about his second marriage and the birth of John and then concluded:

Mr Mander is genial and altogether charming to meet. He is a fluent conversationalist who can talk interestingly and instructively on a wide variety of topics, and is one of the best public speakers representing the Midlands in Parliament today."

On 29th October, Mervyn married Elizabeth Mettlich in Cologne.

A BACK-BENCHER LOOKS BACK

Mr Baldwin started off his election campaign in 1935 at a great meeting in Wolverhampton over which my cousin, Sir Charles Mander, presided. He told me afterwards that while they were chatting together before hand, Mr Baldwin asked him if there was anything in particular he would like him to say and that he had said "say something about Geoffrey." This he proceeded to do in no uncertain terms, the first passages of his speech were as follows:

"I would observe - and it comes to my mind because Sir Charles Mander is in the chair - that his name is not the only association I have with that of Mander. There is a representative in the House of Commons, a personal friend of mine, as many are on the other side to myself, but one in whom all the inquisitiveness of the Manders for the last twenty generations is centred. (Laughter.) When the House of Commons is sitting, my first duty every morning is to look at the Order paper and run through the questions to be asked in Parliament that day and if there be something over which I have tried to draw a curtain of reserve and decency, Geoffrey Mander will tear it on one side and he will tread, honestly and conscientiously, on every corn from China to Peru." (Laughter.)

After the General Election, the first time I saw the Prime Minister in the

Lobby, he asked me what I thought of his speech at Wolverhampton. I replied that it had done me a lot of good on which he commented that he had not thought it would do me much harm.

In the 1935 election the Liberal party returned only twenty one MPs. Thirty three members of the Liberal National party formed part of the new government together with representatives from the National Labour and Independent National parties. The opposition was made up from Labour, Liberals, Independent Labour, the Independents and one Communist. Sir Herbert Samuel lost his seat, and his position as leader of the Liberals was taken over by Sir Archibald Sinclair.

36 Porchester Terrace.
W2
Nov 15 1935
My dear Mander,
I cannot tell you how glad I am about your victory *[in the general election in September]*. It shines out the more brilliantly in the general gloom. You have saved the great tradition of Wolverhampton from being lost and you have kept your own opportunity to speak out clearly in the House of Commons, as you always do, on behalf of peace and progress. And the neat majority of just 4,000! It recalls Lord Showell's description of "the elegant simplicity of the three per cents."
To your wife a very great share of the credit of the victory belongs. I congratulate you both most warmly. And let me thank you for your unwavering and energetic support through this last Parliament. I have always greatly admired the tenacity with which you have held to your course in spite of any opposition - a quality not often found in the House of Commons and one that will continue to make you so useful to the State.
Yours always,
Herbert Samuel
Herbert Samuel was created 1st Viscount Samuel in 1937 and led the Liberals in the House of Lords from 1944 to 1955.
He died in 1963.

THE LIBERAL MAGAZINE
Notes of the Month
THE GENERAL ELECTION
In view of the peculiar handicaps of Liberal candidates in such an election
- such as condemning and supporting the Government at the same time,
though on different grounds - few people of experience expected better
results. The fall from thirty members in the last Parliament to twenty-
one in this is not spectacular. Much more serious is the defeat of such
trusted leaders as Sir Herbert Samuel, Mr Isaac Foot, Sir Walter Rea, Mr
Harcourt Johnstone and Sir Robert Hamilton.

The Party is fortunate in having still in Parliament a group of experienced
and able men to carry on the work, and it will give great satisfaction that
Sir Archibald Sinclair has been elected Chairman of the Party and Sir
Percy Harris,Chief Whip.

THE GREEN CAN
November 1935
CAN ANYONE BEAT THIS?
(We think the following correspondence which has recently taken place
in the Oil and Colour Trades Journal may be of interest to our readers -
Editor.)

Mr Llewellyn Winter Ryland, whose engagement was recently announced,
represents the fifth generation in the well known paint and varnish firm
of Llewellyn Ryland Ltd. A friend asks: "Is this a record?" We don't know,
but it is very interesting. Can anyone beat it?

Yes sirs, we can beat it. My son, Mr Mervyn Caverhill Mander, recently
became a director of this firm, and he is the sixth generation in a direct line
from his great-great-great-grandfather, Benjamin Mander, who founded
the firm in 1792.
Can anyone beat this?
Yours etc.
Geoffrey Le M. Mander
Chairman.

Sirs - In reference to Mr Mander's letter I would like to say that while we cannot at present beat Messrs. Mander's record we can certainly equal it. My son's great-great-great-grandfather, Edward Thornley, was burnt to death while varnish making. He was probably engaged in research in an endeavour to beat Mr. Benjamin Mander.

Yours etc.

Thornley & Knight, Ltd

K. Thornley,

Director

THE GREEN CAN

VOL. IX.   JANUARY, 1929.   No. 1.

Published Monthly for circulation amongst those associated with the Firm of MANDER BROTHERS, LTD., and the Green Can Products of their Varnish, Paint and Ink Business, at home and abroad.

Subscription Rates:
ON THE WORKS   -   3/- PER YEAR.
BY POST   -   -   -   5/-   ,,

Contributions on all topics of interest are invited. A nom-de-plume may be used but the name of the contributor must be submitted to the Editor.
Correspondence and all Subscriptions should be addressed—
"THE EDITOR,"
MANDER BROTHERS, LTD.,
WOLVERHAMPTON.

CANNED TOPICS.

A LECTURE was given in Birmingham on December 14th by Mr. L. A. Jordan, D.Sc., A.R.C.Sc., F.I.C., Director of the Research Association of British Paint, Colour and Varnish Manufacturers, Research Station, Teddington, on his recent visit to America, where he went over many of the Paint and Varnish factories and obtained much valuable information relative to the manufacture of varnishes and paints.   Among those who attended were Dr. Smyth, Mr. C. H. Dunkley and Mr. Wornum.

*   *   *   *   *   *

WILL all readers wishing to have their 1928 copies of "The Green Can" bound let the Editors have them as soon as possible.

*   *   *   *   *   *

On Thursday, January 10th, Madam Parkes Darby is giving a "Dinner Time Talk" on music in the Girls' Mess Room, Heath Town. We feel sure that this will be interesting, and we invite all the girls who stay dinner to attend. If this "Dinner Time Talk" proves successful, as we feel sure it will, further similar talks on interesting subjects may be arranged. We ask the girls at Heath Town to put forward suggestions on what subjects they would like.

A Happy and Prosperous N[...]

We offer our congratulations to N. A. Fanshawe (aged 17), brother to Miss Fanshawe (G.O.), scholar at Wolverhampton Grammar School, who has won the Ogsen Rhondda Scholarship value £100 per annum at Gonville and Caius College, Cambridge.   This is his third success, as previously in May he won the Borough Mayor Scholarship value £50 per annum, and in July the State Scholarship value £80 per annum.

*   *   *   *   *   *

A Joint Conference between the Boards and Management of Mander Brothers, Ltd., and W. S. Low, Ltd., and the Managers and Travellers from the branches of W. S. Low, Ltd., took place in John Street, Wolverhampton, on December 13th, in order that the policy of the firms might be made clear to all.   The deliberations proceeded throughout the day, and a very useful exchange of ideas took place. The party, numbering about 40, took lunch at the Star and Garter Hotel, Mr. Geoffrey Mander presiding at one end of a long table and Mr. W. S. Low at the other.   Mr. F. E. Webb, Managing Director of Aerostyle, Ltd., was also present.

*   *   *   *   *   *

The Annual Meeting of W. S. Low, Ltd., was held in John Street, Wolverhampton, on December 4th.   Mr. W. S. Low (Chairman),

Title page of The Green Can Magazine from 1929...

...and a cover from 1954.

The Green Can

THE HOUSE JOURNAL OF

MANDER BROTHERS LTD.

AUGUST . 1954   Vol. XXXIV   No. 8

1936

On 20th January 1936 George V died. He was interred in the crypt of St George's Chapel, Windsor on 28th January and the following day a leader in the Daily Mail headed "The New Reign." contained the following observations:

> As the coffin went by, drawn by the naval ratings in their dark uniforms, all eyes were turned on the figure of King Edward. All hearts were filled with sympathy for him in the tremendous task which awaits him. Fortunate indeed are we in the fact that so great a son succeeds so great a father. It is to him that the nation now looks with such proud confidence and faith in his leadership.

In February, The Green Can published an account of the funeral by Charles Marcus Mander who was 14 and at Eton. He was the son of Geoffrey's cousin Sir Charles Arthur Mander.

> The whole school walked up to Windsor and we had a wonderful view. We saw everybody, about within touching distance, the poor King, who looked terribly haggard and was biting his lip, walking behind the gun carriage. There were twenty six Princes, and five Kings who were behind Princes George, Henry and Albert. I doubt if I shall ever again see so many of the world's most important men all at the same time.

The Liberal Magazine reported a debate that took place on February 24th on Foreign Affairs. Sir Archibald Sinclair felt that the declarations of the Government had been weak and the League of Nations was now joined in a life-and-death struggle with an aggressor State. Signor Mussolini and others of like mind must be convinced that the League means to stamp out war as a crime against civilisation.

> Sir Archibald asked: Had the present sanctions prevented the despatch of a single Italian soldier or tank or gun, or of a single shell or aeroplane to destroy the independence of Abyssinia and the lives of Abyssinian soldiers, women and children and Red Cross workers?
> Mr Geoffrey Mander said that if they came to a state of affairs when the

League looked like being defeated, there was one way left, which would be effective tomorrow if it were applied: that was by cutting communications between Italy and Africa and preventing Italian ships and munitions of war going steadily forward to carry out their diabolical work in Abyssinia.

WE WERE NOT ALL WRONG

It is significant that Mr Dalton on March 9th stressed the importance of defence against air raids and regretted the lamentable slowness of the Government in dealing with the problem. The Labour Party were deeply interested in the technical questions involved. He said: "They (the Government) do not accept the doctrine that the bomber can always get through, and they are spending large sums of money and undertaking much research in order to defend their populations by other means - by placing in the sky wires, kite balloons, and so on we are entitled to know, are the Government bending all their energies to a consideration of the defence of London and of the population of other great cities. If the Government take the view still that there is no defence except counter-attack, then I submit that they should already be evacuating London. If on the other hand they believe that it is possible to develop other methods of defence, then they should be spending money like water; or the defence of these populations where they are massed together, as they are in what, if they cannot be defended, will be death traps on a gigantic scale."

HANSARD

30th March 1936

Mr Mander asked the Secretary of State for Foreign Affairs *[Anthony Eden]* why the French Government have refused permission to the Abyssinian Government to import arms by the Jibuti Railway; and whether, in view of the terms of the agreement, he will make representations on this subject to the French Government.

Mr Eden: I am not certain to what agreement the Hon. Member refers, but I cannot in any event undertake to answer for the action of a foreign Government

Mr Mander: Would it not be a breach of the sanctions policy agreed upon by the League to prevent munitions going by the Jibuti Railway?

Mr Eden: I do not think it can be so described.

Mr Mander asked what action is being taken by the Government alone or through the League of Nations to protest against and prevent the Italian bombing of Red Cross hospitals and the use of poison gas, contrary to the 1925 protocol?

HANSARD

1st April 1936.

Anthony Eden, Secretary of State for Foreign Affairs, reported on the Italian air bombardment of the Abyssinian town of Harar on 29th March:

The raid had been carried out by 18 Italian aircraft in all approximately three hundred bombs fell in the town. Three bombs fell on the Swedish Mission compound, fifty in that of the Egyptian Red Cross, fourteen on the Catholic Mission, four on the French hospital and Agency and four on the Harar Red Cross, the telephone lines to the British Consulate damaged; the Catholic church and the Abyssinian church of St Xavier were also badly damaged.

In May the war between Abyssinia and Italy ended with the Italian occupation of Addis Ababa.

THE GREEN CAN.

May

THE LONDON DEPOT DINNER

This year's dinner took place, not at a restaurant, but in the august precincts of the Palace of Westminster itself. This unique privilege we must owe to Mr Geoffrey, on whom be all praise.

The setting was delightful. We numbered between forty and fifty, and dined in a long room, giving on to the famous terrace. The last rays of evening were gilding the vane on the Lollard's Tower. The red-brown sail of a barge going down with the tide - a flutter of pigeons, and the powder-blue of the sunset sky, filled out a charming picture.

In May Geoffrey wrote an article on Rearmament for the "Contemporary Review"

Most people will feel, and it is perfectly true, that in a world that is rapidly rearming, and which possesses an almost self-designated aggressor in the person of Germany, rearming more vigorously than all, it is necessary for this country not to be left behind in so deplorable a race, and that any contribution made by us to the maintenance of world order through the collective system must be worthy of, and on a scale consistent with, our great position.

It has been made clear that the Government have no intention of consulting other nations on this subject. This means that each country will remain the sole individual judge of what share it should take in the collective system. Such a situation is little more than the pre-war system of purely national rearmament. I do not believe that the people of this country will ever be prepared to enter into the old-fashioned, obsolete, all-against-all war of the 1914 type, but I do believe they would respond and risk all if it were clear that they were making sacrifices for the organised maintenance of world peace through the League of Nations, and that every alternative had been exhausted.

What causes one to doubt the sincerity of the Government is the fact that in the one practical test that has been available, the Italo-Ethiopian dispute, they have consistently repudiated with horror the suggestion that in any circumstances would they take action which might involve the use of the armed forces of the Crown. Such a risk must be taken if we really mean to make the League triumph over the aggressor now, and so go a very long way towards making certain that force on a vastly larger scale will not have to be used a few years hence.

Extract from a letter sent to Geoffrey from the Ethiopian Minister at the Ethiopian Legation in London on 2nd June 1936

Thanks very much for your letter of the 30th and for the enquiries you very kindly made. I am very grateful for your kind offer to help me and I shall be glad to see you and consult with you when you are able to give me an opportunity.

A BACK-BENCHER LOOKS BACK

One upshot of my constant attacks on the Dictators was that Mussolini took reprisals against my business. My firm held the Warrant of Appointment to the King of Italy as suppliers of varnishes and Mussolini took this away from the Company, stating it was all very well for me to attack him while, at the same time, I was making a large fortune out of my "paint shop" in Milan - actually quite an unprofitable business.

By the summer of 1936,when Geoffrey Mander was fifty four, he was coping with a prodigious level of work.. Between March 16th and April 9th, he contributed to thirty four Parliamentary debates, he attended meetings of Mander Brothers Works Council as President of the Welfare Club, he directed the Annual General Meeting in Wolverhampton and still continued to write innumerable letters on various subjects that interested him. He produced newspaper articles and wrote for the Green Can and other magazines - the April issue of "Printing" contained his "Statutory Force for Wage Agreements" which the editorial described as "a lucid summary of the recent history of this question".

On 11th July Geoffrey and his wife gave a Garden Party at Wightwick Manor for Mander Brothers employees. It was held to celebrate the marriage and entrance into the Firm of Geoffrey's son Mervyn and was reported in The Green Can magazine. Various games and races were organised including musical chairs, bowls and a baffling "tree-pot event," during which, apparently, the men had an advantage over the women: "we wondered whether this was due to the size of their shoes?" Tea was served in the house and the day was rounded off with a concert in the Great Parlour.

In July the civil war broke out in Spain between, on one side, republicans, socialists and communists supported by Western volunteers and opposing them the monarchists backed by the church, led by General Franco and supported by Germany, Italy and Portugal.

In July Geoffrey was helping Mavis to gather evidence for a divorce.

Foreign Office,
S.W.1
27th July 1936
Dear Mander,
Thank you for your letter of July 24th, telling me of your forthcoming visit to Russia *[in September]* I am arranging for Lord Chilston, the

Ambassador in Moscow, to be told your plans, and I am sure that he will be very glad to do whatever he can to help you when you are in Moscow. I am also asking him to warn Mr. Gilliat-Smith, the Consul-General at Leningrad, that you will shortly be visiting that city. I am afraid, however, that we have no consular officers at Kieff or Kharkoff.

I hope you will have an interesting journey.

Yours sincerely,

Antony Eden.

THE LIBERAL MAGAZINE

August 1936

Mr Geoffrey Mander, referring to a recent remark that war is inevitable said: "War is inevitable if the policy of the present Government is maintained unchanged, a policy of weakness, irresolution, failing to carry out our obligations, treachery and cowardice. That means certain war in the world. War is not inevitable and can be prevented. I press upon the Government most earnestly, that, even at this late hour, they should see how far it may be possible, by consulting the leaders of the other parties, to arrive at an agreed programme of Defence and for peace and security."

On August 5th Geoffrey and his wife received an invitation from Charles Trevelyan to stay at Wallington for the night while they were visiting Newcastle. Both Wightwick and Wallington have decorative associations with the Pre-Raphaelites and their friends; there are wall paintings at Wallington by William Bell Scott. During his political career Charles Trevelyan sat first as a Liberal and then as a Socialist MP He was twice President of the Board of Education but the loss of his seat in 1931 ended his political career. He gave Wallington to the National Trust in 1941.

At the end of August Geoffrey continued to travel. He and his wife spent a holiday in the Channel Islands, flying from Southampton to Alderney. A few days later they flew from Alderney to Jersey and landed on the beach. Three days after returning from that holiday they set off again for Brussels where they stayed for two nights and returned to Croydon airport on 5th September.

On 27th September Geoffrey recorded in the flying log book that he and his wife travelled to Moscow and Danzig

An account of the visit to Russia by Geoffrey and his wife was published in The Green Can:

In discussing what my wife and I saw during a recent trip to Russia, when we visited Leningrad and Moscow, I will confine myself to matters that are most directly concerned with the sort of experience we have here.

Men and women under the Soviet regime are treated on a complete equality as regards pay and in other respects too. There is no unemployment, and it's quite usual for both husbands and wives to be at work. If this were not so, many of them would find it difficult to carry on with the low wages earned. This necessitates arrangements for dealing with the children, and at all factories there is a crèche where mothers can leave their children when they come to work, confident that they will be looked after, fed, educated or amused during the day. There were plenty of small beds available for the children to rest. The same system is in operation in railway stations. It is found very convenient by mothers who want to be free to go about the town, see friends or do some shopping. The only payment is a moderate sum for meals.

I wanted to see a factory similar to the one I am familiar with in Wolverhampton, and asked to be allowed to see a paint works. After a few days I was informed that this was not practicable, as the factory was being reconstructed. I said I supposed that meant they did not wish me to see it. They protested that this was quite untrue. I then pressed to be allowed to see a printing ink factory, and on the day before I left arrangements were made for this.

In describing the factory visit he includes a lot of technical information that the readers of The Green Can would understand, while in between he also wrote about the Soviet attitudes to work and efficiency that were so noticeable to a Western visitor.

In various parts of the works, slogans, in the form of broad streamers, were posted up, such as: "Let all Youth rally round the Soviet Power and bring life to USSR." and again: "Greetings to the Revolutionary Youth of all countries. Long life to International Communist Workers."

A deputation of three are coming over to England in the course of a few months to study the latest methods and exchange experiences. The Director who so very kindly showed me round these works will be one of the deputation, and I invited him to come to Wolverhampton and see what we were doing here. When I told him about some of the developments connected with Mander Brothers, such as the Works Council, he was very surprised to learn that anything of the kind existed in England. I had to explain, however, that it was rather exceptional.

The arrangements for the holiday were admirably carried out by Intourist Ltd. We went on a Soviet boat from London to Leningrad through the Kiel Canal, in four and a half days, spent three days in Leningrad, a week in Moscow, and then flew from Moscow to Danzig. We came back by the "S.S. Baltrova" through the Kiel Canal again to London.

THE GREEN CAN

Our thanks are due to Mr Geoffrey for the turf from the lawns at Wightwick Manor which he has very kindly given to the Sports Club. The turf will be of the greatest use this Autumn and Winter for patching the Bowling Greens, and the Cricket Pitch, after the very wet summer we have had.

In London in October 1936 thousands of people clashed with the supporters of Oswald Mosley and the British Fascists.

At the same time as the unrest in the south, thousands of people from the north east began to march from Jarrow to London to protest against unemployment.

The Liberal Magazine printed the unemployment figures for 1936 from "various sources" and at the time of the Jarrow marches, the number of unemployed was 1,611,810.

On the opening of Parliament, on November 3rd, the King's speech included the statement:

The policy of my Government continues to be based upon membership of the League of Nations. They desire to see the League strengthened for its work in the pacific settlement of international disputes, and they have already made known at Geneva their proposals for the improved working and wider authority of the League. My Government will do all in their power to further the appeasement of Europe.

In the debate following the Address, not surprisingly, Geoffrey spoke on rearmament and collective security. His speech was reported in The Liberal Magazine.

Mr Geoffrey Mander said that in so far as Mr Eden was striving to carry into practice his proposals for making the League more effective he would have the support of the Liberal party. They had voted for the rearmament programme in the belief that we as a country play our part in collective security, but at the same time they were profoundly distrustful of the purposes for which the Government might be going to use those arms. They were wholly unconvinced that the Government had any real belief in the system of collective security. It had to be recognised that the Powers were no longer prepared to base the safety of their countries on the collective system of the League. Since the episode of Abyssinia all confidence had gone. Mr Mander said: "I have been at some pains to find out facts concerning the position of our young people of military age, to whom it is desired to appeal with regard to recruiting. As far as I can ascertain, they are divided into three classes. There are those who say they will fight whenever they are called upon to do so by King and country. There are those who say they will not fight in any circumstances. Then there are those who say they do not want to fight, but if it is for something worth while - the League of Nations, which will give security and peace to the world - they are quite prepared to do so. The policy of the Government is driving large numbers of enthusiastic supporters of the collective system - who would fight for it - into the ranks of those who say they will not fight in any circumstances. I do not agree with that particular point of view, but that is what the Government are doing."

Geoffrey then quoted a statement submitted to the League by the New Zealand Government which he felt could revolutionise the whole situation. The statement concluded: "It is our belief that the Covenant, as it is or in a strengthened form, would in itself be sufficient to prevent war if the world realised that the nations undertaking to apply the Covenant actually would do so in fact."

What better test can there be of willingness to promote national defence than the question of supply? In February 1935 the Royal Commission on the Private Manufacture and Traffic in Arms was appointed and its unanimous report was issued on October 31st 1936. One of its recommendations proposed a controlling body presided over by a Minister responsible to Parliament, having executive powers in peace-time and in war-time over all matters relating to the supply and manufacture of orders from abroad. This meant a Ministry of Supply. One paragraph of the report said, "Great difficulties are likely to be met in any attempt to formulate plans for the conscription of industry in time of war, but we are impelled to the belief that these difficulties will have to be faced and we recommend that they should be faced at the earliest possible moment."

Ten days after the publication of this report, the Parliamentary Liberal Party raised the question in an Amendment to the Address, moved by Mr Kingsley Griffith who said, "One is bound to inquire whether the Government really appreciate the gravity of the situation. In the last war we were compelled to take over practically complete control. This had to be improvised at very short notice."

But the Minister for the Co-ordination of Defence rejected the proposal for a Ministry of Supply as unnecessary. He thought to give executive powers to such a Ministry "would involve so much delay and uncertainty that the Government could not contemplate it. When all has been said and done we have a long start over anyone ill advised to meddle with our freedom."

For the Government Sir Samuel Hoare deprecated what he called "any revolutionary change."

The second day of the Debate, November 12th, Sir Archibald Sinclair, winding up for the Liberal party, again asked for a new Ministry, saying that while conscription of industry certainly raised problems, that was no reason for shirking them utterly. Mr Churchill delivered a broadside on the Government.

"The Government simply cannot make up their mind. So they go on in strange paradox, decided only to be undecided, resolved to be irresolute, adamant for drift, solid for fluidity, all powerful to be impotent."

The Liberal Amendment calling for a Ministry of Supply was defeated on November 12th by three hundred and thirty seven votes to one hundred and thirty one. The opposition were united in support of action, the Government stubbornly resisted, Hitler armed.

When he was the Prince of Wales, in 1930, Edward VIII met the married American Wallis Simpson and the blossoming relationship between them had been reported in most foreign newspapers. However people in Britain had been unaware of the story due to censorship imposed by London-based newspaper proprietors.

On 16th November the King told Stanley Baldwin of his intention to marry Mrs Simpson. The death of his father George V made Edward both king and head of the Church of England, which was firmly opposed to divorce and to his proposed marriage. Baldwin agreed with the Church and was supported by the Liberal and Labour parties and when the King began to sound out senior members of the Royal family and the government on the constitutional problems caused by such a marriage, he found that neither they nor any Commonwealth governments supported him.

On 10th December Edward VIII abdicated, announcing his decision in the famous radio broadcast when he stated "I, Edward, do hearby declare my irrevocable determination to renounce the throne for myself and my descendants."

Edward's brother the Duke of York succeeded to the throne as George VI.

On 14th December a message from the new King was presented to the House of Commons by Stanley Baldwin and read to the assembled MPs by the Speaker.

"I have succeeded to the throne in circumstances which are without precedent and at a moment of great personal distress. But I am resolved to do my duty and I am sustained by the knowledge that I am supported by the widespread goodwill and sympathy of all my subjects here and throughout the world.

It will be my constant endeavour, with God's help, supported as I shall be by my dear wife, to uphold the honour of the Realm and to promote the happiness of my peoples."

Geoffrey received a letter in January from the Strathmore Bookshop and Library Ltd. answering his request for any books they might have in stock on William Morris, Charles Kempe and William De Morgan. The letter is the only indication in the archives that Geoffrey and Rosalie Mander were amassing books at the same time as they acquired paintings, carpets, glass, embroideries and wallpapers for the house; books written and sent to them by friends often have cards and letters inside from those authors.

In February The Green Can magazine published an account of a visit to the House of Commons by two Mander employees, Mr Archer and the writer "A.H.G." accompanied by Geoffrey Mander.

A policeman approaches and peers through the windows of our taxi-cab as we draw up at the entrance to the House of Commons. Perhaps he is rather doubtful of Mr Archer and myself, but what momentary doubts he has are at once dispelled as he recognises Mr Geoffrey. We find the Central Lobby. There are policemen at every door and entrance, policemen round the walls and policemen wherever one turns. And then there are the Ushers, kindly and helpful men, who take our hats and coats. Mr Geoffrey is inviting us to refreshment in the Bar, the Bar of which we have heard so much. A small congested place with the marble counter of a railway refreshment room, and buns and cakes under glass shades and a lounging young man who looks rather like a youthful film star, but is really a very able young member of the House. I am surprised by the Bar. I feel as though Tradition and the Constitution and the grandeur of Kings and Queens, Prime Ministers and Ambassadors, have all got inextricably mixed up with an advertisement of Bovril, or that some lunatic has tried to sandwich "Yes We Have no Bananas" between the first two movements of Beethoven's C Minor Symphony.

Then through a narrow doorway that might lead to a belfry and we are in the Distinguished Strangers' Gallery of the House of Commons. And down below, on the floor of the House, the solemn business of governing the Country is proceeding. I find my attention continually diverted from the speakers by the constant coming and going of members who apparently wander in and out at will.

The Prime Minister has just arrived, looking sallow and grey and takes his seat rather wearily. I can see Mr Churchill in a corner seat below the gangway and just below me the member for East Wolverhampton, all attention and nursing his knees, and looking as though at any time he might be expected to interrupt. The pale face of Mr Speaker is outlined by the wig, beneath the vast canopy of the huge chair in which he sits. Mr Churchill is speaking, attacking and questioning this and that. He is producing damaging figures from what looks like a child's exercise book. Mr Baldwin forsakes his restful attitude and is listening with some concern and still the Speaker sits motionless, his face a pale mask for his thoughts. Then we are outside again in a taxi-cab. Sitting back in my corner, I have not the remotest idea where we are and I am not sure that I care because I am enjoying those few comfortable and fleeting minutes when one looks back upon one's dreams.

Old Battersea House,
London SW11
Feb 2nd 1937
Dear Sir,

My husband has handed me your letter, in which, as a sister-in-law of the late William De Morgan, I am naturally interested.

We have been trying to arrange this historical old house as a permanent memorial to William De Morgan and his wife *[Evelyn]* and you may be interested in seeing the enclosed catalogues and card showing you what we are doing here. I am very keen to trace more of my sister's beautiful pictures, but it is difficult, as she kept no record of them, and often when I have laboriously traced one, the owner won't sell! If you ever come across one, I should be so glad to know.

Unfortunately we have no good specimens here of De Morgan mantelpieces *[fireplace tiles]*. I tried to arrange one in a more modern annex to the house, but could not get anything really representative; but I think in the future there will be a very fine collection of De Morgan pottery here, as so many people are leaving their private collections to it.

I have a few pictures here by my uncle, Mr Roddam Spencer Stanhope, otherwise all the collection, apart from period furniture, is De Morgan and Pre-Raphaelite. It would be a great pleasure if some day when you are in London you would come to see it.

Yours faithfully,

Wilhelmina Stirling.

Author of "William De Morgan and his Wife" etc.

By 1937 Geoffrey and his wife had begun to collect De Morgan tiles to add to those originally installed in two fireplaces at Wightwick. Since then a substantial collection of his lustre-ware plates and bowls and tiles has been assembled in the house together with a number of paintings by Evelyn de Morgan and Roddam Spencer Stanhope.

This account by Geoffrey Mander of a visit to Old Place, home of stained glass designer C.E. Kempe, is one of several from a folder entitled "Visits to famous places and people".

REPORT ON VISIT TO OLD PLACE, LINDFIELD, SUSSEX.

February 28th. 1937, by Mr and Mrs Geoffrey Mander.

We went by train from Brighton to Haywards Heath on a very cold day, when the ground was covered with snow.

The house, originally quite small, was built about 1590, and bought by C.E. Kempe in 1875. He added considerably to it from time to time, and was still planning alterations when he died in 1907 at the age of seventy. He left it to his relative, Walter Tower, who succeeded him in his business, and who in 1929 sold the property for £40,000 to Sir Rupert Clark. The present owner is the latter's widow.

There is a park of about two hundred acres beyond the garden.

Unfortunately a great deal of the glass was removed at the time of the sale, as the new owner thought it made the rooms too dark. This is now stored away in the possession of Mr Tower for the most part. Some remains, however, and is of a fine delicate workmanship, chiefly golden in colour.

In the garden the summerhouse has amongst other mottoes: Habitantibus

Summer, by Charles Eamer Kempe.
Stained glass panel in the drawing room at Wightwick Manor.

pax *[peace to those who live here]* being one of the mottoes in the stained glass in the hall at Wightwick. The gardens are extensive, and doubtless in the summer very beautiful. There is much beautifully clipped yew hedge.

In the 1930s Geoffrey added to the existing Kempe collection at Wightwick by buying and installing in the Drawing Room two extra sets of stained glass, probably from the collection stored by Walter Tower.

THE LIBERAL MAGAZINE

April 1937

During the Debate on Foreign Affairs on March 25th - the last Parliamentary day before the Easter adjournment - Mr Mander said, referring to recent events in Spain:

"I am inclined to welcome those events because they have brought us into a sphere of reality, they have stripped all pretence at last, I hope, from the farce of non-intervention that has been going on for so many months. You cannot work or play with people who will not recognise the rules, and both Germany and Italy have made it quite clear in various events during the past few months and years what their policy is. They are advocates of fear politics, and they are going to do all they can, to get by the force of their right arms all that they can in the world."

Guernica, the ancient capital of the Basque country and in 1937 a defenceless country town, was on April 26th subjected to one of the worst air-raids of the Spanish Civil war. On April 28th the rebel G.H.Q. at Salamanca denied all knowledge of the raid.

A possible explanation of this was put forward by the Manchester Guardian correspondent in Bilbao, on April 30th, who wrote:

The general theory here is that Franco protests his innocence of the Guernica bombing because he is no longer informed by his subordinates of what is actually being done in his name. It is suggested by many Basques that the German and Italian general staffs at Salamanca are now simply carrying out experiments in modern warfare on their own initiative without even consulting General Franco.

Elkin Mathews Limited,

Booksellers

78 Grosvenor Street

London W1

5th April 1937

Dear Sir,

We have recently purchased an oil painting which we think may be of interest to you. It is, we believe, a picture of Mrs William Morris, the face of which is painted by D.G. Rossetti and the remainder by Ford Madox Brown. It was originally in the possession of Mr G.A. Rossetti of Bolton, who was, we believe, a nephew of the painter. The picture is in a contemporary gilt frame with a gilt mount, and, in spite of the difference in the technique of the two painters, makes an interesting and not unattractive portrait. The price is £17.10s. and the picture is here for your inspection at any time convenient to you.

Yours faithfully,

W.G. Worthington

The painting was bought for the house and hangs in the Drawing Room. Geoffrey Rossetti was the great nephew of D.G. Rossetti.

Kelmscott Manor,

Lechlade,

Gloucestershire.

May 2 1937

Dear Mr Mander,

I find your letter of the 26th awaiting me on coming home yesterday. I shall be very pleased if you will call here on May 26th and hope you will stay to tea.

I'm much interested to hear about your beautiful half-timbered house with the Morris fittings, and would like to know more about the Rossetti portrait. If Mrs Rossetti Angeli is uncertain about it, I expect I shall be also. I wonder if you have a photograph of it you could show me when you come.

Yours sincerely,

May Morris

May Morris was the youngest daughter of William and Jane Morris. She designed textiles and wallpapers and produced embroideries for Morris and Co.

Mrs Rossetti Angeli was Dante Gabriel Rossetti's niece and the aunt of Geoffrey Rossetti. He originally owned the Mrs Morris painting now at Wightwick which could be the portrait May Morris mentions.

From THE DAILY HERALD
THE CORONATION OF GEORGE VI.
Wednesday 12th May 1937, in Westminster Abbey
Six a.m. in the House of Commons, MPs and their guests, 1,000 in all, eating eggs and bacon. Throughout the corridors and passages, settees and chairs were arranged for them to pass the weary hours until the procession began.

Mr Baldwin wandered around clutching a specially bound programme and a notebook. Occasionally he would sit down and turn a few pages of his notebook. Then he suddenly remembered something important. He pulled out a little stub of pencil with a tin cap on it, opened his special programme and scribbled "Stanley Baldwin" inside the cover. Then he dropped it on a seat with the air of a man who should say "Let anyone take that if he dares," and strolled off for a little chat with Mr Ramsay MacDonald.

Everyone who has witnessed a Coronation must have wondered what thoughts are in the mind of the King as he moves into the centre of this amazing picture. I hear the voice of the Archbishop of Canterbury. "Sirs, I here present unto you King George, your undoubted King: Wherefore all you who are come this day to do your Homage and Service, are you willing to do the same?"

There is a great shout from the nave: "God Save King George!"

Hours seem to pass before this splendid but exhausting ceremony comes to an end. The moment arrives, however, when to a roll of drums and a fanfare of trumpets, King George VI and Queen Elizabeth move down the Abbey church together to face the crowds of London - and History.

A spotlight within their centuries old coach illuminated the faces of the King and Queen on their return drive from the Abbey to Buckingham Palace.

At the German embassy a huge flag, half covered with a swastika, hung down facing the Mall, and in Carlton House Terrace behind, another swastika flag hung from a mast. From the windows, the Embassy staff looked out, and on the roof, there were a score of German servants, standing up and looking on a Mall bordered with scarlet uniforms.

As the King and Queen went by in the great coach, with its golden figures and golden roof, and "God Save the King" was played, and thousands of British people cheered, I saw German hands go up - and give the Nazi salute.

Soon after the Coronation, Neville Chamberlain became Prime Minister following the resignation of Stanley Baldwin.

WE WERE NOT ALL WRONG

The difference between Lord Baldwin and Mr Chamberlain as Prime Ministers was mainly this, that the former rarely bothered to put his horse at a political fence that presented any difficulties; the latter was full of energy, completely master of himself, superbly self-confident, but the fences at which he put his horses turned out to be either booby traps or brick walls. In the event there was not much to choose between them, they both in their own ways, slowly, surely and certainly prepared the ground for war, though nothing, of course, was further from their intention.

A BACK BENCHER LOOKS BACK

Mr Neville Chamberlain was, in private life, a man of the highest integrity who had rendered great services to the City of Birmingham as Lord Mayor. His abilities were at their best in connection with finance, administration, and local government.

His experience of foreign affairs had been very limited: thus it was that when, as Prime Minister, he took over the task of dealing personally with a most difficult international situation he was quite out of his depth. He was inclined to look upon differences between nations as analogous to a difference, say, between the Sewage and Water Committees of the Birmingham City Council, where the obvious thing to do would be to have a joint meeting of the two Committees or their officers, whereupon, by mutual concession, an amicable agreement would be reached. He seemed to think that the same procedure would work with Hitler and Goering.

On June 2nd 1937 Geoffrey and his wife visited Red House in Bexleyheath, the house built for William Morris in 1859. He wrote his usual report.

This house is owned by Mr and Mrs Hills and has passed through many hands since it was built. The house remains very much in its original form, containing some Morris and Burne-Jones glass - only two small pieces of the latter, Morris wall-papers and the famous settle, cupboards and other furniture. In the drawing room are paintings by Burne-Jones. The cupboard in the Entrance Hall has an unfinished painting by Rossetti.

The garden contained plants used in the original design and they were able to take a cutting and some seeds of a Strawberry tree (Arbutus enedo) and also two cuttings from a Maidenhair tree (Ginko) One Ginko cutting was successfully planted and the tree is still growing at Wightwick Manor.

Edward, Duke of Windsor married Mrs Simpson on 3rd June in France.

HANSARD

8 July 1937

Mr Mander asked the Prime Minister whether consideration has been given by the Government and the Committee of Imperial Defence to the problems that would arise in the event of a German-Italian control of Spain and the acquisition of submarine bases and aerodromes by these Powers; and whether, in view of the threat to British communication in the Mediterranean and the British Empire generally, he will state to what extent it will be necessary to increase the Army, Navy and Air Force above the present programme and the cost likely to be involved in the above eventuality?

The Prime Minister: The answer to the first part of the question is in the negative, and the second part, therefore, does not arise.

HANSARD

14th July 1937

On the same day Geoffrey spoke during the discussion on a new clause to the Finance Bill in which it was proposed that there should be exemption from Death Duties in the case of land transferred to the National Trust.

> Mr Mander: This is a matter of great national interest, and we are all very grateful for the acceptance of the proposal by the Chancellor of the Exchequer. I am delighted that he has accepted it, because I am sure it will give great encouragement to a movement, which is developing and may grow considerably in the next few years, for people to hand over property of historic interest or natural beauty.
>
> One of the advantages of the National Trust owning properties in this way is that the public, instead of going into an empty museum or a house with bare walls, are able to go in at intervals and see a house as it is lived in from day to day. It is very nice to be the owner of a historic place and desire to keep it up. If that is not possible, it is at least as attractive a position to be a sort of custodian or trustee for the nation.

A BACK-BENCHER LOOKS BACK

> The policy of setting up a National Home for the Jews in Palestine made a great appeal to me. The Jews have again and again been sacrificed in the interest of the Arabs, and Neville Chamberlain, at a time when he was willing to do almost anything to satisfy Hitler, treated Dr Weizmann with great harshness.

Dr. Weizmann became the first president of Israel in 1949.

In 1917 the Balfour Declaration had promised a national Homeland for Jews and since then the numbers of immigrants arriving in Palestine had increased steadily. The Nazi persecution of the Jews had exacerbated the difficulties that arose from immigration and now there were riots, strikes and violence between Arabs and Jews, who fought not only each other, but the British troops and police who were trying to keep order. A Royal Commission had been set up in 1936 in an attempt to address the problem of Palestine. Its suggestions were reported by the summer of 1937 but the proposal to divide the territory into three areas - an Arab State, a Jewish State and an area under British control - was not accepted by any of the peoples affected.

The Jewish Agency for Palestine

77 Great Russell Street, London. W.C.1

15th July 1937

Dear Mr Mander,

I am very grateful indeed for your letter of the 13th July and its enclosures. What is quite clear is that, before the value of the Negev as a settlement area can be determined, a very great deal of detailed investigation will be required. Of course, we know that there was in ancient times a great civilisation in this part of the world, but that was a long time ago, and the country has since been converted into desert by erosion and the destruction of vegetation. Even with modern methods it would take it a very long time to reconstruct it again.

If I may offer a suggestion, it would be that the most urgent thing is to ensure that the recommendations of the Report shall be carried out promptly, genuinely, and in a proper spirit. There are the problems arising in connection with the proposals for transfer of population, sovereignty, and the transition period, all of which are in my view more immediate than that of the Negev.

Moreover, I see that it is stated in the press that many Arabs would gladly acquiesce in giving us the Negev, providing we give up Galilee. Naturally, such an exchange would be disastrous from our point of view, and this is one more reason why I would be inclined not to press for the inclusion of the Negev within our territory at the present juncture.

Thanking you once again, I remain, with kind regards,

Yours sincerely,

Weizmann.

15 July 1937

Dear Mr Mander,

I have been thinking about your bed and the work you want me to do for it: I find it presents difficulties and on talking about it to Mr Hewett find he agrees with me.

A Hepplewhite bed, being elegant and fragile-looking, wants furnishing in the same spirit. You have put in the room that rich and weighty Acanthus paper and really I don't feel that the bed and paper hit it off. The bed itself would look best with light flowery valance and curtains and a back also decorated (though this might be just a wreath with monogram or whatnot in the middle) but this would fight with the paper! I don't quite see what is to be done about it. Your present idea is to have my motto-valance and then, what? Mr Hewett and I looked at some niceish plain cream material for curtains and back that looked as if it would go with the bed; but even so I am a little doubtful.

Do you know, it would be rather a good thing if you were to get Mr Hewett to come down and see the room and the lighting and see if he could make a suggestion. He is so clever and would take any trouble being genuinely interested in all Morris things. I don't feel I can start anything right away that is not likely to give you and Mrs Mander satisfaction when finished.

Yours sincerely,

May Morris.

The Hepplewhite bed together with the May Morris embroidery remained in the room with the "rich and weighty Acanthus paper" for over forty years until it was moved into a bedroom hung with Honeysuckle fabric - another rich Morris pattern.

In July Japan launched an attack on China and captured Peking. The League of Nations formally condemned Japan's action but no sanctions were applied and a full scale invasion began a few weeks later - marking the start of the Sino-Japanese war.

Earlier in the year Sir Archibald Sinclair had criticised what he called the drifting policy of the Prime Minister and the Government in international affairs. He said the world could be likened to a boat five miles above Niagara Falls. It would only go over the abyss if allowed to drift.

THE GREEN CAN

July 1937

A unique ceremony in the history of Messrs. Mander Brothers took place when seventy five pensioners of the firm were presented with long service certificates by Mr Geoffrey Mander MP

From an account of the proceedings by one of the pensioners:

"The Chairman (Mr Geoffrey Le M. Mander MP) after speaking to us called out the names of those who had the longest years of service. When my name was called (after sitting it is most difficult for me to stand up) to my surprise the Chairman who had left his place, came down the room to me. I was deeply touched by his kindly act (and may he never have legs like mine)."

A letter from Stanley Baldwin

Astley Hall, Stourport-on-Severn.

My dear Mander,

It will be a pleasure to see you. I haven't been in London for a couple of months and a voice from the Big World will be most welcome!

Would it be too early for you if you came about eleven? We should have time for a good talk and you could get back to lunch as you did last time?

Yours sincerely,

B of B

[Baldwin of Bewdley]

THE LIBERAL MAGAZINE

The Second reading of the London Naval Treaty Bill was moved on July 20th by the First Lord of the Admiralty (Mr Duff Cooper)

Referring to the probable feelings of the First Lord towards the Bill, Mr Mander said: "I think he feels it to be rather a poor little thing, but perhaps its smallness is the measure of the complete failure of the foreign policy of the National Government during the last five years. In my judgement the situation in which we find ourselves today is due to the weakness and folly of the British Government since the National Government came into office."

Later Mr Mander said: "The whole of our troubles in Naval affairs are due to the fact that there is in power in Japan, a government, which relies on force as a instrument of national policy and which is unwilling to co-operate with other countries in order to come to a general agreement for disarmament and conciliation on the lines of the League of Nations. But as that is the case, I entirely agree that there is no alternative but to face it."

HANSARD

29th July

Mr Mander asked the Minister of Health *[Sir Kingsley Wood]* whether he will have inquiries made into the position of a worker who has been instructed by the local medical officer of health not to go to work owing to the presence of diphtheria or some other infectious disease in the house, with a view to ascertaining what benefit under such circumstances is available to him? Is it desirable or proper that a man who has been instructed by a medical officer not to go to work because of infection in the house, should stand in a queue outside an Employment Exchange?

REPORT OF VISIT TO WIGHTWICK MANOR BY MR A. HEWETT OF MORRIS & COMPANY LTD.

August 4th 1937

As a result of his life-long experience with the firm, Mr Hewett was able to supply a great deal of valuable information and advice.

He helped in re-arranging the china *[porcelain]* in the Drawing Room and great Parlour. The most valuable pieces are Chinese 17th century Ming and Imari.

Morris and Company

17 George Street

Hanover Square

London W1

6th August 1937

Dear Mr Mander,

Thank you for your letter with the extract from the "Earthly Paradise".

A poem by William Morris. The Kempe windows in the drawing room at Wightwick illustrate a section of the poem and include the relevant quotation.

Yes, the tiles that you refer to are modern Dutch ones.

I am sending you in a separate parcel patterns of tapestries etc. suggested for the frieze, and covering for large settee in the Great Hall. No. 1/1192 "Diagonal Trail" is included to show you how much brighter the colours were originally, and in any case it would, I feel, be much too strong and spotty in effect with the modelled frieze above and the general colouring of the room, which has all naturally toned down altogether with time.

"Diagonal Trail" was already on the wall, below the frieze, and had been there since 1893 when the extension to Wightwick was built; photographs of the room were taken a few years later. He must have been thinking of renewing the original fabric.

I would suggest that you have the patterns pinned up temporarily on the wall just under the modelled frieze and leave them there for a few days to see the effect at various times and in different lights.

The Settee covering depends rather on what you select for the walls, and in view of the multi-coloured materials on the cushions should be rather plain in effect.

I will as arranged get in touch with Miss May Morris about the embroidered hangings for the four post bedstead, and having now seen it and the room shall be better able to advise her as to what may be most suitable in design and colouring.

I am sending, with the samples an illustrated list of the stained glass windows as promised. You will notice that amongst others, one of the important Birmingham windows are illustrated. Also a book on the Merton Abbey tapestries that I think may interest you, and which you may like to put with your other records.

I was very interested to see your house and its contents and much enjoyed my visit.

Yours sincerely,

A. Hewett

In September Geoffrey and his wife spent three weeks visiting Germany, Austria and Poland. While they were travelling the Nuremberg Rally took place, during which Hitler called for more "lebensraum"- living space - for Germany. There are no comments from Geoffrey about the visit to Berlin and Vienna but an account of the tour of Poland appeared in October in The Green Can.

INCIDENTS IN POLAND

In Poland we had the pleasure of meeting representatives in Cracow of two firms who are known to us Dr Dortheimer and Mr Fudokowski.

Mr Bohdanowicz, the President before the 1914-18 war was a customer of our branch - Gebruder Mander at Vienna. We were most kindly looked after by his friend, Mr Fudokowski, a zoologist at the University, whom he had asked to act in his absence. This gentleman was eagerly awaiting our arrival and he spent most of the day showing us the sights of Cracow, which included the Warvel Cathedral and Castle on a hill, the University Courtyard and the famous and beautiful St. Mary Church in the Market Place. From the tower of this, a trumpet has sounded the hour without intermission ever since centuries ago a trumpeter on duty, warning the inhabitants of the approach of the Turks, was shot through the throat by them.

Then there is the firm of Dr Dortheimer, they are suppliers of Printing Machinery, and we are hopeful that business arrangements can be established between us in due course.

Young Mr Dortheimer placed himself entirely at our disposal and took us out in his car to the Salt Mines, some miles outside the city. They have been worked for hundreds of years. A church the size of St Peter's *[in Wolverhampton]* has been beautifully carved by the miners. The whole of this is in salt. Mr Dortheimer then took us to see the Editor of a local Jewish paper, who was much interested to discuss the prospects of emigration of the Jews to Palestine, owing to the difficulty they are experiencing in Poland. He had followed my Parliamentary questions on the subject and from the interest I appeared to take in it, had formed the opinion that I must be a Jew!

We went by train the next day to the Polish mountain resort in the Tatras- Zakopane.

To show the great kindness we experienced, we had considerable difficulty in preventing Mr Dortheimer from himself motoring us there (it took us four hours by train) and arranging for his sister to go up and stay with us, in order to make things as easy as possible.

We are exceedingly grateful to those friends, who - through a somewhat slender business association - did so much to make our stay interesting.

Kelmscott Manor,

Lechlade. Gloucestershire.

3 October 1937

Dear Mr Mander,

Thank you for writing about the cuttings and shrubs from my garden. This will be the good time for them as soon as we get a little rain. The whole ground here is so dried up with this long drought that it would be no good sending. As soon as the weather changes I will see about it.

I'm interested to hear of the success in cleaning the paper in your Great Parlour.

Directly Miss Lobb and I returned from our holiday I had to go to bed with influenza, and now after two weeks of it am beginning to get about. It is owing to this that I have not yet been able to consider a sketch for the bed valance. I was glad to hear from Mr Hewett that he went to see you. He seems to have made some helpful suggestions. I am so hoping that my doctor lets me work a little now so that I can send you something soon.

Yours sincerely

May Morris.

THE TIMES

6th October 1937

From a speech by President Roosevelt deploring the unrest in parts of Europe and Asia.

Without a declaration of war, without warning or justification of any kind, civilians, including women and children, are being ruthlessly murdered with bombs from the air. In times of so-called peace, ships are being attacked and sunk by submarines without cause or notice. Nations are fomenting, and taking sides in civil warfare in nations that have never done them any harm.

Nations claiming freedom for themselves, deny it to others. The peace-loving nations must make a concerted effort in opposition to those violations of treaties and those ignorings of humane instincts which are creating the international anarchy and instability from which there is no escape through mere isolation or neutrality.

A BACK-BENCHER LOOKS BACK

It was announced in November 1937, that Lord Halifax, Foreign Secretary, was to pay a visit to Hitler in Berlin. It was obvious that the peace of the world would be discussed and the known appeasement policy of Mr Chamberlain's government made some of us very much alarmed. Commander Fletcher asked about the nature of the conversations to be held, but he got no satisfaction. Later in the afternoon, I gave notice that I intended to raise the matter on the adjournment of the House when half an hour would be available. This created tremendous interest, particularly on the part of the Press for the whole world was watching the actions of Hitler and the vagaries of the British Government with growing anxiety. The Government Chief Whip endeavoured, unsuccessfully, to persuade me not to proceed with my speech. He then said that he assumed I would be willing in any case to see the Prime Minister before the matter was raised. I at once assented to this and went to Mr Chamberlain's room. He was lying back, looking very tired and dazed. He asked me what my anxieties were and I told him that many of us felt alarmed lest concessions should be made to Germany at the expense of other countries. He then assured me that so long as he was Prime Minister no bargain of the kind would be made and that I could rely absolutely on that. At the time, I felt bound to accept his assurance and called off the adjournment debate. I now regret having done so for, of course, what happened afterwards was not in accordance with what he had told me and one instance of appeasement after another followed until the war broke out.

BIRMINGHAM GAZETTE
Friday 10th December 1937
A GIFT TO THE NATIONAL TRUST
Wightwick Manor near Wolverhampton, it is announced today, has, with its chief contents, seventeen acres of gardens, and an endowment fund, been given to the National Trust by Mr Geoffrey Mander.

Mr Mander and his family will continue to reside at the Manor but the house will be open to visitors one day a week.

Geoffrey had tried to sell Wightwick Manor in 1920; he was able to dispose of much of the land and cottages but failed to sell the house.

From 'THE NATIONAL TRUST - THE FIRST HUNDRED YEARS"
By Merlin Waterson. 1994.

The Trust's new statutory powers made possible a gift which appeared then and since to be highly improbable. Sir Geoffrey Mander offered the Trust Wightwick Manor, a house less than fifty years old. It was difficult to make a case for Wightwick Manor being of outstanding historic interest. The house was mock half-timbered Tudor, on the outskirts of Wolverhampton, with a small but interesting garden designed by Alfred Parsons *[and developed by Thomas Mawson in the early 20th century]*. There had to be special pleading. Sir Geoffrey Mander was an energetic supporter of the Trust in the House of Commons, particularly over unsympathetic planting by the Forestry Commission in the Lake District. He was prepared to offer a substantial endowment in the form of shares in the family's paint and varnish manufacturing business.

Like Wallington, Wightwick is a house with Pre-Raphaelite associations; there are well preserved Morris wallpapers, De Morgan tiles and Kempe glass. The Director of the Victoria and Albert Museum, Clifford Smith, confirmed that it would in time be regarded as decoration of considerable historical importance. Sir Geoffrey and his second wife were already adding Pre-Raphaelite furniture and pictures to the collection. Lady Mander was young, a brilliant literary historian, waspish, witty and very pretty. The Trust was persuaded.

The house was accepted on 10th December 1937, the first to be given in the lifetime of the donor. Later Lady Mander wrote: "He never regretted it, for he liked to think that the public should enjoy what had been his private property."

At the end of 1938 Geoffrey Mander noted that Wightwick had had fourteen visitors. In 2006 there were 25,000.

21 Kew Gardens Road,
Kew.
Surrey
13 Dec 1937
Dear Mr Mander,
Thank you for the little pamphlet that you have kindly sent me. I read an account of your munificence in The Times. I remember when the National

Trust was established and received its first gift of land at Barmouth. How marvellously it has since expanded!

If you are especially interested in Morris and would care to see what I have got connected with him, I hope you will come out here one day when the weather has improved.

Yours sincerely,

Sydney Cockerell.

The friendship that grew between Geoffrey and Sydney Cockerell developed initially through their interest in William Morris; Cockerell had acted as Morris' private secretary and became a collector of Kelmscott Press books. From 1908 to 1937 he was Director of the Fitzwilliam Museum in Cambridge.

Morris & Company Art-Workers, Ltd.,

17 George Street,

Hanover Square

London W1 29th December 1937

Dear Mr Mander,

Thank you for your order for 5 pieces of "Pimpernel" No. 85. Wallpaper. In stocktaking we have discovered that we have a few pieces which have been overlooked and are, therefore, sending the 5 pieces on to you, and are pleased to be able to charge it at the ordinary price of 23/6d per piece. *[This was used in the Billiard Room.]* I am sending you, by separate post today, a few samples of Wallpaper as requested, which I think may be suitable for your purpose. These are all stock papers and can be supplied at once. Should they not be quite what you require, I shall be pleased to send a further selection…

[In the margin Geoffrey wrote 'Lily 367 17/- + 10%'.]

Yours faithfully,

Alfred Hewett

THE GREEN CAN

December 1937

A THORN IN MINISTERS' SIDES

(The following extract from a recent weekly paper, is, we think, a well-deserved tribute to our Chairman's work as a member of Parliament- Editor.)

Mr Geoffrey Mander, Liberal member for East Wolverhampton, is a most persistent thorn in the side of the National Government.

His questions are always to the point and his speeches have just enough venom in them to make Ministers uncomfortable.

Although he does not ask as many Parliamentary Questions as Mr Harry Day, he makes more speeches, and is an adept at "supplementaries."

His predecessor in East Wolverhampton, the late George Thorne, feared that after his death the seat would pass to the Labour party, but he reckoned without Geoffrey Mander, who holds it as an advanced Liberal. He is an enlightened industrialist and runs his factory on the most modern lines.

A BACK-BENCHER LOOKS BACK

About 1938 I received a letter from a French man telling me that he had noticed the very great interest I was taking in the question of Hitler and what trouble he was causing and suggesting he was in a position to offer a solution of the problem. He gave an address in Paris and said that if I would supply him with "les moyennes materieux" *[sic]* he would be quite prepared to take the necessary steps to dispose of Hitler. This was before the War had broken out and as assassination was not one of my political weapons, I thought it undesirable to leave the matter there. It occurred to me that he might possibly kill Hitler and leave a note saying "This is by arrangement with Mr Geoffrey Mander MP", so I handed the letter over to the Attorney General who passed it to the French Authorities. What happened after that I do not know. I hope I took the right course.

Later on, during the War, when the list of those who were to be put in a concentration camp when the German forces landed and took control was discovered, I was interested to note that my name was amongst the number. I consider this a great honour.

Kelmscott Manor,
Lechlade,
Gloucestershire
7 January 1938
Dear Mr Mander,

I have been making a trial-piece of embroidery in silk to see whether silk or wool-work would be better for your bed-hangings. I was at Morris and Co. yesterday, comparing this with one of my wool curtains that were done for an Arts and Crafts Exhibition at Burlington House years ago, against your Acanthus paper; both Mr Hewett and I concluded that the wool-work was rather more in keeping. As the wool-work goes quicker and uses less material, the estimate will be less, as follows:

Bed hangings wool-work on linen - i.e. pair of curtains 7.5ft long by 4.8ft wide.

Valance 1ft deep.

Back cloth (a medallion perhaps).

Inside valances, linings, making etc. £140.

Silk work on linen £165.

The silk on linen looks very brilliant and charming if you prefer it, but the other is my choice. I wait to hear whether you accept either estimate. The curtains mentioned above are a set of four short window-curtains. Looking at them afresh I thought they looked very jolly. I wonder if you could place them anywhere. I would let you have them at a very reasonable price.

Yours sincerely,

May Morris.

Although the Treaty of Versailles had forbidden union (Anschluss) between Germany and Austria, in February at a meeting with the Austrian chancellor Kurt von Schussnigg, Hitler announced that he had decided to absorb Austria into the German Empire. Previously von Schussnigg had made unsuccessful appeals to European countries for help in his attempts to guarantee the independent integrity of Austria. Now he was forced to sign an agreement that made Austrian foreign and economic policies subservient to Nazi Germany.

HANSARD

21 February 1938

Mr Eden: I stand before the House today to give the House in a few brief sentences an account of my reasons for having resigned the office of Foreign Secretary. Recent months, recent weeks, recent days have seen the successive violations of international agreements and attempts to secure political decisions by forcible means. We are in the presence of the progressive deterioration of respect for international obligations. This is a moment for this country to stand firm. Of late the conviction has steadily grown upon me that there has been too keen a desire on our part to make terms with others rather than that others should make terms with us. This never was the attitude of this country in the past. I do not believe that we can make progress in European appeasement, more particularly in the light of the events of the past few days - and those events must surely be present in all our minds - if we allow the impression to gain currency abroad that we yield to constant pressure.

HANSARD

22nd February 1938

Mr Mander asked the Prime Minister whether the recent action of the German Government with regard to Austria was discussed in the conversations between the Lord President of the Council and the German Chancellor; and were the conversations affected thereby?

The Prime Minister (Mr Chamberlain): The answer to the first part of the Hon. Member's question is No Sir. The second part does not therefore, arise.

Mr Mander: Is it really proposed to go on with these negotiations as if nothing had happened in Austria? May I ask the Prime Minister whether Herr Hitler has informed the Government whom he wishes to be appointed as British Foreign Secretary?

On 11th March Nazi troops entered Austria and a few days later Hitler was given an enthusiastic welcome from many of the Austrian people when he entered Vienna; the occupation of Austria now left the Czechoslovakian frontier exposed to an advance by Germany. Two weeks after, Hitler told Konrad Henlein, the leader of the large German population in the Sudeten region of western Czechoslovakia that the "Czechoslovakian question" would soon be settled. This border area had been controlled by Czechoslovakia since 1919 and gradually the resentment of the German inhabitants had grown, helped by Nazi propaganda.

In March 1938 Chamberlain noted that "You only have to look at the map to see that nothing France or we could do could possibly save Czechoslovakia from being overrun by the Germans if they wanted to do it. I have therefore abandoned any idea of giving guarantees to Czechoslovakia or the French in connections with her obligations to that country."

In May Hitler and Mussolini met in Rome and agreed that there should be lasting support between Italy and Germany.

Hitler and Mussolini.

WE WERE NOT ALL WRONG

An important debate on Air Defence took place on May 25, 1938, when Mr Dalton moved for a complete and searching inquiry into the state of our air defences. In the course of his remarks he said: "If the worst should come, I shall not envy the Prime Minister or his colleagues when they look back upon the vote which they will give today, if they vote against this inquiry. If the worst should come I shall not envy them when they remember that today they voted against holding an inquiry - independent, expeditious, competent and confidential as we propose - into our air defences, while there is yet time, though perhaps not much time."

The motion was rejected by 329 to 144.

In June, in Austria, all Jews in employment were dismissed.

A BACK-BENCHER LOOKS BACK

Lady Astor was one of the sincerest, bravest, and liveliest Members of the House. As a rule she seemed to me to be fundamentally right in her outlook on public affairs, but not, I am afraid, on the following occasion. She was an appeaser... This did not, of course, prevent me from having a great admiration for her qualities of heart and head.

I think that perhaps a good illustration of the way in which a back-bencher MP can call attention to matters of great importance, if he uses all the opportunities available to him in the form of questions, debates on the adjournment, and similar ways, is through an episode that caused a world sensation at the time.

One day in 1938 information was conveyed to me from an authoritative source that at a luncheon given at Lady Astor's private house on the 10th May, the Prime Minister had given information to a number of American and Canadian journalists as to what his policy was with reference to the threatening situation in Europe caused by Hitler.

THE LIBERAL MAGAZINE
CHAMBERLAIN V. MANDER

There was a three-cornered duel in the House last month, in which the principals were the Prime Minister, Mr Geoffrey Mander and Lady Astor.

The drama began on May 14th, when Mr Joseph Driscoll, the London correspondent of the Montreal Daily Star, cabled a story about British foreign policy to his home journal. Similar stories were published in the United States and Canadian Press. It explained that this country was favourably inclined to what looked suspiciously like a Four Power Pact, to which Russia might be admitted at some time in the future "if she behaves."

Mr Mander had good reason for thinking that this cable bore the hall-mark of genuine official inspiration, and on June 20th he asked the Prime Minister for further information about it. If the reasons for this "fundamental disagreement" were to be given at all, they should be given to the House and not to the American Press.

The Prime Minister, by way of reply, twitted Mr Mander with a liking to pose as the "enfant terrible" of the House, and charged him with "endeavouring to stir up mischief, if possible, with other countries with whom he ostensibly desires that this country should retain friendship."

Unmoved by this onslaught, Mr Mander had the temerity to ask whether the Prime Minister saw the journalist himself, and Mr Chamberlain said he would neither deny nor affirm anything "in connection with a statement in this paper or a statement in any other paper at this time or any other time on matters of this or any other kind."

Having thus forearmed himself against any similar criticism until his dying day, he remarked acidly:"That is my final word, and I do not think there is any more to be said."

But there was, as it happened. Next day Sir Archibald Sinclair *[Liberal party leader]* returned to the attack and pressed the Premier again, saying he was entitled to argue that the Prime Minister should make his statements on foreign policy, "not to parties of American journalists, but to representatives of the people in this House."

Mr Mander returned to the assault. Was it not a fact that this interview took place on May 10th at a luncheon given for the purpose by Lady Astor?

The Noble Lady repulsed the attack. "I would like to say that there is not a word of truth in it," she declared.

This disclaimer proved to be too sweeping. On June 27th Lady Astor rose to her feet to make a personal statement.

She had been told that her refutation of Mr Mander's allegation had been taken by some as a denial of the accuracy of the contents of the article. This seemed to surprise her, for she hastened to add that such was not the case. "As to a further point of misunderstanding, I never had any intention of denying that the Prime Minister had attended a luncheon at my house. The Prime Minster did so attend, the object being to enable some American journalists who had not previously met him to do so privately and informally, and thus to make his acquaintance."

What she did deny, and continued to deny, was that an invitation for journalists to meet a public figure was an interview, since an interview is "a meeting arranged with a view to the communication of information intended specifically to be made the subject of articles in the Press." She trusted that now all misapprehensions would have been removed.

What is abundantly clear is that Mr Driscoll's story was not denied, and that Mr Mander emerged from the duel unscathed.

The arguments between Mr Chamberlain and Geoffrey were followed with great interest by the Press and the public. Articles were published and cartoons appeared in Punch and daily newspapers and the overwhelming verdict was in favour of Geoffrey and the questions that had been asked.

NEWS CHRONICLE

June 1938

Mr Lloyd George said this among other things of the Prime Minister:

"He has placed himself in a position where his own personal reputation is in conflict with the interests of the British Empire."

Mr Mander whose "mischievous curiosity" is a valuable Parliamentary and public asset, asked a question of the first importance. Mr Chamberlain declined to answer.

Instead he abused Mr Mander. I hope Mr Mander will continue the "fishing inquiries" which the Prime Minister so greatly abhors.

FROM JOHN'S AUTOBIOGRAPHY.

One night - I must have been about five - my father brought into my bedroom a Low cartoon of him in the Evening Standard, bringing 'a nice basket of lemons' to a convalescing (and wincing) Neville Chamberlain. My father's question time assaults on Chamberlain - especially on his soon notorious lunches with Ribbentrop at Nancy Astor's - may indeed have brought on spasms of indigestion. My father became for a short time a national figure. I think it was his proudest moment.

EXCERPTS FROM LETTERS RECEIVED BY GEOFFREY IN JUNE 1938 FROM MEMBERS OF THE PUBLIC:
I feel that this is a time when I may write to say, as I hope many others are saying, how very glad I am to think that you are a member of the present Parliament. I am one of those who are grateful to you every day for your fine efforts, which I hope will not cease, to expose the wanton irresponsibility of the Government.

Congratulations on your persistence in harrying this vile Government with awkward questions. Why not reveal all you know when Neville Double-face won't tell the truth? The Government must fall if the Opposition would only pluck up courage to tell all they know. No more shadow boxing - take off the gloves for a real hard K.O!

May a Conservative congratulate you on your determination to continue to shew up the unconstitutional methods employed by the Prime Minister in his efforts to bolster up the Fascist countries. Not content with selling Great Britain and the Empire in an (unsuccessful) attempt to buy off Mussolini, he now refuses to answer any question which he considers may place him in an awkward position!

A friendly personal letter from a member of the Government, the Secretary of State for Air, Sir Kingsley Wood, ended with:
I suppose you are occupying the holidays in thinking of more questions you can put to the PM!

In July, following Germany's example, Mussolini began to adopt anti-Semitic policies.

THE LIBERAL MAGAZINE
A report on a Foreign Affairs debate in Parliament - 26th July

Mr Geoffrey Mander thought that in regard to Czechoslovakia, Herr Hitler's game was to protest strongly at every concession that it was not enough, and that he must have more until the time came when he would have everything he wanted. Having made all the concessions they possibly could, having regard to the safety of the State, the Czechoslovak Government should then say that they could go no further, and that they were prepared to stand, alone if necessary, against any attack from an aggressor. He believed that an attitude of that kind would rally round Czechoslovakia those forces which stand for law and order in the world.

FLYING LOG BOOK
August 17th. Pilot - Sutcliffe. Machine type - Puss Moth. John's first flight. *[He was six.]*

THE GREEN CAN
The Royal Academy 1938

A visit to the Royal Academy this year was of special interest, if only to have the opportunity of studying item 312 in gallery No. 5, namely, a portrait of our Chairman, "Geoffrey Mander, Esq, MP" by Clarence White, a delightful piece of work carried out in a natural style and with easy execution, which gives us a truthful reproduction of our Chairman without flattery or the use of high lights and dark shadows.

Clarence White visited Wightwick Manor in July 1937. His portrait of Geoffrey now hangs there in the entrance hall.

A BACK-BENCHER LOOKS BACK
My constant agitation against the Government's foreign policy made both members of the Government and their supporters often extremely angry with me and an old Conservative friend of mine - Sir Samuel Roberts MP - told me that he had to spend quite a lot of his time explaining to his colleagues that I really was not quite as bad as they thought.

In dealing with political matters and particularly foreign affairs, I would say that Mr Chamberlain was extremely ruthless and no doubt would have justified various methods he employed, by the importance he attached to his own abilities to solve international differences.

Mr Chamberlain was of a reserved character and did not mix much with members generally. His usual procedure was to go straight to his room after Questions unless, for some reason, he had to be present at the ensuing debate. He had a photographic mind and on receiving a document could remember clearly its contents. He was not easily upset and I quote, as an example, the suggestion made by Lord Quickswood that, as a Unitarian he was not well placed to advise the Crown on the appointment of Bishops. When he was asked at Question Time what notice he proposed to take of this suggestion, he said "none whatever."

On August 20th Geoffrey and his wife flew to Holland for a short holiday; in August and September visitors to Wightwick included Philip Toynbee, and Frank and Elizabeth Pakenham, later Lord and Lady Longford.

In September negotiations began between the Czech Government and the Sudeten Germans who were demanding full autonomy for the region. Some progress had been made when the talks were suddenly suspended because of alleged "brutal" action against Sudeten Germans by the Czech police.

A BACK-BENCHER LOOKS BACK

On 7th September, 1938, I moved a resolution on the subject of censorship. "That this House attaching the utmost importance to the maintenance of British liberty of expression, both in the Press and in public meetings, and in other media such as cinema films, would greatly deplore any action by the British Government which attempted to set up any form of political censorship or which exercised pressure direct or indirect."

There had been a feeling amongst many of us that the Government had been endeavouring to manipulate the Press in connection with various aspects of their foreign policy.

The British Board of Film Censors is not an official but a private organisation though subject to Government pressure. In the '30s the board indicated to those who were thinking of making new films that it would not be possible to convince the Italian Government that the

British Government were not responsible. Whenever cuts in these films were made, they included anti-government and anti-fascist material while anything favourable to the Government policy was allowed. Direct instructions were not given, but indication sufficed.

The situation in Czechoslovakia simmered away and in an attempt to bring peace to the region, the Czech Government made a number of concessions to the Sudeten Germans.

On 12th September at the Nuremberg Congress, Hitler stated that he "would not suffer the oppression of the Sudeten Germans."

Foreign observers in the Sudeten areas reported that Hitler's Nuremberg speech appeared to have been a prearranged signal for demonstrations and violent attacks on police posts and public buildings. This disorder led to the Czech Government bringing in martial law in certain districts; they refused to give way despite demands from Herr Henlein that the laws be revoked.

A BACK-BENCHER LOOKS BACK

During the crisis of 1938 four of the five newsreel companies played down the Czechoslovakian point of view, but Paramount gave it space. The showing of this film was not tolerated for more than one day. Paramount had invited Wickham Steed, the famous editor of "The Times", and Mr A.J. Cummings of the "News Chronicle" to speak during the reel. The film was issued on the evening of 21st September and it was withdrawn on 22nd September. A telegram was sent by British Paramount News to all its theatres saying: "Please delete Wickham Steed and A.J. Cummings speeches from today's Paramount news. We have been officially requested to do so." Later on they denied they had been officially requested to do so and said they had done it at their own discretion.

Unfortunately later, in reply to a question in Parliament from Geoffrey, Sir John Simon, the Chancellor of the Exchequer, contradicted Paramount's denial and stated that the Government considered that passages in the newsreel might have had a prejudicial effect on the Prime Minister's conversations with Herr Hitler and decided to make "certain excisions from the news-reel."

There you get a perfectly clear and open case of political censorship by the Government of the day in the interests of the foreign policy that they were pursuing, and it was a foreign policy which was detested by probably half the nation.

Assurances of support for Czechoslovakia from Great Britain, France and Russia, in the event of German aggression, were made several times during the last weeks of September. At this stage the Czech Government stated that Hitler's demands were "absolutely and unconditionally unacceptable" while Hitler refused to believe in any promises Czechoslovakia might make.

On the evening of September 27th Mr Chamberlain broadcast a message to the Empire in which he said "How horrible, fantastic, incredible, it is that we should be digging trenches and trying on gas masks here because of a quarrel in a faraway country between people of whom we know nothing."

David Thomson in his book "England in the Twentieth Century" commented: "It was the authentic voice of the insular-minded Birmingham business-man."

A BACK-BENCHER LOOKS BACK

The Munich debate which took place on September 28th, 1938, was a lamentable illustration of a great opportunity missed. The occasion is well known and is notable for the introduction, in the middle of Mr Chamberlain's speech, of a telegram from Hitler, inviting him to meet him at Munich. The production of the cable was cleverly staged and took the House by storm. Speeches of good wishes for success were delivered at once by the opposition party Leaders. When the famous telegram arrived, nearly the whole House rose in enthusiastic acclamation - but not the whole. There were some of us on the Liberal and Labour benches who retained our seats as we did not believe for a moment that a man with Mr Chamberlain's views could be left to deal with Hitler: and so, of course, it proved. I turned to Col. Wedgwood who was sitting behind me and we discussed the desirability of continuing the debate, but before we came to a conclusion, the House rose. I blame myself very much for not having, with others, kept the debate going for a while, as I am sure an entirely different atmosphere could have been created and the fiction of national unity destroyed. This was an example of a failure to make use of the rules of the House by which there would have been about five hours available for debate.

Neville Chamberlain arrives in Munich for the Munich Conference. September 1938.

The Munich conference was attended by Hitler and the heads of government of France, Great Britain and Italy. Czechoslovakia was not represented and Chamberlain's chief concern was not to protect Czechoslovakia but to avert war at any cost.

The settlement resulting from the conference included the transfer of almost one-third of Czechoslovakia to Germany by October 1st. The Czech president, Eduard Benes resigned in protest.

On his return to London Chamberlain claimed he had brought back "peace with honour".

In the House of Commons Winston Churchill declared "England has been offered a choice between war and shame. She has chosen shame - and will get war."

WE WERE NOT ALL WRONG

The crime of Munich lay not in the events of that day, because things had been allowed to come to such a pass that there may well have been no alternative to the abject and humiliating British surrender that took place. The crime lay in things done and left undone, weeks, months and years beforehand; in reluctance to understand Nazi mentality, and the failure to place this country in a position to meet its menace. The crime lay in being continually taken in, in weakness and hesitation, and in the inability to grasp what was going on in the world. The shame lay in claiming the settlement as "Peace with Honour."

The report from a Royal Commission on Palestine, in 1937, had proposed a threefold partition of the territory, but it failed to please any of the people involved and a further Commission in 1938 went on to reject partition.

On October 11th Geoffrey and his wife flew, via Rotterdam, to Prague for a three day holiday. The only record of the visit was the basic information in his flying log book.

21 Kew Gardens Road, Kew, Surrey
4th Nov 1938
Dear Mr Mander,
The assembly of Parliament has reminded me that I never wrote to thank you for your kindness in securing a seat for me on 6 October, and

especially for planting me for the afternoon in such a perfect position for hearing and observing. It was a place that I had not occupied since my first visit to the House of Commons on 29 March 1889 and it was a notable experience that I shall never forget.

Yours sincerely,

Sydney Cockerell.

When Sydney Cockerell was William Morris' secretary he met many of Morris' friends, including Ruskin and Wilfred Scawen Blunt, and his friendship with the Manders provided Geoffrey's wife, Rosalie Glynn Grylls, with an authoritative insight into the lives of the Pre-Raphaelites and their circle which was to prove invaluable later when she wrote "Portrait of Rossetti" (1964).

On 9th November a German official at the Paris embassy was murdered by a young Polish Jew. This was used as a signal by the Nazi propaganda minister, Joseph Goebbels, to order "spontaneous" acts of violence in Germany against Jews, by members of the S.S. and the S.A. (Nazi stormtroopers). During the following twenty four hours thousands of Jewish owned shops and businesses were destroyed, synagogues were burned down, One hundred Jews were killed and many more were injured, or arrested and sent to concentration camps. The streets in German cities were covered in so much broken glass that the night became known as Kristallnacht (the Night of Broken Glass.) However, because their actions were met with some disapproval in Germany, the Nazi party continued to pursue its anti-Semitic policies but with greater circumspection.

THE LIBERAL MAGAZINE

The Nazi party, said Sir Archibald Sinclair at Northampton on November 11th, had made the shooting in Paris of a German diplomat the pretext for a "foul persecution" and the "most ferocious pogrom which Europe has witnessed since the Middle Ages."

The Chancellor of the Exchequer on November 18th said into the better prospect since Munich, had been thrown a development which had deeply shocked and stirred the world.

13 Kensington Palace Gardens,

London. W.8.

7th December

My dear Mander,

On Monday, the 19th December, I am arranging a Farewell Dinner in honour of Jan Masaryk who, as you will know is resigning his position as Czechoslovakian Minister to this country.

I would be delighted if you are free to join me on this occasion and hope I may look forward to the pleasure of entertaining you as one of my guests. The time is 8.15.

Yours sincerely,

I. Maisky.

Richard Smith,the Assistant Curator of the Walthamstow Museum in London, wrote to Geoffrey congratulating him "on the fine stand you have been making in the House of Commons in defence of the great ideals of liberty and freedom." He was certain that his exposures of the beginnings of authoritarianism in Britain was supported by "the great mass of British people."

Mander Brothers' Works Joint Committee Meeting was held on December 12th 1938. Recorded in the minutes was the Nightwatchmen's Report.

The Chairman *[Geoffrey Mander]* stated there were four cases to report. Also one peculiar incident, that a cow was found roaming about the Works at Heath Town, and on the police being informed, and a van brought for its transfer, it decided to escape by swimming the canal and disappeared under the Bridge.

HANSARD

22 December 1938

Mr Mander asked the Home Secretary whether he is aware of the existence in England of a branch of the German Workers' Front extensively organised and compelling every German subject in this country to belong to it; and whether he will take steps to deport the persons responsible for this system which is contrary to the interests of this country?

Sir S. Hoare: I am aware that there is a branch of this organisation in this country. There can be, of course, no question that German nationals have under our laws complete freedom of choice in this matter and the use of intimidation with a view to compelling them to join against their will would be a punishable offence. If, in any case, there were evidence that intimidation had been used, appropriate action would be taken.

Mr Mander: Is the Home Secretary aware that many of these German nationals feel afraid not to belong to this organisation because of what might happen to their relatives in Germany, and will the right Hon. Gentleman seriously consider closing down the whole organisation?

Sir G. Fox: Does the right Hon. Gentleman think it is in the national interest that German servants employed in this country should be compelled to go to this organisation and give information of what they have heard in the houses where they are employed?

Sir S. Hoare: I should certainly disapprove of any action of that kind.

1939

In 1939 the Spanish Civil War was still raging and in January, with the support from German and Italian troops, the Nationalists captured Barcelona

THE LIBERAL MAGAZINE

February

Speaking on the proposed loan of £10 millions to Czechoslovakia, Mr Geoffrey Mander pointed to "the difficulties of distinguishing between what will and what will not be useful to Germany from a military or economic point of view." He added: "The Czech Government are obliged to do what they are told, but I am sure of this, no kind of propaganda, however long continued, will have any effect on the minds of the Czech people. I believe they will keep alive their own ideals until the hideous nightmare of Nazi-ism will be brought to an end once and for all."

On 22nd February the Government authorised the formation of a British Expeditionary Force to be sent to France in the event of a war with Germany

In March, with the collapse of the Republican forces, the Spanish Civil War came to an end as Franco's army took Madrid. One of his first actions on gaining power was to hold mass executions of many of the Republicans and their sympathizers who had opposed him during the war.

It was in March that Mr Chamberlain announced that he believed "Europe was settling down to a period of tranquillity" - five days later Hitler took over the rest of Czechoslovakia and entered Prague.

In the spring, Britain and France formed an alliance with Poland and Romania in the hope that a united stand would persuade Hitler to modify his actions.

Report from THE LIBERAL MAGAZINE of a debate in Parliament held on 3rd April.

Mr Churchill referred to the "solid identity of interest" between the

Western democracies and Soviet Russia.

Mr Lloyd George spoke of an alliance with Russia as "a military matter of the very first importance. If we are going in without the help of Russia we are walking into a trap."

A BACK-BENCHER LOOKS BACK

Mr Chamberlain could make himself agreeable when occasion demanded, as I found on the occasion of the Wolverhampton Wanderers being in the Cup Final in 1939. Owing to the illness of Sir Robert Bird, the Senior Member for Wolverhampton, it fell to my lot to make the arrangements, as the finalists are always received at the house of the Prime Minister *[10 Downing Street]*. This was somewhat humourous in view of my constant furious attacks on Mr Chamberlain. When I saw the Chief Whip, Capt. Margesson, about it he said with a twinkle in his eye, "You see, we return good for evil." On the day, Mr Chamberlain, whose interest in sport did not range much beyond fishing and shooting, managed to appear as a keen follower of soccer. Coached by his Parliamentary Private Secretary he asked some relevant questions and referred to the Wolves captain's recent success in scoring some very successful goals, and made an admirable impression.

THE LIBERAL MAGAZINE

May 1939

Conscription

In less than a month after Mr Chamberlain had repeated his pledge that he would not introduce conscription in peace-time, he, without warning and without consulting the Opposition parties, demanded its adoption by Parliament. Undoubtedly the actual reason for Mr Chamberlain's action was the knowledge that "our friends in Europe" were not convinced that we meant business. Having regard to the Government's record, that conclusion was hardly surprising.

During the debate that followed on the 9th May Geoffrey spoke about the proposal to call up Reserve and Auxiliary Forces without declaring that a state of emergency existed. The Prime Minister had stated that "it is desirable to take certain precautions without the publicity and shock which would be caused by the issue of proclamations."

HANSARD

Mr Mander: I regard the introduction of this Bill with a great deal of suspicion. It is placing increased power in the reactionary and incompetent hands of a number of well intentioned gentlemen who happen to be his Majesty's Government. The Government have seemed to be most anxious in the last few years that nothing should be done to which any exception could be taken by either of the Fascist States. It may be thought that it is more effective to do things quietly and stealthily, without making it clear what is being done, whereas the best thing that we could do would be to state in the most open and clear way precisely what action we are taking in order to protect ourselves.

He and other members of Parliament also were concerned that the wording of the Bill, as laid out by the Government, would not safeguard the jobs,wages and pensions of returning servicemen. These points and a number of other concerns were discussed in a long debate that lasted into the evening.

A BACK-BENCHER LOOKS BACK

There was an occasion, under the Ten Minutes Rule *[also on 9th May]* when I introduced a measure called "Conscription of Wealth (Preparatory Provisions) Bill". The measure certainly had its humourous side but it had a serious purpose. It was the time in 1939 when conscription had been introduced and my bill was to try to apply exactly the same conditions to the conscription of wealth as to that of human life. For instance, just as age groups were called up for the forces, so wealth, in certain categories, could also be called up, and there was even a provision that enabled conscientious objectors to go before a tribunal and ask that their money, if taken, might be applied to some other purpose than paying for war. The ideas put forward caused a great deal of hilarity and when I sat down Mr Maurice Petherick arose and spoke in opposition. After this the Speaker asked the "ayes" and "noes" to declare themselves. Much as many Members were opposed to the measure they did not like the idea of appearing to their constituents as opposing it and poor Mr Petherick could get no one to support him in the Lobby.

REPORT, *written by Geoffrey,* of visit paid by Mr and Mrs Geoffrey Mander May 16th to Mrs A.M. Gill, 20 Molyneux Park Road, Tunbridge Wells.

Mrs Gill is the youngest sister of William Morris, she was born in 1846 at Woodford Hall. Remembers the Water House and paying a visit to Red House. She rarely leaves her room; she suffers badly from rheumatism, but sits up in her chair, and is mentally very vigorous, and takes a great interest in all that is going on. She resembles her brother and May Morris, details of whose will she was anxious to obtain. *[May Morris died in 1938.]* She remembers Burne-Jones (whom she says W.M. made) but never visited Kelmscott or met Rossetti. She married a Devonshire squire who was killed in the hunting field.

Remembers W.M. bringing in flowers and leaves from the garden and drawing designs for his wallpapers etc. Incident of W.M. buying a handkerchief in Bond Street and being taken for a sailor as he laughingly told them. She has with her a maid of fifty years service and a nurse; has numerous Morris relations. Spoke of the odd beauty of Mrs W.M. Anxious to know what I thought of a speech by Lloyd George. A gracious old lady.

In May, as usual, Geoffrey continued to participate in debates on widely differing subjects including the Japanese bombing of Chinese civilians, old age pensions, the Official Secrets Acts, the League of Nations and Civil defence; on 24th May he drew attention to the troubling fact that the British Ambassador had attended the Spanish Nationalists' victory march in Madrid.

John Mander was seven years old in May. He was attending Gibbs School at 134-5 Sloane Street, presumably travelling from 4 Barton Street each day. He wrote:

"I have the impression that I liked Gibbs and learnt more there than at later and more eminent establishments." *He was at Eton from 1945 to 1949.*

His father continued to juggle his life as an MP and his position as Chairman of Mander Brothers and other committees.

Every month the Green Can magazine included items of general interest for the Manders' employees; one in June headed "A Special Use for Varnish" written by a member of the sales staff, told of his visit to a firm in London, W.E. Hill & Son, founded in 1762 as specialists in the sale and repair of violins and now using Mander's varnish to touch up repaired violins.

Increasingly, in the summer of 1939, other articles appeared echoing general concern about the unstable situation in Europe with titles like "Air Raid Precautions", "High Explosive Bombs and Protection" and "On Keeping Your Head."

PUNCH
19 July 1939
A correspondent asks whether, in view of Mr Mander's many questions in the House 'De' could not be prefixed to his name.

THE LIBERAL MAGAZINE reported Geoffrey's part in a debate on 20th July 1939 when he spoke on Palestine.

He said, "I turn to the question of immigration. It seems to me that the policy of the Government, in effect, though not in intention, is working out to one of encirclement of the Jews. They are being encircled now. Hunted from Germany and other countries, they are not welcome anywhere else in the world."

The editorial comment in the magazine continued:

We should make it clear to the Palestine Administration that their first object should be to build up a National Home where Jews could live inside a Federal State. We should make it clear that we intend to tolerate no disorder there either from Germans, Italians, Arabs or Jews. By a policy of that kind we would build a bulwark of British strength in the eastern end of the Mediterranean, steady and reliable, which might be of infinite value to us in the days to come.

A POST CARD of Le Chateau, Cheonceaux, written by Elizabeth, was posted in Paris:

We were taken round this by a real Mrs Woodhouse *[the housekeeper at Wightwick was Mrs Woodhouse]* and it felt exactly like Wightwick, only much better furnished. The same Flemish tapestry. Saturday Mavis, C*[arl]* and I walked 11 kilometres. Today we've only walked 2 but we are going to a ball tonight.

Heavenly day. This chateaux is built in the middle of the river. Lovely. Love Liz and Mavis.

A BACK-BENCHER LOOKS BACK

An illustration of the effective use of questions was in connection with the Anglo-German organisation known as The Link in the days before the War. It was run in my opinion as an organisation of Nazi propaganda in this country. A number of quite innocent people were taken in and I did what I could to expose it.

One day, towards the end of July 1939, the Home Secretary, Sir Samuel Hoare asked me to go to his room in the House and told me that he was now quite satisfied as to the real objectives of the Association and asked me to put down a question, which I did, as follows:

"On August 3rd Mr Mander asked the Home Secretary 'Whether he is aware that the so called Anglo-German organisation known as The Link is in fact an instrument of the German propaganda service financed by Germany and whether he will take action to put an end to these activities?' Sir Samuel Hoare: 'The professed object of this organisation is to promote understanding between England and Germany but it does nothing to enable Germans to understand the English view and devotes itself to expressing the German point of view the organisation is being used as an instrument of the German propaganda service and money has been received from Germany by one of the active organisers. As regards the last part of the question, I have no power to intervene unless an organisation breaks the law.'"

The session was adjourned and I had gone to the South Coast. The reply became available after I had left London and a terrific press bombardment took place at my hotel from journalists anxious to have further information about this piece of Nazi offensive.

John Murray published "Claire Clairmont" the biography of Mary Shelley's step-sister, by Geoffrey's wife, Rosalie Glynn Grylls.

A BACK-BENCHER LOOKS BACK

A proposal was made by the Mandates Commission just before the War, that a limit should be placed on the immigration into Israel. This had been carried by a majority only but had to go before the Council of the League of Nations where unanimity was required. I did my utmost to bring the seriousness of the matter to the attention of the Ambassadors of those powers most likely to be helpful with a view to securing the hostile vote that was necessary to stop the plan, and spent one morning driving to the Soviet Embassy, the Chinese and Czechoslovak [Embassies] where I had personal friends but the situation had become too serious to hope for action at that time.

Hitler and Stalin announced a non-aggression pact on 23rd August.

On the 1st September German troops entered Poland. In the House of Commons that evening Mr Chamberlain made a statement:

"I do not propose to say many words tonight. The time has come when action rather than speech is required. Eighteen months ago in this House I prayed that the responsibility might not fall upon me to ask this country to accept the awful arbitrament of war. I fear I may not be able to avoid that responsibility."

He then outlined to the House of Commons the events that led up to the crisis now being faced and read to the MPs text of the document that the Ambassadors of Britain and France had handed to the German Government after the German troops had crossed the Polish frontier that morning. It ended with the statement:

"Unless the German Government are prepared to give His Majesty's Government satisfactory assurances that the German Government have suspended all aggressive action against Poland and are prepared promptly to withdraw their forces from Polish territory, His Majesty's Government in the United Kingdom will without hesitation fulfil their obligations to Poland."

After the tense debate following the Prime Minister's announcement, Parliament then carried on with the business of the day which included a number of debates concerning the preparations for war.

The Armed Forces (Conditions of Service) Bill led to a debate during which Geoffrey asked whether consideration had been given to the desirability of maintaining local regiments, such as the South Staffords, so that these soldiers would remain with friends from their own locality. He felt regiments like these fostered esprit de corps and produced better soldiers.

THE LIBERAL MAGAZINE

September 1939

Broadcasting at 11.15 a.m. on Sunday, September 3rd, Mr Chamberlain said: "This morning the British Ambassador in Berlin handed the German Government an official note stating that unless we heard from them by eleven o'clock that they were prepared at once to withdraw their troops from Poland a state of war would exist between us. I have to tell you now that no such undertaking has been received and that consequently this country is at war with Germany. The situation in which no word given by Germany's ruler could be trusted and no people or country could feel safe has become intolerable. Now we have resolved to finish it I know you will all play your part with calmness and courage."

HANSARD

3rd September 1939 12.6 p.m.

The Prime Minister made a statement in the House of Commons after his broadcast. He read out the complete message that the British Ambassador had handed to the German Foreign Secretary that morning and went on to say, "This is a sad day for all of us, and to none is it sadder than to me. Everything that I have worked for, everything that I have hoped for, everything that I have believed in during my public life, has crashed in ruins. There is only one thing left for me to do; that is, to devote what strength and powers I have to forwarding the victory of the cause for which we have to sacrifice so much."

In his reply Arthur Greenwood, the deputy leader of the Opposition, praised the bravery of the Polish people in their fight against the German invasion, while the leader of the Liberals, Sir Archibald Sinclair, declared "Let the world know that the British people are inexorably determined, as the Prime Minister said, to end this Nazi domination for ever, and to build a world order based on justice and freedom."

After the declaration of war, until April 1940, very little appeared to be happening in Western Europe, (the Phoney War) but this was the period when Poland was being invaded, and on the 3rd September an Allied passenger ship was attacked and sunk by a German submarine. Many children who were evacuated in September, returned to their families during the next few months. A propaganda war was begun and tons of leaflets were dropped over Germany in an attempt to counteract Nazi misinformation.

THE LIBERAL MAGAZINE
It was officially announced on the evening of September 3rd that the Prime Minister had decided to reconstitute the Government and to set up a War Cabinet on the lines of that established in December 1916. It was announced that the Prime Minister invited Sir Archibald Sinclair to accept a Cabinet office but that after consulting his colleagues Sir Archibald replied that he and his friends considered that "in the present circumstances they could render better service to the nation and the Government by supporting all necessary war measures from an independent position."

Hitler's advance through Poland was a powerful demonstration of Blitzkrieg or lightning war: eight days after the invasion,German troops had driven a path right across the country and were camped outside Warsaw. During the early part of the war this tactic was repeatedly employed with great success - a Blitzkrieg usually began with an attack across a border using tanks, followed by mechanized infantry and then foot soldiers supported by the air force.

On 17th September the Soviet Union attacked Poland from the east and the country was then divided between the two invading countries.

A letter to John from his father contains the interesting information:
I had lettuce and tomato sandwiches in Parliament today and my Abyssinian friend had a ham s [sandwich].
Emperor Haile Selassie had been in exile in England since 1936.

THE GREEN CAN
WORKS MAGAZINES IN WAR-TIME
As the question of how best to keep the Green Can going in war-time is being considered, our readers may be interested to read the following letter from the Industrial Welfare Society - Editor.
"The Industrial Welfare Society approached a number of editors to learn

their views and has also been in touch with the Ministry of Information and other authorities. The majority of editors of works magazines approached, are planning to carry on though some anticipate publication in a restricted form. Three or four magazines are to cease publication, an action very much to be regretted. It is interesting that in a number of cases the magazines were started during the Great War to act as a link between the firm and members of its staff serving in the forces.

All newspapers, trade papers and periodicals have been urged by the Government through the Periodical Proprietors Association to maintain publication and circulation as far as possible subject to economies.

Editors will need to be circumspect in publication of articles and illustrations which might be of use to the enemy. This applies to articles on the factory itself and from members of the Forces. Indication should not be given of the whereabouts of troops or ships, nor on the specific type of war work on which the factory is engaged."

On the same page as this serious article there is a notice of a fictional meeting: included on the agenda are: 'Shooting prospects' and 'The Pre-Raphaelite School of Camouflage'.

Together with their victories on land, German submarine warfare against British shipping at this time was highly effective (in October H.M.S. Royal Oak was sunk in harbour.) The Soviet Union continued to advance and occupied Estonia, Latvia and Lithuania. In November they invaded Finland and met spirited opposition.

THE LIBERAL MAGAZINE

Diary of the Month

Dec 1 - The King signed a Proclamation calling up military service men aged 20...

Dec 15 - Mr Chamberlain arrived in France, on a visit to the British Expeditionary Force.

The B.E.F. and the French First Army had advanced into the Low Countries in an attempt to defend Belgium from the German advance. They were in position behind the Maginot Line, a series of fortifications running along the eastern frontier of France, built between 1929 and 1936 and thought to be impregnable.

At the beginning of the war, a number of secret sessions of the House of Commons were held and no records were kept by Hansard. As well as this, to avoid any possible breaches of security, speeches were checked by interested Ministries before they were delivered.

After five years, in December 1945, Parliament agreed "that no proceeding in this House during the last Parliament held in Secret Session be any longer secret."

Mavis and Roger Partridge were divorced in the mid 1930s and in January 1940 she married Fitzroy Phillips.

By Spring 1940 John had been removed from Gibbs School in London and was attending Wolverhampton Grammar School. At this time local grammar schools were private fee-paying establishments for children of secondary school age, often with kindergartens and junior departments as well.

FROM JOHN'S AUTOBIOGRAPHY:
I had various governesses, but the age of the governess was departing, and that of the post-war au pair advancing. The governesses taught me little, and were ephemeral phenomena. The only one I remember with any distinctness came when I was about seven, a German Jewish refugee girl, Ilse. One story she told me on a walk was about her life in pre-war Germany: you had to put the kettle on if you thought the Gestapo might hear you talking, because that put their 'bugging' machinery out of action. I think this was the first time I realised that we were not at war with the kind of enemy one had read about in school-books.

At Wightwick Manor in July 2007 an unexpected email arrived from an American, Gary Kaufmann:
My 82 year old mother escaped Germany on a Quaker ship known as one of the Kinder Transports. At age fourteen she was taken in by Sir Geoffrey

John and Ilse.

Mander and his family and became their governess for their children. My mother has fond memories of her stay and care by the Manders while she called Wightwick Manor her home. At the time her name was Ilse Herz. When my mother became old enough the Manders even sent her to nursing school and she cared for many of the soldiers who were wounded in WW11.

In a second email Mr Kaufmann explained that his mother had told him that she arrived in England in 1940 or '41 when she was 16, not 14. She lives now in Connecticut, USA. The Kindertransport programme was run by a charity, the Central British Fund. It raised money to send unaccompanied Jewish children to England.

At about this time Geoffrey began to send John letters and light-hearted verse from London and, while he was so young, always written in capital letters:

EDWARD BURNE-JONES
ALWAYS EAT [S] STONES
AND STEWED FIR CONES
WITH GRAVY OF BONES
LOUD WERE THE MOANS
OF EDWARD BURNE-JONES.

In March 1940, Finland was forced to surrender to the USSR. Despite being massively out numbered by the Soviet troops, the Finns had fought hard and managed to hold up the invasion for several months.

THE LIBERAL MAGAZINE
Points from Parliamentary Debates
Wholesale and retail price increases of about one-third and sixteen per cent respectively were mentioned by Mr Geoffrey Mander on April 2nd. He asked for consideration of an iron ration, or basic ration, containing the necessary vitamins of life and made as cheap as possible, and for family allowances outside the wage structure.

A Polish Army had been established before 1939, in France, based on a French concept enabling it to integrate quickly into the French command structure on the outbreak of war.

In April 1940, a parliamentary visit was organised to meet the Polish Army in France. We flew to Paris where a sumptuous luncheon with many guests had been prepared for us by the Poles. At this, to my surprise, shared I am sure by my colleagues, I found myself placed next to General Sikorski, the Commander-in-Chief *[Prime Minister in exile]*. Apparently I was regarded by them as a VIP. The explanation was rather a touching one. When war broke out, arrangements had been made for an Anglo-French Council to concern itself with Military co-operation. I suggested in a Question (in Parliament) that the exiled Polish Government should be included on this Council particularly in view of the fact that we had been able at the outset to do little to help them. They were very grateful for this token acknowledgement of their country (and I am afraid that they credited me with more responsibility for the action taken than was justified.)

We motored from Paris through Tours and further west where the Polish Army units were stationed during that period of the "phoney" war, and visited them in their camps. We spent a Sunday morning with them at a religious service in the open in beautiful weather a few days before the attack on the Western front began. In front of us sat the President *[in exile - Count Raczkiewicz]* and Commander-in-Chief before a pulpit which had been built out of green branches gathered on the spot. The sermon was delivered by their Chaplain-General of the Forces with great vigour and broadcast to all the troops. As it was in Polish I could not understand it but learnt afterwards that it was an impassioned appeal, not only for victory, but for a victory for democracy. The whole proceedings were most impressive.

A few weeks later Geoffrey received an emotional letter from General Sikorski, the Polish Prime Minister, thanking him for his visit and for a letter he had sent afterwards.

Between April 5th and April 9th the German army entered and occupied Norway and Denmark, and British forces began to withdraw from Norway.

The Green Can started to publish helpful information at the start of the war under headings such as "What You Should Be Doing Now" and "Incendiary Bombs and Fire".

Incendiary bombs can be tackled by anyone with a cool head. Enter the room carefully. Do not open the door with a rush. A draught makes a fire burn more fiercely. Keep near the wall and down on the floor. Smoke does not worry you if you crawl. Remember, in an emergency - Horses should be taken out of the vehicle and fastened up in the nearest shelter. Remember your dog. Give it shelter and if you are not sure of it do not forget to put its muzzle on. Finally - Baby respirators will be issued as soon as received. In the meantime and as a substitute, have a box (wood) which will hold baby comfortably, ready. If gas is used you can place baby in this and wrap the box in a blanket which must be kept damp. Baby will be quite safe.

A BACK-BENCHER LOOKS BACK

Neville Chamberlain's profound error of political judgement came at the end of the great debate in 1940, when, insensitive to the gravity of the situation, he made an appeal to his friends in the House to support him.

During the three day debate in May on the Conduct of the War, Herbert Morrison had said:

"I listened as we all did, with attention to the Prime Minister yesterday. This was not a confident Prime Minister. It seemed to me that the Prime Minister was himself conscious of shortcomings on the part of the Government and very uncertain of the case which he was presenting to the House of Commons."

He went on to accuse the Government of suffering from misplaced optimism, criticised its lack of understanding of Hitler's psychology and asked why no information on the invasion of Norway seemed to have been either received from the Intelligence Service or acted upon. He spoke for fifty minutes putting forward a number of serious points that he and other MPs felt should be answered.

HANSARD

The Prime Minister (Mr Chamberlain): It may well be that it is a duty to criticise the Government. I do not seek to evade criticism, but I say this to my friends in the House - and I have friends in the House. No Government can prosecute a war efficiently unless it has public and Parliamentary support. I accept the challenge. I welcome it indeed. At least we shall see who is with us and who is against us, and I call on my friends to support us in the Lobby tonight.

He spoke for two minutes.

A BACK BENCHER LOOKS BACK.

As he sat down, I moved over to ask Mr Richard Law what he thought of it; his comment was "That has killed the Government" and so it proved. The shock produced by the evidence, that, at the height of a world crisis in which the fate of the country was involved, the best he could do was a party and personal appeal, was too much. When he left the Chamber that night it was to the echo of Leo Amery's quotation of Cromwell's words: "For God's sake go."

But he had no intention of going if he could help it, though it was clear that he himself was the greatest obstacle to national unity. The next day a small group of his friends went over to Downing Street to try and persuade him to stay. On the other hand, Mr. Macmillan [a Conservative] went down to the Labour Party Conference, then meeting at Margate, to urge them to refuse to serve under Chamberlain as Prime Minister.

The debate had started as an adjournment motion, not generally feared by a Government (unlike a Vote of Censure when defeat is fatal). It was only gradually during the three day debate that the seriousness of the crisis was realised and that the motion had in fact become a Vote of Censure.

On the last day, 9th May, of the Conduct of the War debate Geoffrey was one of the final speakers:

The First Lord of the Admiralty [Winston Churchill] referred to the Prime Minister's appeal to his friends and said that the Prime Minister had friends when things were going well. I would like to know when things were ever going well under the present Prime Minister. I have never heard of any period during the time he has been in charge when we were not going from one tragedy and disaster to another. I want the Prime Minister to go, not because I have any personal animosity to him; I have nothing but the kindest feelings towards him as a human being, but to him as a statesman I am very hostile indeed. It is purely in the political sense and for political reasons that we want to see him go.

On 10th May 1940 German forces invaded Holland and Belgium and Mr Chamberlain resigned as Prime Minister. The new Prime Minister was Winston Churchill.

A BACK-BENCHER LOOKS BACK

Mr Neville Chamberlain hated the idea of giving up the Premiership and so did a great many of his supporters. After Mr Churchill's succession, when he entered the House he was very coolly received by the Conservative benches while Mr Chamberlain received an ovation from his diehard supporters, some of whom never accepted whole-heartedly the leadership of Mr Churchill.

On 13th May the Germans broke through the Maginot line into France and the BEF began to retreat towards the sea. On the same day the new Prime Minister, Winston Churchill, spoke in the House of Commons:

I would say to the House, as I said to those who have joined this Government; "I have nothing to offer but blood, toil, tears and sweat."
You ask what is our aim? I can answer in one word: it is victory, victory at all costs, victory in spite of all terror, victory, however long and hard the road may be; for without victory, there is no survival.

At the end of the debate that followed Hansard recorded:

Question put - "That this House welcomes the formation of a Government representing the united and inflexible resolve of the nation to prosecute the war with Germany to a victorious conclusion." The House divided: Ayes, 381; Noes 0.

THE LIBERAL MAGAZINE
TREACHERY BILL

Supporting the Treachery Bill, which imposes the death penalty for grave cases of espionage and sabotage, Mr Geoffrey Mander said on May 22nd: "In normal peaceful times, I am strongly in favour of the abolition of the death penalty. But what on earth has that to do with the situation in which we find ourselves today? The mere fact of going to war means that we are obliged deliberately to kill large numbers of men, and when we think that not only men, but women and children, are being deliberately machine-gunned in a most ruthless manner by the enemy, surely it is not too much to ask that the people who facilitate that and make it possible for such outrages to be carried out should suffer the death penalty which they themselves are inflicting on large numbers of people."

This debate was held in Parliament during the week that the German forces advanced and captured Amiens and reached the sea at Abbeville. The retreating Allied forces were trapped on the beaches near Dunkirk.

On 26th May Operation Dynamo began with the rescue of the first soldiers from the beaches and during the few days more than 338,000 British and French troops were removed from Dunkirk in boats of every size and description.

Some letters printed in the Green Can magazine now came from former employees who were serving in the forces:

My ship took part in the evacuation of the BEF at Dunkirk. In all we made five trips, bringing back to England approximately 4,000 soldiers. Every trip we were attacked by large numbers of German aircraft and at one time I counted 47 planes overhead. We had four torpedoes fired at us from submarines. We sank one floating mine on the Wednesday, our third trip. On arrival at Dunkirk we came within the range of the German guns, and it was like hell let loose. Our final trip was on the Friday, and when we were about six miles off Dover a Dournier came over at 10pm and dropped a bomb so near us that it lifted us right out of the water, putting out all lights and disabling our engines. A few plates in the ship's side had sprung and we were taking in water. Our captain made an SOS and a destroyer came up and escorted us into Dover. We got into port suffering only two casualties. Surely we must bear a charmed existence.

A BACK-BENCHER LOOKS BACK

One of the most memorable of secret sessions was that which took place a few days after the Dunkirk evacuation. No records, of course, were kept of any of the speeches made, for no reporters were present. Those who published their speeches now have to rely on manuscript notes eked out by memory, which may not be always accurate. On this occasion the sitting was extremely dramatic. A number of members took part in the debate, who but a few hours before, had been on those famous beaches. No wonder they were excited and that we, who had been on English soil, were moved. I recall another very moving incident when the House was in the process of going into Secret Session. Mr Quintin Hogg (Lord Hailsham) rose to raise objection to matters being discussed in the presence of Mr Willie Gallacher who was a Communist. As soon as Mr Gallacher grasped the point that was being made, he rose, deeply disturbed, and said that he would not for a moment desire to remain during the proceedings if any of his colleagues objected and immediately left the Chamber.

It was not realised, I think, at the time, that Mr Gallacher's son had recently lost his life fighting in the air for Great Britain.

A BACK-BENCHER LOOKS BACK

Mr Churchill was very astute in the use he made of the political material, at Cabinet level, that he found lying about when he took over. The men of Munich were well looked after but only in positions where they could have no influence on Government decisions and were not free to criticise. Thus Sir John Simon became Lord Chancellor. Sir Samuel Hoare was posted as Ambassador to Madrid, and in due course Lord Halifax became British Ambassador in Washington. I believe they all did very good work but none of them were in direct control of the day to day policy decisions about the War.

Among Winston Churchill's new appointments were Archibald Sinclair who was appointed Secretary of State for Air and Anthony Eden who became Secretary of State for War. In his first speech in office, Anthony Eden called for men to come forward and join the Local Defence Volunteers: "You will not be paid, but you will receive uniforms and you will be armed. In order to volunteer, what you have to do is give your name at your local police station, and then, when we want you, we will let you know."

A few weeks after this, the name "LDV" was changed to "Home Guard" because Churchill felt that the original name was uninspiring.

A BACK-BENCHER LOOKS BACK

At home during this period, I became a private in the ranks of the Home Guard in the neighbourhood of Wolverhampton, but it was most difficult for me to perform any useful service because of my parliamentary duties. Finally a proposal was put forward by my Commanding Officer, Colonel Beddows, that I should take on special duties as a Liaison Officer between the Home Guard and the Netherlands Army, which was stationed in Wrottesley Park near the town. The point was this - in 1940 there was a very real possibility that airborne German troops might land in the country west of Wolverhampton and march on the Black Country. The idea was that I should familiarise myself with the officer personnel of both the Home Guard and the Dutch Army, and in the event of German troops marching westward I was to go in a car, near the front of the Dutch, so that if we met the Home Guard, I could explain to them that they were Dutch, not Germans, and ask them not to shoot!

This was quite a sensible idea but how it would have worked out in practice I do not know.

In June Italy officially declared war on Britain and France and then invaded southern France. On 14th June the German army marched into Paris and on 22nd June the French formally surrendered. It was then that Hitler focused his attention on Britain.

From June to September German and British air forces fought each other over the English Channel and along the south coast of Britain. Equipped with superior fighters, Spitfires, and an early form of Radar, the RAF inflicted considerable damage on the Luftwaffe.

70 Lancaster Gate,
London W2
June 14th 1940
Dear Mr Mander,
The Morris firm is as I think I told you in my previous letter in the hands of an Official Receiver to wind up and dispose of everything as quickly as possible. There seems to be no one to take it on, or carry on in the future, and it looks as if all Morris' work and endeavours are to be lost, and in any case I am afraid no one would trouble in these times to produce them in the same way.

The stocks are being sold at the Shop, and I presume anything left over will be jobbed off to some small dealer.

Yours sincerely,

Alfred Hewett

FROM A SPEECH ON RUSSIAN FOREIGN AFFAIRS given to the Supreme Council of the Soviet Union in August:

True to her policy of peace and neutrality, the Soviet Union is not taking part in the war. Our relations with Germany remain entirely as they were laid down in the Soviet-German Agreement. This agreement removed the possibility of friction in Soviet-German relations and has assured Germany a calm feeling of security in the East.

At the beginning of the war the government began the "Dig for Victory" campaign encouraging everyone to grow their own fruit and vegetables and to become self sufficient; now lawns were dug up and planted with potatoes, playing fields were sown with vegetables, and cabbages were grown in Kensington Gardens. The flower beds in the gardens at Wightwick Manor were dug up and planted with vegetables.

The Minister of Food announced that "every extra row of vegetables in allotments saves shipping "

During the first year of the War, all foreign nationals were interned. This meant, for example, that Germans who had fled from Nazi Germany and Italians who had worked for years for firms with factories based in England (i.e. Pirelli) and had homes and families here, were interned with people who had entered the country illegally or were possible spies or enemy agents. Later many were judged to be no danger to the Allied cause and were released.

Belgian evacuees were billeted in the Malt House at Wightwick during the war. This building had been used as a farmhouse during Geoffrey's youth.

FROM JOHN'S AUTOBIOGRAPHY.

The house was full of refugees - he [Geoffrey] had been active in helping to get many refugees out of Germany and Austria - and 18B (the regulation under which alien refugees were shipped off to the Isle of Man - where, incidentally, they did fine work in sorting out the archaeology of the island) replaced the 'Means Test' as the most abusive word in his otherwise non-expletive vocabulary. I felt these strange figures, with their often pathetic store of English, took up too much of my parents' time. That I resented this is suggested by a story in which I said to my mother, concerning some unfortunate Czech professor, who had unwittingly taken up most of my playtime, "Why don't you send him to bed?" The remark suggests something of my underlying resentment as my parents became gradually more and more taken up with war work, and I tended to see less and less of them.

At the beginning of the war evacuating children from cities, often from deprived areas, suddenly focused attention on poverty and ill health in infancy.

In July it was decided that mothers and young children should get free or cheap milk.

HANSARD

21st August

Mr Mander: I understand that this gentleman [Prince Starhemberg] is actually serving in General de Gaulle's army at the present time. How is it that he, undoubtedly a man of great courage, is able so easily to find service in one of the Allied armies whereas large numbers of humble people, strongly anti-Nazi,who were driven out of Austria, have discovered that all we can do for them is to throw them into internment camps?

REPORT OF VISIT PAID BY MR GEOFFREY MANDER MP TO PREES HEATH INTERNMENT CAMP. AUGUST 30TH 1940.

There were in the above camp altogether about 1,100 persons; 787 Germans, 185 Austrians, 81 Italians, 17 Poles, 22 Czechs and a few other nationalities.

In considering the position at this camp, I have in mind the fact, as already announced, that it was proposed to close it before long, and that it would not be reasonable, therefore, to propose changes which certainly ought to take place if it were going to be on a permanent basis. The day I went was one of brilliant sunshine, entirely suited for camping conditions, but it is obviously impossible for these people to remain under canvas during autumn and winter, and even now on wet and cold days the conditions are far from comfortable, particularly for the older people and those in poor health.

Doctor Beckett appeared to be active and doing everything he could, but there had been, and still is, a considerable lack of medical supplies and equipment. In this and in other respects the REs [Royal Engineers] appear to be to blame for inexcusable delays - they should be instructed by the Government that work of this kind must be carried out when it is decided on. The washing arrangements have recently been improved by the erection of fences and covering around the ablution centres, otherwise they had to do all their washing, as is still the case in part of the Camp, entirely in the open without any sort of protection or covering, and until a few days ago there was no hot water at all.

THE GREEN CAN

Our readers will be interested to know that Mr Martin Mander [Geoffrey's uncle] who has lived for many years in New Zealand, has sent instructions that the interest on his Preference Shares in Manders (Holdings) Ltd. are to be paid in future to the Red Cross fund or to any other similar war fund. This most generous gesture from the other side of the world will be deeply appreciated in this country.

Germany's bombing raids escalated and in September the Blitz began with bombing raids on London (eventually lasting, without a break, for over fifty nights.) Industrial areas like Coventry and Liverpool also suffered and it was estimated that, at this time, there were about three hundred to six hundred civilian casualties every day.

FROM JOHN'S AUTOBIOGRAPHY.

I have the impression that their's was a supremely happy 'political marriage'. The circumstances that she was a good generation younger than my father meant that the group that began to form around their salon in Barton Street were young Liberals and Socialists who shared his views on the appeasement of Hitler and used him to some extent as their mouthpiece in the Commons. Among these young men several have achieved fame: Dingle Foot (son of my father's great friend Isaac), Archie Sinclair, David Low, A.L. Rowse, Frank Pakenham, and many others.

It was a charming house, bombed in 1940, fortunately the bomb did not explode, since it arrived in the kitchen while Ronald Fuller was sheltering in the scullery.

Ronald Fuller was an old friend of Geoffrey and Rosalie; at Wightwick, in the Day Nursery, there is a framed illustrated poem written in celebration of John's birth in 1932. In 1939 he published a book on Francis Dashwood, "Hell-Fire Francis".
A year later he wrote "Ballade of the Bomb on Barton Street" with these last lines:

> All those in shelters bored and bent,
> all those who scan the sky with fearful gaze,
> all those who have been long in city pent
> the shrapnel shatters, the time bomb slays.
>
> The worms hold revel where the corpse decays;
> O very nice indeed! O very neat!
> Don't kid yourself that terror always pays,
> Nazi, who dropped the bomb on Barton Street!
>
> Hitler, your hordes may chant triumphant lays
> while your vain carnage is still incomplete,
> but rue will mingle with your shoddy bays-
> You went and dropped a bomb
> on Barton Street!

THE GREEN CAN
1940
We understand that Mr Mervyn Mander has been appointed to a position as Air Gunner in the Transport Auxiliary which is organised under the Air Ministry for the purpose of ferrying aircraft from factories to aerodromes in different parts of the country and other similar work. He leaves at once for the necessary instructional course, and will ultimately be transferred to the flying side as Pilot.

SECRET SESSIONS SPEECHES

Compiled by Charles Eade. Published 1946.

On Tuesday, September 17, 1940, while German Bombers raided London unceasingly throughout the night, the House of Commons went into Secret Session to hear from Mr Winston Churchill how Parliament would carry on with its duties during the Battle of Britain and in face of the heavy bombardment from the air which was going to be inflicted on the capital during the months ahead. The notes used by Mr Churchill on that occasion were, fortunately, so full as to form an almost exact record of what he said.

He warned the House of the ever-growing dangers of an invasion attempt and reported on what was known about German preparations. These included upwards of 1,700 self-propelled barges and more that 200 ships gathered and ready at German occupied ports. When some of these ships were bombed by the RAF there were tremendous explosions proving that these vessels were fully loaded with munitions. Then he said:

"I wish to speak about the sittings of the House and how we are to discharge our Parliamentary duties. Here we are sitting on the target. This group of prominent buildings and towers between three major railway stations, with the river as a perfect guide by night and day, is the easiest of all targets. This building is not well constructed to withstand aerial bombardment. There is an immense amount of glass about the place, and the passages are long and narrow before the blast and splinter-proof shelters can be reached. There is no certain defence against the attacks which might so easily be made."

He went on to propose measures he felt could diminish the attractiveness of the Palace of Westminster as a target. The hours and dates of Parliamentary sittings should not be made public and thus an element of uncertainty introduced. It would be safer for all MPs if they were at home or in shelters before night time air raids began, so business was to be concluded at four in the afternoon. Finally, he asked the House to support the idea of fewer sittings, at least for the next month or two.

A BACK-BENCHER LOOKS BACK

It had been intended, as is now well known, that if London had to be evacuated at any point during the War [MPs] would go to a named station, get into a train and proceed to an unknown destination. This was actually Stratford-on-Avon and Parliament would have sat in the Shakespeare Memorial Theatre.

Fortunately this necessity never arose though after the House was bombed we were obliged to move into the Lords and Church House, where many sittings were held. In many ways Church House was not at all convenient, as the general lay-out of committee rooms, lobbies etc. was not in accordance with Westminster traditions. But it worked well enough. I went once to see Parliament opened by the King at Church House, in the place where the House of Lords sat, which was the Bishops' Chamber.

The fact that this event was to take place was kept secret for obvious reasons but it was interesting to have seen it.

I used to sleep in one of the corridors of the House of Commons with various members of the staff. One could not get breakfast, but a hot bath was always available in the morning. There was a feeling of complete security as the noise of aeroplanes overhead could not be heard. This was, in fact, quite illusory because the various ceilings overhead were insubstantial and could easily been penetrated if a bomb had fallen.

There were other occasions when I used to sleep in a Committee Room as part of the arrangements for Fire-Watching and my companions were on occasions, Lord Fermoy and a Labour member, Mr Taylor. My objective was to get to sleep as soon as possible but they carried on a long conversation and a debate took place between them concerning the employment by Fermoy's wife of a lady's maid. Taylor could not understand at all why she should require the services of someone in this capacity, but Fermoy put up the most successful case he could in the most loyal manner on behalf of his wife. As far as I know, the difference of opinion remained unbridged at the close of the war.

Lord and Lady Fermoy were the grandparents of Diana, Princess of Wales.

THE GREEN CAN
October 1940
ARP DEVELOPMENTS IN OUR FACTORIES
The most serious effect of aerial bombardment would be the loss of time and production caused by sitting in shelters for hours on end when every

effort should have been made to 'keep the wheels turning'. It was with this in mind that the roof spotter or "Jim Crow" as Mr Churchill called him came into being.

The procedure at the moment is as follows: When the town alert sounds, the look-outs proceed to their respective positions, where, with their finger on the alarm bell, watch and listen intently for approaching craft or hostile action. Immediately - and this is very important - they detect anything of this nature, they must give intermittent rings on our alarm bells for all employees to take cover. There is a type of dive bombing from a great height which is too quick for the roof watcher to anticipate; in a case of this kind we have issued instructions for every member of the firm to have a place of temporary safety. For example, in the offices, under desks, on the floor close to the brick walls, lying on one's tummy with hands clasped behind the head to protect the ears as far as possible. Or in the works, under machines under benches etc. When we are suddenly attacked without warning, be prepared after hearing an explosion, to drop where you work.

From the start of the war, every Wednesday, Jan Masaryk gave a radio talk from London to Nazi-occupied Czechoslovakia. His broadcasts countered misleading Nazi propaganda and gave the Czechs information on the progress of the war.

October 16th 1940: The people of London are very angry - of fear there is no question. The inhabitants of the capital city are following the wild and unsystematic bombing undertaken by German planes with scorn and anger.

I have been to the north of England where our soldiers arranged a concert for our and the English Red Cross. It was a great success. Our lads sing very well and they arranged and sang a number of English songs really excellently. Of course they also sang our own songs, and I felt very homesick.

I know and I know joyously that the vast majority of our people at home stand firm as they did on March 15th 1939. Deception, lies, robbery and sadism - those are the philosophical foundations of your temporary tyrants. Believe nothing they tell you.

Jan Masaryk's talks were published towards the end of the war under the title

"Speaking to my Country." There is a copy at Wightwick signed 'to Geoffrey le M. Mander, Jan Masaryk'.

On 23rd October a long and lively debate took place in the House of Commons on Exit Permits (Mr H.G. Wells). The MP for Horsham and Worthing, Earl Winterton, raised the question of the exit permit granted to H.G. Wells to go on a lecture tour to America. He spoke passionately and at great length about what he described as "Mr Wells' views"

HANSARD

He has in fact for years past suggested or said openly that the Throne is a medieval and useless institution, the Christian religion a senseless, Judaic superstition, and the whole structure of society rotten. What I am solely concerned about is the wisdom of granting such a man an exit permit in the certain knowledge that he will use all the publicity and power which he possesses to denigrate his country abroad. Mr Wells is reported, soon after his arrival to have given a series of interviews. He made a number of wounding remarks about a number of politicians. He referred to them as sly, second-rate politicians who make ambiguous, non-committal speeches.

Earl Winterton continued at great length - the debate filled 11 pages of Hansard. At one point Mr Shinwell observed that, "It is, in my judgement, a great pity that my Hon. friend should have used so much eloquence, and, I may add, so much vituperation, on so poor a case. It seemed to me that the speech was more fitted to the Reichstag." Other points were interposed by other MPs and Geoffrey joined in with:

I would like to ask the Under Secretary [for the Home Department, Mr Peake] what is the policy of the Government. As I understand it, the practice at the present time is to say to anyone before he or she goes abroad, "Will you give an undertaking not to say anything which will affect the war effort of this country?" I should have thought it entirely wrong to put any prohibition on a British subject going to the United States and saying what he liked about the British Government.

Earl Winterton then asked Geoffrey if he would allow Fascists out of prison and send them to America? Geoffrey replied:

If there are any Fascists who are dangerous to the country, and they have

The Czechoslovak Government in Exile during the Second World War. Jan Masaryk, Deputy Prime Minister and Foreign Minister is on the right.

been wrongly let out, they ought to be locked up. Suppose the Noble Lord had been himself in the United States early in May, or perhaps April, and some journalist had asked him about his views about the late British Government, for example, did he consider the right Hon. Gentleman the Member for Edgbaston [Mr Chamberlain] the statesman best fitted to lead the country to victory, the Noble Lord would have been in a very embarrassing position. He could hardly have said "Yes." We all know how strongly he opposed the late Government and assisted, rightly, to throw them out of office.

Later in the debate he was able to read out very patriotic quotations from newspaper articles written by H.G. Wells. Earl Winterton was not convinced by any opposition arguments and shortly before the House adjourned he asked sarcastically if anyone would give serious consideration to letting Sir Oswald Mosley be sent to the United States to give a series of lectures?

Golders Green
N.W.11
Dear Mander,
Thank you for sending me the copy of Hansard with the Wells debate.
It gave me a good laugh. I really think something must be done about
Winterton. My compliments to Mrs Mander and our hopes that you are
both keeping cheerful in these blue times.
Yours sincerely,
David Low

David Low was a political cartoonist. He became famous in the 1930s and 1940s for cartoons attacking fascism and oppression. He was given a knighthood in 1962.

In the new government formed by Winston Churchill in May 1940, Neville Chamberlain was appointed as Lord President of the Council, but he resigned on October 3rd after an operation. Churchill wrote a letter to him that concluded:"I trust that having put down your pack you will find your health and strength restored and that we shall rejoice together in the better days that are to come."

Just over a month later Chamberlain died aged seventy one.

Among the tributes paid to him in Parliament, Sir Archibald Sinclair said "The Liberal Party opposed his policies but respected his character and integrity."

David Low.

THE LIBERAL MAGAZINE

November 1940

THE HOME GUARD

The existence of the Home Guard was one of the reasons why invasion did not take place in the summer, said Mr Geoffrey Mander on the 19th. "We all feel the deepest gratitude to them" he said. They have been working under a very great strain for the past months. The members have their own jobs to do, and very often they are up all night once or twice a week. I am sure the country appreciates what they have done."

At Wightwick Manor there is a book recording the war time service of the local Home Guard battalion. The HQ of No. 13 platoon was at Wightwick, in the Squash Court. This was in the 17th century Malthouse, one of the old buildings that were part of the estate bought by Geoffrey Mander's father in the 1880s. In 1928 a large upper room was divided to create two rooms, one of which was a squash court.

Transport was adequate. Lord Dartmouth lent us his shooting brake, an invaluable addition. In July, 1940, four Morris 8s were "borrowed" from Mander Bros. for the use of Company Commanders.

The Area Commander came to see a demonstration on a field at Wightwick in the early summer. The flamethrower designed by Captain Wood and made by CSM Nuttall functioned amazingly well. Its seventy five feet flame was fearsome and lasted for three minutes. The fifty-gallon tank containing the mixture was mounted on an Austin 7 chassis which was towed behind a car.

The Green Can received and printed a hostile newspaper cutting sent to the magazine by Mr Gandolfo, the manager of Mander's Milan branch:

In the House of Commons the Liberal Member Mander said that after the war "something" will have to be done to prevent further aggressions against Finland. According to him this "something" ought to take the shape of a rejuvenating of the League of Nations. Mr Mander is a Varnish Manufacturer and also has a branch in Italy. He evidently thinks that everything can be mended with a coat of Varnish: the League of Nations, the map of the world and one's conscience."

Captain Wood and CSM Nuttall's flamethrower.

Home Guard.

HANSARD

21 January 1941

WAR AND PEACE AIMS

Mr Mander asked the Prime Minister whether he is now able to make a statement with reference to the war and peace aims of the Government?

Mr Churchill gave a noncommittal answer ending:

"I am not, however, able to add anything at the present time to previous answers on this subject."

Stockport

Jan 30 1941

I see in the Manchester Evening News that it is your intention to make an effort to persuade the Government to state its "Peace Aims". I would like to add all the support possible. I congratulate you on being a live member and not a "yes" man.

With every good wish,

I am yours faithfully,

Ernest Taylor.

Astley Hall,

Stourport on Severn

1st February 1941

Dear Mander,

It would be a real pleasure to see you.

What about next Saturday or Sunday: either would suit me. You come by way of Kidderminster and Stourport.

It is a pleasant road to Kidderminster, one which I used to take often going to our little works in Swindon. After Stourport (over the bridge) ask your way.

As to time, I suggest your arriving about eleven and getting home to lunch or arriving about noon and staying to lunch - whichever is more convenient to you.

It is a way of acquiring merit to visit the aged.

Yours sincerely,

Baldwin of Bewdley

A BACK-BENCHER LOOKS BACK
From a chapter on Stanley Baldwin

During the War great unpopularity fell upon him and he spent most of his time at his country house, Astley Hall, Worcestershire, without a secretary and without any neighbours or friends to talk to. Hearing he was most interested to get news direct from the centre, I motored to see him on a number of occasions from 1941 till he died in 1947 and never did he say a nasty or unkind thing about anyone. He received the often unjustified criticisms of himself with silent dignity. There was an Evening Standard article attacking him. He said, "I have kept my mouth shut." I continued, "With great dignity", and he said, "many thanks."

Well known are his speeches on the Abdication of Edward VIII and, before that, during the General Strike when he asked the country to trust him.

With regard to the Abdication, he did admit that it was an occasion when he was able to render some service to the state as effectively as anyone available at that moment.

With regard to the question which had arisen earlier in the '30s as to the inclusion of Mr Churchill in his Government, he said he felt that if you had a lion about it was better to have him chained to the hearth than roaming at large, and so took him into the Cabinet.

The Speaker's Office,

House of Commons.

11th Feb 1941

My dear Mander,

The Speaker asks me to acknowledge your letter of the 10th Feb.

He thinks that the risk of a new Member being elected to a constituency, and the former Member, whose death had been presumed, turning up again, happily alive, is very small, but legislation would be introduced at once, should such a case arise.

Yours sincerely,

Ralph Verney.

In March 1941 British troops launched an attack in Italian-controlled Ethiopia.

Geoffrey spent the month up to 13th March 1941 taking part in over forty debates on subjects as diverse as incendiary bombs, medical man-power, fried fish industry, Tangier, bricklayers' labourers, Russia, and feeding stuffs (pigeons). His contribution to a debate was sometimes simply one comment or question. He persisted in asking for clarification on the Governments' War and Peace aims.

As well as his Parliamentary duties in London, he continued to travel to Wolverhampton regularly to attend, as the chairman, Manders' Works Joint Committee Meetings.

In April 1941 British troops entered and took Addis Ababa, in Ethiopia.

Some MPs were anxious to know if a persistent rumour concerning the Government's territorial ambitions in Abyssinia were true. The short Parliamentary discussion, recorded in Hansard, concluded with Geoffrey's question:

> Mr Mander asked the Secretary of State for Foreign Affairs whether he will give an assurance that any political officers now being appointed to take over centres of administration in Abyssinia are doing so with the consent and approval of the Emperor Haile Selassie?
>
> Mr Butler: Yes, Sir.

High Commissioner for Ireland,

33-37 Regent St.,

SW1

3rd April 1941

Dear Mr Mander,

Thank you. May we fix Tuesday, 8th April at 12.15pm when I will be glad to see you?

Yours sincerely, W. Dulanty

John Whelan Dulanty was a journalist and one time Irish Ambassador to London. Geoffrey's meeting with him was probably sanctioned by the British Government. He received a long letter afterwards from Viscount Cranborn, the Secretary of State for Dominion Affairs:

Confidential

April 12th 1941

Thank you so much for your letter and account of your interview with Delanty. He seems to have said to you very much what he has said to me. So far as wheat, tea, petrol etc. are concerned, the difficulty of course is that we need them all ourselves, and we cannot, I think, be expected to let our stocks run dangerously low in order to make ourselves pleasant to a neutral. I think that Delanty himself recognises this, though very naturally he is out to get what he can for his country.

The position with regard to arms is somewhat different. Here we have to supply not only ourselves but our allies, who have desperate need of anything that we can give them. Of course, if Eire came into the war on our side, the situation would be radically altered. But, while they remain neutral they must expect that we satisfy our allies first...

Finally, there is the question of a united Ireland. Any approach to this very thorny subject must, for us, take account of two vital considerations - It must have the approval of Ulster, and it must guarantee, once and for all, our strategic security. Nothing that De Valera has said up to now goes to show that he would be willing to satisfy these considerations. I am not unsympathetic towards the difficulties of Eire. At the same time, the honest truth is that, so far as the battle of the Atlantic is concerned, they stand or fall with us.

A BACK-BENCHER LOOKS BACK

During the course of the War several small books were published of a controversial nature, dealing with its origin and progress and they had a very considerable circulation. Among the best known was "Guilty Men" *[by "Cato": Frank Owen, Michael Foot and Mervyn Jones]* and my contribution was the one called "We Were Not All Wrong." The reason I came to write it was this. I found that the story being spread around in conversation, in speeches, and in letters to the Press, by those who had supported the foreign policy of the National Government from 1931 onwards, was that we were all wrong: we had all made mistakes and misjudged the position. My purpose was to show that the reverse was the truth; that both the Labour and Liberal parties, and a number of Conservatives too, were right and whose policy if it had been adopted, would have prevented the outbreak of the Second World War which, as Sir Winston Churchill has stated, could so easily have been avoided.

If the Conservative Government had had the courage to do what became necessary when war broke out, at an earlier stage, that is, to take joint action with such other powers that would help us, we could have nipped the Nazi regime in the bud and prevented its development, but there was a lack of faith and a lack of courage in the Conservative Government in the pre-war years which made them blind to the menace of Hitler and unwilling to carry out the obligations for joint action to which we were pledged under the League of Nations. We know now that the pathway to the beaches of Dunkirk lay through the wastes of Manchuria, the Rhineland and the desert and mountains of Ethiopia.

A reply to these books was published called "The Left was Never Right" by that tempestuously delightful figure Lord Hailsham, then Quintin Hogg, and later my colleague at the Air Ministry.

"The Left was Never Right" by Quintin Hogg was printed by Faber and Faber in 1945. He described Geoffrey as "the talented author of a widely advertised little book" and continued "As a piece of impertinence Mr Mander's book needs some beating." At one point he [Hogg] referred to "Mr Winston Churchill, that absurd, diehard Tory". A chapter ended with his judgement that "the Labour Party drifted towards war niggling, carping, and dividing against the Government's efforts to prepare for war. Let us leave them dividing."

NEWSPAPER CUTTING

"We Were Not All Wrong." by Geoffrey Mander, MP (Gollancz 2s. 6d.)
Mr Mander's thesis is simple. He discovers a tendency to excuse what he calls "The Municheers", on the ground that not only they but practically everyone else were wrong about both Nazi intentions and Nazi rearmament. That suggestion he seeks to quash by quoting textually columns of speeches by Labour and Liberal MPs and others, and some who, like Mr Winston

170

Churchill, were neither Labour nor Liberal, warning the Government of the inaccuracy of its information, the obscurantism of its attitude and the folly of its policy. On the whole, he makes his case, for what it's worth (which depends on how such things matter at this moment).

This is a useful and competent piece of political pamphleteering, valuable, among other things, for its citation of more than one strong assertion of faith in the League of Nations by the present Prime Minister.

419 Park West. W.2.

19th April 1941

Dear Uncle Geoffrey,

I have read your book at one sitting. I think it is extraordinarily trenchant writing and quite devastating in its attack. Certainly equal to "Guilty Men" in its readability, convincingness and vigorous writing.

Am most interested in your various Peace Aims activities which I read about in the Press.

Yours affectionately,

Peter Neville.

HANSARD

23rd April

PIGEONS

Mr Mander asked the Secretary of State for Air the number of pigeons from the United States of America accepted for use overseas, and the countries in which they are going to be used ?

Sir A. Sinclair: It would not be in the public interest to give the information asked for by my Hon. Friend.

Mr Mander: Will my right Hon. Friend bear in mind that there are vast numbers of pigeons in this country which will have to be slaughtered because of the present restrictions as regards feeding-stuffs, and will he see that these birds have the preference wherever possible.

Many budgerigars and exotic birds kept as pets in Britain died during the war because suitable seeds were unavailable.

HANSARD

29th April

British War and Peace Aims

Mr Mander asked the Prime Minister whether he will provide facilities for discussing the Motion in the name of the Hon. Member for East Wolverhampton approving the declarations of British war and peace aims, made in March by his Majesty's Ambassador to the United States in New York, since published as a White Paper?

Following on from this question the Motion was set out in Hansard. It proposed future economic cooperation between nations, mutual defence if necessary, the possibility of utilising the British Commonwealth as a bridge to greater world unity, the maintenance after the war of sufficient armed strength "to make effective the will of the nations resolved to preserve peace and freedom; a refusal to negotiate for peace with Hitler, and a declaration that we desire neither a vindictive peace nor territorial gains, but are going to see that steps are taken to ensure the world against the repetition of a war at the hands of Germany." Mr Churchill refused to allow time for discussion.

Geoffrey's questions about War and Peace aims were not the only ones with which he doggedly persevered. During the session from 22nd April to 29th May he returned several times to the question of Fire Watchers rations.

Mr Mander asked why it has been decided that neither tea nor any other rationed food shall be used in the supplying of meals to fire watchers?

He was concerned generally about the distribution and supply of food in wartime and wanted to know whether his proposals to deal with the special needs of young children requiring such food as eggs and fruit had been addressed; he asked if there were any arrangements for schools and clinics to give out oranges to children whenever possible; he felt that it should be possible to prevent most nutritional deficiencies by distributing a biscuit that could contain many of the important minerals and vitamins.

Air Ministry,
Whitehall SW1
2/5/41
Dear Geoffrey,

Thank you so much for your book. I am very much touched by the inscription. The fault of the book, if you will allow me to say so, is that there is much too much of me in it and not nearly enough of you, one Liberal MP you are grossly unfair to! The man who spoke up in season and out of season, who badgered the life out of successive foreign secretaries at question time, who trod on every aggressors' corns - and the only thing you say about him is he kept quiet (almost you suggest pusillanimously - but in my opinion quite rightly) in the Munich debate!

Incidentally the whole Liberal Party (with not more than one or two exceptions) remained seated during the ovations to Chamberlain and Attlee in the Munich debate.

Thank you so much,

Yours ever,

Archie.

[Sir Archibald Sinclair]

In May the deputy leader of the Nazi Party, Rudolph Hess, arrived by plane in Scotland to "start peace negotiations".

Mander Brothers kept in touch with former employees, then in the forces, by sending them monthly copies of The Green Can magazine. In return the editor received, and printed, photographs and letters from unidentified places with accounts like this from one soldier who wrote

Quite a lot has happened to me since my enlistment. Bombed, machine-gunned and blown out of bed etc.

On 5th May Haile Selassie returned to Abyssinia from a five year exile in England.

The National Anthems of unoccupied war-time allies were played every week by the BBC.

Ministry of Information
10th May 1941
Dear Mander,
With reference to your letter of the 7th May you will be pleased to hear that the Abyssinian National Anthem is now to be played by the BBC every Sunday until further notice.
Yours ever,
Duff Cooper
Please excuse pencil

By this time a number of rooms at Wightwick Manor were being used as headquarters by the 11th Anti-Aircraft division of the Royal Artillery; the rooms they occupied were all in the 1893 extension to the house. Two hundred and seventy other ranks worked there, most of them were clerks. A number of officers lived in; the Great Parlour filled with extra tables and chairs was a general office, the Billiard Room (with its useful table) became the map room and the Dining Room was the officers' mess. These rooms are all inter-connected. Members of the ATS worked in the kitchens and lived out at Wightwick Hall nearby. In the Old Manor House, where the Home Guard had their HQ in the Malt House, a second smaller group from the Royal Artillery was stationed.

The German navy's most powerful warship was the Bismarck. When it was sighted in Norway in May 1941, the British North Atlantic fleet went into action, at first unsuccessfully, and the battle cruiser Hood was sunk. The Bismarck eventually was sunk on 27th May by the cruiser Dorsetshire.

From a letter printed in THE GREEN CAN.
We have just returned from sea after a little more excitement. We were in company with the "Hood" right until the night before she engaged the "Bismarck." As we had run out of fuel we had to call in and fill up. We had hardly completed this operation when we were ordered out with all dispatch. We raced to the spot where the engagement had taken place, to find the "Hood" had just sunk. All we saw was a few pieces of wreckage and an officer's chest of drawer. I was aboard the "Hood" only a fortnight ago. I met two old shipmates, one of whom had been aboard her nearly

four years. I asked him if he'd like to change with me, but he wouldn't hear of it, saying he liked her.

Now I suppose I must consider myself very lucky. It seemed very hard for us aboard here to believe she had been sunk, after having escorted her almost to the last. I think I am correct in saying there were only four survivors from the whole ship's company

The Hood was hit by a salvo in the foremost magazine which had been full of high explosive shells. Only three men survived out of a crew of 1,418.

At the end of 1940 Hitler had begun the preparation for Operation Barbarossa, the planned invasion of Russia. This started with a series of campaigns in the Balkans that ensured any advance into Russia would be on a wide front.

In the early hours of 22nd June 1941, the planned attack began with an air strike, and then a vast army made up of the German army and its allies advanced into Russia.

A long and detailed debate was held in Parliament on 24th June on the German invasion of Russia.

It began with the a statement by Secretary of State for Foreign Affairs, Anthony Eden, in which he said:

Through his attack upon Russia Hitler hopes to break the military power of that vast State, and thus to free himself from any contemporary or subsequent Eastern anxiety when he turns to his duel with our own land...
As the outcome of the events of the last few days, conversations have, of course, been proceeding between the Russian Government and ourselves. The House will appreciate that I am not able to reveal the full results of those discussions, but I can tell the House that I have now heard from His Excellency the Soviet Ambassador that his Government have accepted our offer to send military and economic missions to Russia to coordinate efforts in what is now, beyond doubt, a common task - the defeat of Germany.

The following debate was wide ranging. Some uneasiness was expressed by MPs over what was bound to be a closer relationship with a Communist state and this appeared to be echoed in the country. Aneurin Bevan said:

I overheard a conversation on a bus yesterday between two working men, one of whom said, "now we shall see whether the British Government prefer to fight the Soviet Union or Nazi Germany. Now we shall see where their real interests and their real affections are".

The MP for Norwich, Mr Strauss, was anxious that nothing should appear to condone the past aggressive actions of Russia towards the Baltic States. Geoffrey felt that it would be reasonable to allow the British Communists:

To get their breath and seriously consider what their position is, without our going back too much upon what we all know has happened in the past.

Mr H. Strauss: They have not waited to get their breath. Already, yesterday, they put out an announcement associating the attack upon Russia with the dirty work that had been going on since the arrival of Hess in this country. When my Hon. Friend asks us to give the Communist party a chance it is only fair to point out that the Communist party in this country did not wait to think the position out before making that announcement.

Mr Mander: I think they must have been out of breath, and I am prepared to wait until they have had time to give the matter proper and serious consideration and to let us know where they do stand, which I imagine will not be the position which they occupied a week ago.

In his speech today the Foreign Secretary paid a well- deserved tribute to the Polish Government in the very difficult position in which they find themselves, in view of the struggle that is going on. I hope that my right Hon. Friend the Foreign Secretary will, during the coming weeks and months, use all his diplomatic and persuasive abilities for the purpose of trying to reconcile those two great countries, Poland and Soviet Russia.

A BACK-BENCHER LOOKS BACK

I remember vividly a luncheon given by the Polish Government at the Dorchester, when General Anders was present. At the beginning of the War he had been arrested by the Russians and placed in solitary confinement under not too pleasant conditions. When the Soviet[s], however, came into the War [as allies] discussions took place between the Polish and Soviet Governments as to the provision of a Polish Army to co-operate on the Eastern Front. One of the first essentials was the provision of a Commander-in-Chief in the Field and one day General

Anders, to his astonishment, found himself removed from his dungeon and in the twinkling of an eye, converted from his then status to that of Commander-in- Chief of the Army. The change was, indeed, breathtaking.

EXCERPT FROM A LETTER from Ivan Maisky, Ambassador for the USSR.

14th July 1941

With regard to the playing of "The Internationale" I find the situation very anomalous. One might like or dislike it, and irrespective of what else it might be associated with, it is our National Anthem just as "God Save the King" is yours, and therefore should be treated as such. In playing all the National Anthems of other Allied countries I don't think such discrimination is justified. Therefore I cannot approve the attempt to substitute our Anthem with a Red Army marching song or any other music, which in themselves may be admirable but are not the Soviet National Anthem.

HANSARD

23rd July

Mr Mander asked the Minister of Information whether, in arranging for the broadcasting on Sunday evenings of songs of our Allies, he will, as a matter of courtesy, consult with their representatives in this country with a view to selecting representative items acceptable to them.

Mr Bracken: The BBC will select the programme, but the representatives of our Allies will be consulted to ensure that it is acceptable to them.

The July edition of The Green Can included the Treasurer's yearly report on Mander's Welfare Club. The magazine made a loss in 1940/41 as more employees joined the Forces and subscriptions fell; this coincided with the additional expense of supplying free copies to the absent members.

Mr Geoffrey then reviewed the work of the Club during the past year. He said the Green Can was certainly doing very good work by acting as a link between the works and our colleagues in HM Forces.

From a letter published in the same edition of The Green Can:

> As you know my husband is prisoner of war in Germany, and I am not
> allowed to send him any books or any printed illustrations whatever, so
> I am saving the copies of 'Green Can' for him when he gets home. He
> was taken prisoner in June 1940 and I didn't receive his first letter until
> January this year, but I am pleased to say they have been fairly regular
> every month since. He writes very cheerful, and says he's keeping his chin
> up in hopes he will be home soon.

On 6th August 1941 the Lord Privy Seal, Mr Attlee, opened a debate in Parliament
with a report on the progress of the War. His statement included information on
the fighting in what he called "that enormous battle area" from the White Sea to the
Black Sea, the Battle of the Atlantic, the situation in the Middle East and assurances
that the Government was maintaining the utmost vigilance on the conduct of Japan
in Indo-China.

The debate was long and detailed and MPs raised a number of points including
questions about the American loan to the Great Britain (Lease-Lend), censorship of
the Press, and the possibility of harsh, and therefore risky, reparations after the War.

Geoffrey was concerned by the attitude of some MPs and members of the public
to the pact between Russia and Poland; he spoke from personal experience:

HANSARD
> It is sometimes said by those who, I think, do not altogether appreciate
> what has happened, that the Polish Government is just the same as the
> Government in that country before the war - that it is reactionary and of
> the Right. I venture to think that is quite untrue. Let me give one example
> to prove what I am saying. Some years ago when I was in Poland [1938]
> I was in a little mountain resort called Zakopane. I had an introduction
> to a certain Cracow professor who was one of the leaders of the Peasant
> Party, which, though representing 70% of the nation, was then entirely
> unrepresented in the Government. He had recently been in prison for
> political reasons - because the national peasants had held some big
> meetings. Finding that he was in that resort I endeavoured to get in touch
> with him. I had to go secretly by roundabout ways, to his hotel, looking
> all the time to see that nobody was about. Finally I had an interesting
> discussion with him in his bedroom, with the windows carefully closed.

That professor, Professor Kot, is now one of the leading Ministers of the present Polish Government in London. It shows the remarkable change in the political orientation of the Polish Government, a point which ought to be made clear.

Professor Kot and Geoffrey had met for lunch, in London, a few days earlier.

Czechoslovak Ministry of Defence,
134 Piccadilly, London W1.
12th August 1941
Dear Mr Mander,

  Soldiers of one of the Czechoslovak regiments that fought in France in 1940 and who are now in Great Britain have compiled the enclosed booklet on the first anniversary of their arrival to this country.

It would give me great pleasure if you would kindly accept the enclosed copy of this book and I know how honoured our soldiers will feel at the thought that perhaps you will find a moment of time to look through it.

Yours very sincerely,
Lt. Gen. Sergěj Ingr,
Minister of Defence.

The first formal statement of war and peace aims, the Atlantic Charter, was issued jointly by Britain and neutral America on 14th August 1941 after Winston Churchill travelled in great secrecy to meet Franklin Roosevelt in Placentia Bay, Newfoundland. Their statement had mixed origins - it included Roosevelt's Four Freedoms, freedom of speech and of worship and freedom from fear and from want. The British emphasised the need for economic development and greater social security. These aspirations were eventually adopted by all the Allied Governments. The German High Command was particularly disturbed by the declaration that both countries would seek to carry out the main aims of the charter "after the final destruction of the Nazi tyranny" which they interpreted as a thinly disguised declaration of war from the USA.

Parliament's summer recess in wartime was short. In 1941 it lasted from 7th August until 9th September; at the same time most schools had summer holidays lasting for about eight weeks.

Geoffrey returned to Parliament full of his usual energy. On 10th September, during Oral Answers to Questions, he contributed to a discussion on Abyssinia; this was followed straight away by a question about Vichy France (British Diplomatic Relations) when Geoffrey asked the Secretary of State for Foreign Affairs "whether he will now consider the advisability of now breaking off diplomatic relations with Vichy France and according full recognition to General De Gaulle and those associated with him on behalf of Free France." A lively exchange of views followed between him and Anthony Eden.

Later he enquired about the progress of negotiations between representatives of Poland and Czechoslovakia and then, after other questions and answers, started a lively debate about the lack of payment for part-time employees in the House of Commons kitchens during the Recess.

In the summer of 1941, when he was nine, John Mander left Wolverhampton Grammar School. In September he started as a boarder at the preparatory school Summerfields near Oxford, attended by his father nearly fifty years before. He wrote about it years later:

> I hated sleeping as a small boy in a dormitory of twenty other boys. There was never anywhere to retreat to, in order to read in peace and quiet, although the grounds were large and one had ample free time. Indeed, my experience in English boarding schools was not that one's life was over-organised, but rather that one had more time to oneself than one would have had at home. This would not have applied to me since during the war I had the run of Wightwick, to my great delight.
>
> I do not think my father had any particular ideas about the best kind of education for children. He was highly sentimental about the Harrow School Songs. He was in these and in many other respects, a profoundly conservative man. School was simply part of that eternal process. My father and his father had been through it all. What objection could there be?

A LETTER, ORIGINALLY WRITTEN IN FRENCH, TO JOHN FROM HIS FATHER.

November 16 1941

Dear little John (but not so little)

Here is a letter in the beautiful French language which you are learning so well. Later on I shall send you a letter in Greek when you begin to learn this famous language. You have done very well to be top of your class. Congratulations!

Your devoted father,

G. le Mesurier M.

Following Geoffrey's parliamentary question in April about food for carrier pigeons, in November an article appeared in THE GREEN CAN with the title 'PIGEON HERO OF THE BLITZ':

Bombers and fighters are not the only wings that are filling the skies in increasing numbers. More and more carrier pigeons are being used by the British Army to take their part in maintaining vital links in the chain of communications at home and abroad. The pigeons already have a wounded 'hero,' a blue chequer cock, which arrived in London with a leg missing during a heavy raid, having flown from a town in the Eastern Counties. It was thought that the bird was struck by a fragment of shell. It was nursed back to health and showed no signs of wishing to retire on a pension of maize. This pigeon is now doing excellent work.

HANSARD

25th November 1941

Mr Mander asked the Prime Minister whether he will make it clear to the enemy that, in any settlement of peace terms, full restoration will have to be made of machinery and other property removed from an occupied country and arrangements made for the reconstruction of property destroyed, further more that any Germans settled in territory outside Germany must be removed?

The Prime Minister: We must not count our chickens before they are hatched.

University College, Oxford

Dec. 1 '41

Dear Mrs Mander,

I must apologise for not writing to you before this to thank you for sending me your husband's book but I wanted to read it first. Now I have done so, and, as a result my thanks are enthusiastic and sincere. I have rarely read a book which has interested me so much. It is a brilliant presentation of a case which it is essential for as many people as possible to understand. Recriminations are useless, but a scientific analysis of what caused the disaster is necessary if we are not to make the same mistakes again. One of the things that struck me was how well Attlee came out of the whole thing - his speeches were almost the best of the quotations.

I do hope that we shall meet soon again. Our cook is leaving us but I am very good at opening a tin of sardines.

Yours sincerely,

Arthur Goodhart

Arthur Goodhart was Master of University College and editor of "The Quarterly Review".

Geoffrey's continuing interest in the possibility of a Jewish Homeland was shown by his question recorded in Hansard on 4th December 1941

Mr Mander asked the Prime Minister whether, in view of the broadcast made by Field-Marshall Smuts, the Prime Minister of South Africa in which he said that the case of the Balfour Declaration had become overwhelmingly stronger, the British Government will make a similar declaration?

He received a noncommittal answer from the Lord Privy Seal.

On Sunday 7th December 1941 Japan attacked the US Pacific fleet in Pearl Harbour. In less than 30 minutes they bombed 13 ships and destroyed about 200 aircraft with the loss of more than 3,000 personnel. On 8th December the United States declared war on Japan and this was swiftly followed by Japan's allies, Germany and Italy, declaring that both countries were now at war with America.

On the same day - 8th December - the commander of the British fleet in Singapore, Vice-Admiral Tom Phillips, discovered that the Japanese were about to land on the Malayan coast and despite the fact that the navy had hardly any support from fighter aircraft, he put to sea with two ships, the cruiser Repulse and the battleship Prince of Wales Two days later they were attacked and sunk by Japanese bombers; thousands of men were killed.

1942

HANSARD

8 January 1942

Mr Mander asked the Minister of Pensions whether his attention has been called to the statement in a recent issue of 'The Midnight Watch,' the wall sheet of Britain's fire-guard and Civil Defence workers, issued by the Ministry of Home Security, to the effect that women do the same patrols as men, lose the same amount of sleep, etc, and only receive four-fifths of a man's compensation when hurt; and whether he will rectify this position by giving equal compensation to both sexes?

The Minister, Sir Walter Womersley, gave a negative reply.

Mr Mander: Is not my right Hon. Friend aware that this policy is advocated in the journal issued by the Ministry of Home Security, and will he not give more attention and sympathetic consideration to a policy put out by one of his colleagues in the Government?

Sir Walter began by saying that, "I have had the pleasure of reading the document which my right Hon. Friend has just flourished." and then continued with a second negative reply and the business of the House moved on.

Later that day Geoffrey asked Anthony Eden whether any progress had been made in negotiations with Haile Selassie over full recognition of Ethiopia's independence. Mr Eden said he hoped to make an announcement before long.

This letter to John, in English but using the French version of his name, has no address or year on it - references to a dormitory places it after 1941 although where Geoffrey is sleeping is a mystery. It does not sound good.

Jan 25

Dearest Jean,

Great News. Two mice killed in traps last night in our room. Noise woke me up. Cat did nothing but sleep when shut in. Three set tonight.

We walked on aerodrome for a change!

Has our luggage come? Who are you sitting next to? Send plan of dor[mitory]

Love from Dad

HANSARD

27 January 1942

The Prime Minister (Mr Churchill): From time to time in the life of any Government there come occasions which must be clarified. No one who has read the newspapers of the last few weeks about our affairs at home and abroad can doubt that such an occasion is at hand. I have come to the conclusion that I must ask to be sustained by a Vote of Confidence from the House of Commons. A Debate on the war has been asked for. I have arranged it in the fullest and free-est manner for three whole days. Any Member will be free to say anything he thinks fit about or against the Administration or against the composition or personalities of the Government, to his heart's content, subject only to the reservation which the House is always so careful to observe about military secrets.

Half way through the first day of this debate Geoffrey spoke at even greater length than this excerpt would suggest.

There are two forms of criticism in this House. One is friendly, in which I hope to indulge a little myself, and the other is hostile, even bitter, criticism. Some of it is criticism to which the Prime Minister really ought to give most careful consideration, such as that from Sir William Beveridge. He is a man who speaks with the widest experience and with a full knowledge of what happened in the last war, and his criticism is put forward entirely in the public interest. I think he made four suggestions. One was that the Prime Minister should not continue to be Minister of Defence. Sir William Beveridge rightly says that the job of the Prime Minister is to say to the Minister of Defence, "What are you doing about so and so?" But there is no one in a position to say that to the Minister of Defence at the present time, and I should have thought that that was a source of weakness.

Then there is the question of having a Minister of Production. I do hope that whatever comes out of this Debate we shall get carried into effect a proposal which I believe commands the support of all parties in this House and approval throughout the country, and that is that there should be one individual Minister in charge of the three production Departments Six or more months ago we were told by the Ministers concerned that during the autumn and winter there would be terrific, unimaginable attacks on Germany, including Berlin. They have not taken place and it is very disappointing. I think that obviously it must be because we have not got the aircraft with which to do it, and that shows there is something thoroughly faulty with our organisation.

An explanation should be given of our attitude towards Vichy. Why did the Prime Minister ask the Government of Canada to remain in diplomatic relations with Vichy at a time when the British Government have deliberately broken off those diplomatic relations? I should have thought that we knew exactly where Vichy stand, and we ought to have nothing whatever to do with them. Let us break all contacts with traitors of that kind

In February 1942 Air Marshall Arthur Harris was appointed head of Bomber Command and under his direction the "terrific, unimaginable attacks" touched on by Geoffrey did take place, but later in the spring. The RAF began controversial night-time bombing of civilian targets in an attempt to lower the morale of the German population.

On 15th February 1942 130,000 British and Allied troops were defeated and Singapore surrendered to the invading Japanese.

Astley Hall, Stourport on Severn.
20th February 1942
My dear Mander,
I am so glad you are getting over that beastly influenza and propose coming here on March 1st. That is wholly agreeable to me.
By all means bring Molson with you if you are happy in his companionship and he would like to come.
Yours sincerely,
Baldwin of Bewdley

In 1942 I visited him with Mr Hugh Molson, MP, who unsuccessfully tried to persuade him to write his reminiscences. He made it clear that he had no intention of doing so. Mr Baldwin was, of course, closely associated with the Pre-Raphaelite group and their descendants through his mother who was one of the beautiful and talented daughters of the Rev. G.D. Macdonald - a well known Methodist Minister. They all made most interesting marriages: one became Lady Burne-Jones (whose granddaughter was Angela Thirkell, the novelist) and another was the mother of Rudyard Kipling. The third married Sir Edward Poynter, later President of the Royal Academy, at the same time as his own mother married Alfred Baldwin, at St. Peter's Church, Wolverhampton, in 1866. It was to have been a triple wedding but Macdonald's son unfortunately was ill. Mr Baldwin remarked that for the occasion the family drove in a coach with postilions to St. Peter's Church, though this astonished him, coming from what he called a "humble home".

S.B. in his younger days used to see a great deal of his cousins. In later years William Morris, his beautiful and impassive wife Jane, and others of their group were well known to him. He once told me a story about them. Morris was standing, laying down the law in his vigorous way to some of his friends when Val Prinsep came up to him from behind and struck him a heavy blow. Morris paused in his flow of rhetoric for a moment and without looking round said, "don't do it, Janey." This afterwards became a standing joke in the Baldwin family and the sentence was used whenever it could be appropriately applied.

Val Prinsep was a painter who had worked in Paris for a few years. George Du Maurier said that he based the character Taffy, in his novel "Trilby" on Val Prinsep.

THE GREEN CAN
February 1942

The prospect for the paint trade and in particular the printing ink trade is, to use a Churchillian epithet, "bleak and sombre." Raw materials are in short supply and must inevitably in the national interest be more and more reserved for Government uses. Articles which now are generally painted should have the numbers of coats of paint reduced or entirely eliminated. When there is not enough to go round it is obvious that, for instance, aeroplanes and battleships must be protected with dope and paint while wooden toys and similar articles may safely go without paint. The Board of Education are advising Local Authorities to give up interior painting in schools, and where necessary substitute soap and water for paint.

Dope was a cellulose paint used to waterproof and strengthen aircraft wings constructed from fabric.

THE GREEN CAN carried an account of Mander Brothers' Works Joint Committee held on Monday 2nd March in Wolverhampton, conducted by Geoffrey.

The Chairman remarked that it was interesting to those who had been connected with this Council so long to learn that Mr Bevin [Minister of Labour] had ordered all ordinance Factories to set up similar Councils and hoped to extend this to other Factories in the near future.

HANSARD

4 March 1942

The Secretary of State for Air, Sir Archibald Sinclair, made a long statement about the Air Estimates for 1942 including information on the support given by the RAF to the other services and the expansion of training facilities for all Allied air crews.

In the middle of the debate that followed, Geoffrey spoke knowledgeably and at length:

It seems curious that when the monoplane has been adopted for all operational purposes not only in this country but almost everywhere abroad, and is used very largely for the later stages of training, that when airmen first learn to fly they should be trained on biplanes - Tiger Moths. It obviously delays their training because the two types of machines are so different in many ways. It is the case, I believe, that some time ago a prototype Magister was got out which had flaps and brakes and various other things which would be useful in the training of those who will later have the experience of larger machines. I should like to know why we are still using biplanes and have not proceeded with that prototype.

Casselton Elliott & Co.

4 & 6 Throgmorton Avenue,

London EC2

11th March 1942

Morris & Co. Art-Workers Ltd (In Liquidation)

Dear Sir,

I am in receipt of your letter of the 9th instant. I did not purchase the tapestries, fabrics etc. formerly the property of Morris & Co. but have acted as Liquidator of the above company. As Liquidator I have now disposed of the whole of the Company's stocks, so I am afraid there is nothing which I can offer to you. The Company's stocks of wallpaper were purchased by Messrs. Sandersons Fabrics Ltd. of 56 Berners Street, London, W1, while the remaining stock of fabrics was purchased by Mr G. Surman of 226, Ulster Chambers, 168 Regent Street, London W1. Possibly one of these firms might be able to assist you.

Yours faithfully,

T.A. Ryder.

Liquidator

A BACK- BENCHER LOOKS BACK

During the War, Back Bench MPs found they had time to spare owing to the fact that normal political controversies had ceased. When, therefore, Sir Archibald Sinclair invited me, in March 1942, to become his Parliamentary Private Secretary in place of Mr Wilfred Roberts, who had resigned, I was very glad and accepted the position.

Sir Archibald, as Secretary of State for Air, attended most Cabinet meetings and controlled a service vital to victory. He was also leader of one of the three parties making up the War Cabinet. It was further a great pleasure to be associated with a Statesman for whom I had such a high regard.

Cutting from EASTERN DAILY PRESS.

27 March 1942

CHAMPION QUESTIONER

Mr Mander's appointment as Parliamentary Private Secretary to Sir Archibald Sinclair, the Air Minister, will rob the House of Commons of some of its gaiety. He had developed into the champion questioner of Ministers on the Front Bench. It is estimated that every question addressed to a Minister costs the country something like £1. What Mr Mander's almost daily catechism of the Treasury Bench must have cost the nation from first to last is a matter for statisticians to ascertain.

Mr Mander, who had experience of the RAF in the last war, will have much to interest and occupy him in his new role, but it is doubtful whether he will enjoy it half as much as he enjoyed the job of putting awkward questions to embarrassed Ministers.

A Parliamentary Private Secretary rarely engages in the hurly-burly of political life. His job is to be in constant attendance on his departmental chief and to fetch and carry for him. But a Parliamentary Under-Secretaryship has always been regarded as a stepping-stone to higher things.

The Mount,
Wolverhampton.
March 29
My Dear Geoffrey,
Congratulation from us both on your government appointment. Mother [Geoffrey's aunt] is so pleased altho' we shall miss your so pertinent questions which have so often wakened up the unthinking fools. I suppose the new moustache is in honour of the advancement?
With best wishes for an interesting career.
Your affectionate Cousin,
Daisy.

Cutting from BIRMINGHAM POST
MR MANDER'S NEW ROLE
His Wolverhampton constituents will be amused to learn that Mr Geoffrey Mander today has been the subject of much good humoured chaff on his appointment as Parliamentary Private Secretary to the Air Minister. Mr Mander's colleagues in the Commons have not forgotten that he was a member of the Committee on Offices of Profit under the Crown and a signatory to a report not exactly complimentary to Parliamentary Private

Secretaries generally and distinctly disapproving their multiplication. The member for East Wolverhampton will not add to the number of PPSs and if he brings to his new duties half the industry he is wont to apply to baiting Ministers at question-time he may play a useful part. His chief is so deeply engrossed in administrative work at the Air Ministry that he rarely appears in the Commons. Mr Mander's task will be to keep him informed about currents of opinion. Acceptance of this honourific - yet highly honourable - post bars participation in debate on air matters, but leaves Mr Mander entirely free to carry on his characteristic tilting at the work of other Government Departments.

A BACK -BENCHER LOOKS BACK

The position of Parliamentary Private Secretary was usually occupied by some young member who wished to obtain experience of Parliamentary work, but as all the young members were away engaged on war work, more senior members were glad to offer their services. The appointment is one made by the Minister himself and not by the Prime Minister. I was, therefore, perfectly free, in theory, to continue my usual practice of asking questions, but it was not easy to walk over to the other side of the House from the bench behind the Ministers and be in my place to ask a question after I had finished helping Sir Archibald with his. Indeed, after one day when Mr Eden had asked me to postpone my three Foreign Office questions, I gave up the practice.

The result of this decision can be seen in Hansard's index. In the month before the 1942 Easter Recess Geoffrey took part in forty two debates, in the first month after his appointment when Parliament returned - April 13th to May 14th - he is recorded as speaking only on fourteen occasions. In later years, possibly becoming used to his new position, he increased his involvement in debates.

Thus it was that I spent three years at the Air Ministry, sharing a room with Sir Louis Grieg, friend and confident of George VI. He was, of course, full of interesting stories and a number of distinguished visitors used to call to see him in his room, among them the Duke of Kent, and Prince Bernhardt of the Netherlands. The chief difficulty with the latter was to keep him on the ground as he was always liable to rush off to fly the latest type of RAF machine, to the anxiety of those responsible. I think in the end he was forbidden to do so.

THE GREEN CAN

We have had under consideration the possibility of introducing part-time work for women in our factories. Schemes of this kind have been working very well elsewhere, and in view of the shortage of labour and the importance of the war work we are doing, the time may come when some plan of this kind may be essential. In these circumstances we should be glad if our readers would kindly consider whether there are any women members of their families who might be prepared to put in regular half days.

The women employed by Manders before this all worked in the firm's offices.

On 23rd April, the House of Commons went into secret session to hear a statement by Mr Churchill on the situation in the Far East and the fall of Singapore.

He stated that in seven weeks a third of Britain's fleet had been crippled or lost and added "the violence, fury, skill and might of Japan has far exceeded anything that we had been led to expect."

A BACK-BENCHER LOOKS BACK

Nothing causes so much anxiety as the controversial P[arliamentary] Q[uestion]. Just as the questioner had carefully thought out his form of words so also the officials of the Ministry get together in order to produce a reply which will expose the smallest possible surface for attack. At the Air Ministry when I was with Sir Archibald Sinclair one of my duties as Parliamentary Private Secretary was, on the day when he was answering questions, to receive in the Inner Lobby from an Air Ministry messenger, a locked despatch case which contained not only the reply itself but a considerable list of possible or probable supplementaries [questions] that might be put by MPs interested in the subject, together with suitable replies to those imaginary questions. Much ingenuity was exercised on both sides. It was worse for the Minister, for a foolish or inaccurate answer might receive immense publicity and do the Minister and the Government much harm. Sir Archibald was always capable of holding his own.

In May the intensive bombing of civilian targets by the RAF under "Bomber" Harris culminated in the destruction of one-third of Cologne in a single night. As a result of the huge numbers of incendiary bombs that were dropped at one time, a new phenomenon appeared, the fire storm, which sucked in oxygen from surrounding areas suffocating any people near by - the resulting devastation outstripped anything seen before.

A BACK-BENCHER LOOKS BACK

I feel no doubt that "Bomber" Harris precisely possessed the qualifications that were needed at that particular moment in Bomber Command. As a matter of fact, he had to spend a lot of his time trying to prevent his bombers being taken away from him and used for other purposes. He conducted what were called "Conduction Courses" at his house near High Wycombe. Distinguished individuals would come down and spend a night there while he endeavoured to prove to them the immense importance of leaving the bomber force with him, rather than divert it for Naval transport or Military purposes. In this task he was very successful.

On one occasion when I took down Lord Winster to one of these courses, I was informed that one of my bedroom doors opened on to a bathroom which was also accessible to the Air Chief Marshall and I was greatly alarmed lest I should find myself in the bath with Harris banging at the door to be let in. I therefore spent considerable time in wandering around the house in pursuit of another bathroom not threatened with an attack from this quarter.

This account was written in the 1950s after Reginald Fletcher became Lord Winster. In 1942 he was PPS to the 1st Lord of the Admiralty, A.V. Alexander.

In North Africa in June, after a battle between the Allies and the Axis forces under Rommel, the British were driven back into Egypt until they eventually reached El Alamein.

Flying Log Book: During the summer of 1942 Geoffrey flew with Archibald Sinclair to air fields all over the country - in June - Glasgow to Hendon via Irish Sea,

192

Isle of Man, Rhyl, Worcester. On August 14th their course covered Bobbington (near Wolverhampton), Stourport, Windsor, Gainsborough, Shrewsbury and back to Bobbington again.

August 22nd seems to have been the most exhausting day: they landed four times taking in Moreton-in-Marsh bomber OTU, then on to St Athan (Wales), Fairwood Common and then Abingdon where they landed at midnight.

THE GREEN CAN reprinted an article Rosalie Mander wrote for The Star newspaper about part-time work in factories.

> There are still many machines idle which could perfectly well be manned by part-time labour, for in the country in general we have been very slow in mobilising this large reserve of man-power. In the large Midlands town with which I personally have most acquaintance, part-time work is very much on the map. An advertisement in the local paper brought in over 1,000 applications and as it had been anonymous it could not be known to those offering their services that the work was comparatively clean and the factory very up-to-date with excellent welfare arrangements. The actual work seems tiring first of all to anyone not used to standing much or using their arm muscles, and it is also a little frightening - like bathing the baby for the first time: but machines, like babies, don't really break so easily.

On 19th August British and Canadian commandos suffered heavy losses in a disastrous raid on Dieppe. They lost tanks, aircraft, landing craft and thousands of troops.

Two of Geoffrey's cousins were married in August. The wedding of Anthony Mander was held in Shepperton, Surrey and a light hearted account of Philip Mander's wedding in Hove was printed in The Green Can, and obviously written by the groom.

> One can get some idea of the ceremony by referring to the prayer book; but there were one or two unrehearsed touches (no, the wedding-ring did not fall down a grating) for the parson, an ex-naval chaplain, seemed to have lost the names of those whom he was joining together, and the organist gave an encore extra verse that wasn't there (but it was nevertheless bravely sung).

A BACK-BENCHER LOOKS BACK

It is, of course, the custom for ministers when they have to make a public speech to have some sort of draft placed before them on which they can work. This is the task of one of the Private Secretaries. Occasionally, I would be asked to contribute a passage on foreign affairs and finally the Minister would work the whole speech out in his own particular form. On one occasion when the construction of gliders on a large scale was the subject of interest, I tried to persuade Sir Archibald to introduce a passage, making some reference to the first glider in the world's history - the Pterodactyl, an animal eighteen feet across from wing tip to wing tip, which lived some ninety million years ago and could not fly, but took off from heights and glided downwards as a means of catching fish. In order to make sure of the facts, I paid a visit to the Director at the Natural History Museum but I regret to record that my suggestion was not adopted!

In August Claude Auchinleck, who had been in command during the retreat to El Alamein, was replaced by General Bernard Montgomery as commander in the field under General Alexander.

Geoffrey recorded in the flying log book that he spent three hours on a night flying course which took him from Bobbington, near Wolverhampton, to Andover and Cambridge.

Among his letters received at this time was a thank you from Stanley Baldwin after Geoffrey had attended what was described as "our festival"

A BACK-BENCHER LOOKS BACK

During the War I was one of three members, one from each party, who kept in touch with Dr Weizmann and his friends. The other two were Mr Hammersley (Con) and Mr Barnett Janner (Lab) We used to dine at regular intervals with the supporters of the Movement [National Homeland for the Jews] and kept in the closest touch with their changing prospects. The only members of the Government on whom the leaders of Israel could with certainty rely in the Churchill Government, were the Prime Minister himself, Mr Amery and Sir Archibald Sinclair.

Following his appointment in August, Montgomery concentrated on building up the Eighth Army and its equipment until he was sure that it was at full strength. During this time Allied air and submarine attacks had made it difficult for Rommel to obtain supplies and when, in October, Montgomery launched his attack, the numbers of Allied men, tanks and aircraft were far greater than those of the Axis forces. During the long drawn out offensive however, the British again lost many of their tanks but by November 2nd it was clear that Rommel had lost the battle and he and his army retreated.

Later Churchill said "Before Alamein we never had a victory. After Alamein we never had a defeat."

By the summer of 1942 German troops had reached the outskirts of Stalingrad. The battle that followed was bitter and continued into the dreaded Russian winter.

In 1941 the Government had commissioned a report on the direction Social Services should develop after the war and a former director of the London School of Economics, William Beveridge, was put in charge of the inquiry. The report was published at the end of 1942.

For the first time since his appointment as Archibald Sinclair's PPS, Geoffrey spoke at length in a debate:

HANSARD

2nd December

Reference has been made to the Beveridge Report which has been in the hands of Hon. Members since yesterday. I accept with enthusiasm the general principles of that momentous Report. I must say that the proposals which will abolish want and provide free doctoring, a wives' charter, pensions for all, children allowances and the abolition of the means test are social aims about which we should come to a decision in the very near future. In addition to the Beveridge proposals, we require a national statutory minimum wage below which it will be illegal for any person to be employed.

After two speakers interrupted him and Lady Astor complained, "nobody else will get a chance to speak" Geoffrey continued:

I should like to make a few remarks on the international situation. We want some permanent arrangement which will eliminate for all nations the possibility of war in the future. I gather that the idea is - and it seems to me to be a thoroughly sound one - that the United Nations should be taken as the basis of the new world order, that they should take over from the League of Nations such of its work as was valuable - and that we should develop it under the banner of the United Nations. The vital thing in the future is that we should know that military power in overwhelming force can be operated the moment an aggressor starts, or even makes preparation to start.

A matter that is talked about a good deal now is the re-education of the minds of German youth. It is very difficult to see precisely the manner of doing it. You want some kind of spiritual castor oil which will purge the minds of the Nazis and all those whom Hitler has brought under his heel.

He then touched on a number of other subjects including a brief statement on Works Councils - a subject very close to his heart - and in concluding stated:

I would say that we have a very difficult task before us in the days of peace. We ought to devote to it the same passionate devotion that we are giving to the war.

HANSARD

17th December

WAGE RATES

Mr Mander asked the Minister of Labour the lowest rate of wage fixed by any trade board at the present time?

Mr Bevin: The lowest general minimum time rates are 1/4d per hour for adult male workers in the fustian cutting trade and 7d. per hour for female workers in the drift net mending trade. I should, however, point out in both trades piece work predominates and minimum rates for piece work have also been fixed.

Mr Mander: Will my right Hon. Friend consider the advisability of adopting a minimum rate and making it the national statutory minimum for the whole country below which it would be illegal for anyone to be employed?

Mr Bevin: I should want notice of that question.

Using the Retail Price Index, 1942's 1 shilling, today (in 2009, the time of writing) would buy approximately £1.48p's worth of goods. On the same day

Geoffrey asked the Paymaster-General whether any plans were being considered to avoid unemployment after the war and despite his persistence he received a noncommittal answer.

In December the Prime Minister commented about the war and cooperation with the Allies, "If you keep in your mind the supreme object, namely the destruction of Hitler and Hitlerism, there is no room for small points of national self-assertiveness. As long as the job is done it does not matter much who gets the credit."

1943

This comes from the " Visits to Famous People and Places" folder. Most of the people Geoffrey visited had some connection with the Pre-Raphaelites and William Morris.

> REPORT OF VISIT BY SIR GEOFFREY MANDER TO MRS
> GLADYS JOSEPH daughter of William Holman Hunt at Hampstead
> on January 3rd 1943.
>
> I found Mrs J. a delightful and vigorous person very much like portraits
> of her father. She remembered all the Pre-Raphaelites and their associates
> and made these points.
>
> Violet Hunt. She felt sorry for her - she was her own worst enemy. She
> always had some grievance and enjoyed *Success de Scandale*.

Violet Hunt lived with the author Ford Madox Hueffer, later Ford Madox Ford, who was a married man. He spent eight days in prison in 1910 after he failed to comply with a decree for restitution of conjugal rights and then in 1912 a newspaper featured Violet Hunt in a report as 'Mrs Ford Madox Hueffer' and this led to a notorious court case brought by his wife. Ford Madox Hueffer was the grandson of Pre-Raphaelite Brotherhood associate and painter, Ford Madox Brown.

> She remembers Morris at Kelmscott playing back gammon with his
> daughter Jennie.
>
> Mrs Morris had a strange and striking beauty, she was cold and aloof, a
> bad housekeeper. Morris idealised her. She liked a good gossip.
>
> Ruskin. She remembers reading to him at Brantwood "A Fleet in Being"
> during which a flash of remembrance came to J.R. and he asked after her
> father. They went to the window to watch a rainbow.
>
> De Morgan. She found him most delightful, he talked just like his books.
> *Latterly William De Morgan became a successful writer of fiction.*
>
> Swinburne. She never spoke to him, but met him often as he was walking
> up the hill for his daily tramp on Putney Heath. He used to walk along
> on his toes muttering. The public-house he visited, according to her, was
> "The Green Man".

She knew Mr and Mrs Watts-Dunton very well and was often at the Pines.

Found the latter very congenial, always inviting in friends to meet W.D. Theodore Watts-Dunton (1832-1914) was a solicitor and novelist who was friendly with many writers and artists including Whistler, Ford Madox Ford and the Pre-Raphaelites (Rossetti painted his portrait). He took Swinburne into his house, The Pines, Putney, and looked after him for the last years of the poet's life, restricting his drinking and generally keeping him out of trouble.

In 1939 at the sale of the contents of The Pines, Geoffrey and Rosalie Mander had bought a large painted cabinet, a cupboard that contained a folding bed, and two mirrors - the cupboard with bed was £4 and the cabinet cost £5. All the pieces were elaborately painted with pictures based on Rossetti works by his pupil Henry Treffry Dunn.

At the Wannsee Conference held in 1942, Nazi and SS leaders had decided to deport all Jews to camps where eventually they could be exterminated. In areas that they controlled Jews were rounded up and taken to holding areas in Eastern Poland before transportation.

Some Jews who had been moved already to Treblinka managed to escape and return to the Warsaw ghetto carrying confirmation of the treatment that awaited them all.

When the SS entered the Warsaw ghetto on 18th January 1943 they faced unexpectedly fierce resistance from the inhabitants and after four days of fighting in the streets they withdrew.

HANSARD

27th January

POST-WAR EMPLOYMENT

Mr Mander asked the Prime Minister whether he will consider the advisability of inviting Sir William Beveridge to conduct an inquiry into the most effective means of preventing unemployment after the war?

Mr Attlee [Deputy Prime Minister]: The prevention of unemployment cannot be dissociated from Government policy over the whole field of economic affairs. Examination of this matter must therefore form an integral part of the study of post-war policy by the Government, and it is undesirable at this stage that it should be entrusted to any single individual.

Panel on the folding bed bought from The Pines, painted by Henry Treffry Dunn.

Geoffrey and three other MPs continued to question Mr Attlee but they received no conclusive answer from him.

On 31st January 1943, despite Hitler's orders, the German army surrendered at Stalingrad. The losses incurred on both sides during the battle were immense and this turned out to be one of the most significant turning points in the war.

A BACK-BENCHER LOOKS BACK

It is not generally known that during the War a factory was situated in the lower part of the Houses of Parliament, where members of Parliament, messengers, policemen, and other officials and their wives, connected with House, spent their evenings in making quantities of small arms of different types. Three members were appointed as a link between the House and the factory but it so happened that I was the only one who was able to keep in close touch. There was difficulty in the first place in getting the consent of the Lord Great Chamberlain, then Lord Ancaster, to the installation of the factory on the ground that it would mean having Home Office officials inspecting the premises. He retired to some inaccessible place in Scotland to escape our importunity and finally, when it was brought home to him that the Home Office inspectors had for long been in the habit of visiting the House of Parliament, he gave way.

Offices of the Minister of Production,
1st February 1943
Dear Mander,
You will be glad to learn that the Lord Great Chamberlain has now given his permission for the scheme for a small munitions plant in the basement of the Palace of Westminster, and has asked Lord Esmé Gordon-Lennox, and the secretary to the Lord Great Chamberlain to get in touch with the promoters of the scheme so that work can be started as soon as possible.
Yours sincerely,
Oliver Lyttleton
He was Minister for War Production.

2nd February 1943

Munitions

Dear Mr Mander,

The Minister of Production's secretary informed me yesterday that in answer to Mr Lyttleton's personal appeal, the Lord Great Chamberlain has given consent for the munitions unit to start production in the Palace of Westminster.

I an therefore writing to express to you, on behalf of the volunteers, our most grateful thanks, for without your intervention this consent would not have been obtained.

Yours sincerely,

T.G.B. Cocks.

A BACK-BENCHER LOOKS BACK

Thereafter could be found every evening in the lower parts of the Palace of Westminster a mixed gathering which often included one of Winston Churchill's daughters. The whole arrangement worked very happily and effectively and turned out much useful ammunition for the Forces. If the Germans had known, they would have been fully justified in bombing the Houses of Parliament - but they had done this already!

At the end of February Geoffrey took part in a number of debates covering such diverse subjects as distribution of sickness benefits, India and Mr Gandhi's fast, midwives, and the United Nations and post-war co-operation.

THE GREEN CAN

March 1943

It has been the custom of the Firm for some time to make small loans to various of their employees who are able to make out a special case for assistance. It was always their intention that such a loan should be of a semi-permanent nature, but the custom has grown up in some case of frequent repayments and further loans, sometimes several in the course of a year. We would point out that this was never the intention, and we would ask those affected to bear this in mind, as a great deal of extra work is involved in book-keeping when a number of transactions have to be dealt with.

We have pleasure in announcing that at the Board Meeting on March 8th, Captain Philip Mander was unanimously elected a Director of the Company, and we trust that this will be a happy lifelong association with the business.

Eventually Philip Mander became the Chairman of Mander Brothers; he was the last member of the family to hold the post.

In March, as usual, employees' correspondence from all over the world was published in The Green Can. This is an excerpt from a letter from H. Chambers who was stationed somewhere where the weather at the time was "grand."

I want to ask you if you will kindly thank Mrs Mander very much indeed for the grand variety of books which she sent. I got them quite safely and they are being passed round and read by all our chaps here. I was using some of Manders paint the other day, it looked like old stock, and I was wondering if I had had a hand in its manufacture. Anyway, it was good stuff.

The Imperial Palace, Addis Ababa,
15th April, 1943
Dear Mr Mander,
I thank you for your letter of February last. I am sorry I was not able to send as much gold as I should have wished for the benefit for [sic] the heroes of the Royal Air Force whose co-operation in the present struggle for human liberty and everlasting peace is beyond praise. It gives me great pleasure to hear that the heroes of the Royal Air Force appreciate the gift. Your sympathetic acts in giving the cause of Ethiopia the necessary support in her dark days are well remembered by all of us with unforgetful gratitude. I also remember the occasions at which you raised in the House of Commons about [sic] the fate of Ethiopia. By the aid and the undaunted courage of the British Army and the British public Ethiopia was liberated from the Fascist yoke and her independence again restored. It is my wish also that Great Britain and Ethiopia will remain for ever the closest friends and allies.
Yours sincerely
[Unclear]

Haile Selassie.

The Ethiopian Embassy was asked for help in deciphering the signature at the end of this letter. They sent a very helpful reply: "we cannot verify the signature on the letter but it is signed 'Haile Selassie, Emperor', in Amharic." Amharic is a Semitic language spoken in North Central Ethiopia.

THE GREEN CAN

CHRISTENING

A very interesting and happy party was given at Wightwick Manor, on Saturday afternoon, April 17th, the occasion being the christening of Nicholas Mervyn Mander, son of Mr and Mrs Mervyn Mander, and grandson of Mr Geoffrey Le M. Mander, MP, Chairman of the Company, who was born on January 22nd, 1943.

Before tea, which was dispensed in the Great Parlour, a photograph of Baby Nicholas and his Godparents was taken; also one of the family and guests, amongst whom were representatives of Mander Brothers.

There were present four generations of the family:

Mary, Lady Mander (Great-Aunt) [the sister of Geoffrey's mother Flora], Mr Geoffrey Le M. Mander MP (Grandfather), Mr Mervyn Mander (Father) who is 2nd Officer in the Air Transport Auxiliary, and last Nicholas Mervyn Mander, the younger generation.

We offer our congratulations to Mr and Mrs Mervyn on the birth of their baby son, and wish him health and happiness in a world at peace.

HANSARD

22 April 1943

NATIONAL FINANCE

Children's Allowances

Mr Mander asked the Chancellor of the Exchequer the approximate cost at the present time of instituting a system of children's allowances on the lines of the Beveridge Report at the rate of 5/- per week, taking into consideration the economy that would be effected by the consequent reduction in the cost of service children's allowances?

Sir Kingsley Wood referred him to details issued in a White Paper in 1942, where, he said, it was concluded that the impracticalities of such a system would allow few savings.

Mr Mander: In view of the very great interest in children's allowances, could not my right Hon. Friend consider introducing them in the near future, so that people can have some of their Beveridge jam now?

Sir K. Wood: That is quite a different question from the Question on the Paper asking the cost.

On the night of 16th May the Dambuster raids took place during which three dams in the Rhur valley were attacked. Power stations were crippled and over 1,000 people killed.

On 19th May there was a long discussion in Parliament about the refugee problem.

Speaking for the Home Department, Mr Osbert Peake made several points about the vastly increased numbers of refugees in the world since the 1930s and the difficulties in helping such people. He said:

> For many years the refugee problem has been a matter of deep concern, and has received the most earnest attention of His Majesty's Government. Before the war, apart from the situation in China, it was, from the advent of the Nazi regime until October 1938, mainly if not exclusively a Jewish problem and a problem confined to Europe. After 1938 there was the added exodus from Czechoslovakia and from Poland.

He touched on what had been attempted by many countries and what had been achieved, and reviewed suggestions (he described some) for rescuing civilian internees and prisoners of war - as "fantastic".

> The burden on these neutral States who have generously received these people may become unduly heavy if the refugee population continually increases.

All the MPs who took part in this debate spoke thoughtfully and at length. Geoffrey had a number of comments to make:

> It has been suggested that we should enter into negotiations with Hitler and with Laval. I believe that would be an entirely wrong policy. These people are never moved by any dictates of humanity, and any such negotiations would only be used by them as blackmail against us. I noticed only yesterday in the newspapers a statement to the effect that the German Director of Labour had told Laval that he should stop the removal of children from areas endangered by air raids. That is typical of

the type of mind with which we should have to negotiate if that suggestion were adopted.

He went on to talk about anti-Semitic propaganda being put forward by "our enemies".

I believe that the people of this country, in the main, would support action by the Government to help refugees who are Jews, and I give just this one example. From my constituency there came quite spontaneously, and was sent to me, a petition signed by a large number of the leading citizens of all parties and creeds urging very strongly that the Government should take action, and making it quite clear that they did not intend to be animated by any fears that appear to exist in some parts of this country.

THE GREEN CAN
June 1943
COMMUNICATED BY THE BOARD

As the victorious Allied Armies advance it is interesting to see the emergence of our former Agents. We have just had a letter in the most friendly terms from an Italian who has represented us for the last twelve years throughout all Sicily, and whom we have known altogether for forty years. He recalls with pleasure his visit to London. In due course we hope he will resume his activities on our behalf. The goodwill which undoubtedly existed in Italy for our goods does not appear to have been adversely affected. We hope to receive similar news from France as our victorious troops advance. Only recently we received a letter from a member of the Levy-Finger family who has escaped to this country bringing us news of M. Roger, the head of the Firm who for so long were our Agents in France.

A BACK-BENCHER LOOKS BACK

At one stage during the war when the use of gliders was very much to the fore, the War Office arranged for a number of MPs of all parties to go down to an aerodrome in the South of England and see for themselves what developments were taking place; I attended as representing the Air Ministry and the events of the day did not go to plan.

The weather was unfavourable with low cloud and General Browning, who was in command, in his opening address to the visitors said breezily that the conditions were such that he was not inclined to risk the lives of his pilots and that the only persons who would be in peril would be the assembled MPs.

The provision of gliders and their use was a subject of acute controversy at the time and when, at a conference in a hanger, questions were asked for, this came well into the open. It was Lord Winterton who asked how many gliders the General wanted. He answered two hundred. Winterton then asked how many he had got and the answer was two.

We then went off in two parties for glider flights. The one I was in, after taking off, flew a few feet above the ground for several hundred yards and then crashed. The only damage that was done, however, was the destruction of the rear portion of the glider. We thought this was a good story to tell to the other party but on emerging from our plane we found waiting for us General Browning with his arm in a sling. He was able to inform us that our colleagues had also crashed and that several of them, including Ellen Wilkinson who had broken an ankle, were on their way to hospital. All this, of course, had marked repercussions in the War Office and Air Ministry and I had to present a report of the day's proceedings to the Secretary of State that night, for the information of the Cabinet.

Ellen Wilkinson was Parliamentary Secretary to the Ministry of Home Security. General Browning was the husband of the author Daphne du Maurier.

In July, after a series of military defeats, Mussolini was dismissed from his post as Prime Minister of Italy.

James Lees-Milne kept detailed diaries from 1942 to 1947 while he was employed by the National Trust. He travelled round the country visiting and assessing the historic buildings offered to the Trust and advising on proposed acquisitions for its houses. His diaries were published in 4 volumes; this extract comes from "Ancestral Voices" covering 1942-1944.

21ST JULY 1943

I looked at a portrait of Violet Hunt in red crayon that Geoffrey Mander wants the Trust to buy for the Wightwick collection. A pretty thing but I consider the Pre-Raphaelite association too remote.

Presumably Geoffrey and Rosalie Mander persuaded him that a wider view of the group and its associates could be more productive - the portrait of Violet Hunt hangs now in the Honeysuckle Room at Wightwick. This change of heart was demonstrated in 1946 when he wrote while visiting Oxford:

> Looked at a portrait by Watts of Mrs Senior nee Hughes, sister of Tom Hughes, author of 'Tom Brown's Schooldays.' A fine full-length, c.1868.
>
> I have written to Sir Geoffrey Mander to ask if he would like it at Wightwick. It is enormous.

It was accepted and the portrait now hangs in the Great Parlour.

This letter was sent to Geoffrey in his capacity as Vice-Chairman of the Anglo-Polish Parliamentary Committee

> 24th July 1943
>
> Dear Mr Mander,
>
> I am sure you will understand the delay in replying to your kind letter. I wished to write personally to you for I was very touched by your friendly words of sympathy in the sad loss which Poland has sustained in the tragic loss of General Sikorski and those accompanying him on his last service to his country and the Allied cause. Would you please convey to the members of the Anglo-Polish Parliamentary Committee my sincere thanks for their condolences.
>
> It is a double grief to us that we have also lost in the same tragic accident the trusted and valued friend of Poland of many years' standing in the person of Colonel Cazalet, which we deeply deplore.
>
> Yours sincerely,
>
> Wladyslaw Raczkiewicz

General Wladyslaw Sikorski was the President of the Polish Government in exile. He was killed when the RAF bomber in which he was returning to England, crashed into the harbour in Gibralter. Over the years a number of theories about the crash have grown - it has been suggested that Sikorski had been assassinated either by the British Government or the Russians. Although a court of enquiry in 1943 found the crash was caused by mechanical failure, later investigations revealed that security at Gibralter was lax, so it was possible that sabotage had occurred. Victor Cazalet was one of two British MPs on the plane.

Letters published by The Green Can from former employees in the Forces:

As we travelled the road, it was our good fortune to sample the many oranges that were then in full season. In Palestine there are countless acres of nothing but Orange, Lemon and Grapefruit Groves, and to us after our long period of abstinence (as part of the British War effort?) we were in seventh heaven.

...the same position where I had camped when I had first arrived in the district, and where I had spent Christmas. However, the place was much changed as the paddy fields had now all dried and it was no longer necessary to walk along the banks between each field. The jungle was very dry and now quite easy to see through.

As you can guess am now back aboard a minesweeper. We have a routine job of "sweeping" to do and the only exciting thing that has happened aboard since I joined her was when the ship's dog went mad with the heat and chased the crew all over the ship.

During the three weeks up to 5th August, Hansard lists Geoffrey's usual varied mixture of questions, subjects included Company dividends, Stock feeding-potatoes, Accidents while on leave, Town and Country planning, and Agriculture - rabbit traps.

THE GREEN CAN
September 1943
An interesting item of news is sent by Leonard Smith, late of Burnley Branch, now stationed in Sierra Leone. At one time having nothing particular to do, he went on a shooting expedition alone, and got lost in the bush. After wandering around for some time he at last came upon a very desolate and deserted looking hut, he decided to try his luck walking to the door, he knocked and after a short wait to his great surprise the door was opened by a man who was carrying a Winslow Paint can.
Winslow paint was produced by Mander Brothers.

After secret negotiations, on 8th September Italy officially surrendered to the Allies. The Italians had been offered favourable terms on the understanding that they joined in the war against Germany, who, at that time, had eight divisions in control in southern and central Italy. It was also in September that German Special Forces rescued Mussolini from prison.

In October British troops entered Naples and Italy declared war on Germany.

In 1943 nearly all mines in the country were privately owned companies and it was estimated there were about 1,500 in operation. During the war the Ministry of Fuel and Power had operational control of the mines while, at the same time, managers were still responsible to their boards of directors. This dual control gave rise to some criticism.

On 12 October a debate was held in Parliament on the Coal Mining Situation. It began with a long statement by the Minister of Fuel and Power, Major Gwilym Lloyd George. He acknowledged that there was some unease about the ability of the Ministry to increase production to meet consumption, and concern over unrest in the coal industry.

HANSARD

I come to measures which the Government propose to take immediately for the improvement of coal production. We have reviewed the position of miners in the Armed Forces. Substantial numbers of ex-miners have been returned to the mines during the past two years. In the last two years over 60,000 ex-miners have been returned to the industry. We are taking steps to institute a comb-out of miners in the Army, particularly the older men, with a view to their return to the mines.

He then talked about strikes occurring in the industry and of the problems faced by both the managers and miners to whom he had spoken. A number of speakers felt that to be efficient the mines should be nationalised and that this was what miners had been demanding for years.

Mr Mander: We have managers serving two masters. They are serving the State and the mine owners. The managers, being human, and having to envisage a situation in which the mines come back to the mine owners, are wondering, naturally, what will then be their position if they have not carried out exactly what the owners desire That is creating a very unsatisfactory position, because they have to look to the situation when the mines may come back under private enterprise. I think there is a strong case now for going a step further and taking the mines over completely for the State, making them into a great public service.

From my personal experience of industry, I would say that the wider you open the door in giving facilities to the workers to discuss any problem that is relevant to the particular business concerned, the better and happier will be the results.

I agree also with another suggestion, which is that any direction given to individuals to go down the pits should be applied to all classes, whatever old school tie they may wear. If it should be done all round I am sure that it would produce a very happy psychological effect, because people would realise that there was equality of treatment.

On 5th November Geoffrey recorded in the Flying Log book that he and Archibald Sinclair visited Staverton (Cheltenham) for a meeting

On 11th November a debate on the Moscow Conference, begun on 18th October, was opened by the Foreign Secretary Anthony Eden. He proceeded to report on the sessions and informal meetings held between the British, Russian and American delegates:

HANSARD

Mr Eden: We all agreed to start the talks with a discussion of measures for shortening the duration of the war. I can say about our military discussions, that I believe that they did more good to our mutual relations by the frank and exhaustive examination which was made of them than any other phase of the Conference. Now I would say something about the first of the published decisions of the Conference. The importance of this declaration is in the emphasis it lays on the decision of our Governments to continue our co-operation and collaboration after the war.

He went on to explain how they had set up an advisory commission to study and to make joint recommendations on any future problems.

As regards the remainder of the agenda, it is sufficient to say there was no major political question in Europe which was not the subject of discussion between us in some form or other.

Geoffrey was among a number of speakers who responded to Mr Eden's report.

Mr Mander: He has remedied one of the main faults of the League of Nations, which was, of course, that the obligations were loose and the arrangements for firm action were not arranged in time. We are going to remedy that. Some reference has been made to the position of Poland. Her great hope and the only hope for the peace of the world is that there should be good will and complete understanding between this country and Russia and America as well. Another interesting point in this connection arises out of the new machinery set up. My right Hon. Friend has made it clear that the three Powers, including Russia, are going to decide the fate of Italy and other European Powers, and it seems to follow automatically that the same conditions will apply in considering countries in the East, such as Poland and others, and that the three Powers will discuss matters and come to agreed decisions. That again is a hopeful step forward.

1944

The Green Can magazine continued to be produced, but the bound copies for 1944 and 1945 are missing from Wightwick. They start again in 1946.

In January 1944 the Allies were fighting in Italy and advancing slowly towards Rome. The monastery of Monte Cassino was part of a strong German defensive line in a mountainous area that became the site of the largest European land battle.

   In Parliament Sir Herbert Williams asked the Prime Minister whether some statement could be made about the progress of operations in Italy because it was felt that General Montgomery had raised feelings of false optimism by talking to his troops about the early capture of Rome. Mr Churchill replied "I do not know about false optimism but there has been a lot of bad weather."

> Headquarters. 21 Army Group
> 14-1- 44
> Dear Mander,
> I have your letter of the 12th Jan. Will you send the following message from me to the residents of Wednesfield.
> Your sincerely,
> B.L. Montgomery
> MESSAGE
> I commend the "Salute the Soldier" campaign to the residents of Wednesfield. The soldiers of the Empire are doing their duty on the battle fronts, and they are worthy of the best possible support from the home country. If you will provide the weapons and munitions we will do the rest.
> B. L. Montgomery. General.
> C-in-C 21 Army Group

Salute the Soldier was a campaign in which towns were encouraged to raise funds for military equipment through National Savings. Towns had a target and competed with each other to raise the most money.

A debate in Parliament on 19th January followed the second reading of the Education Bill (always known later as the 1944 Education Bill) by the President of the Board of Education, Mr Butler. While the Bill touched on a number of new initiatives including raising the school leaving age (to fifteen) and planning further education opportunities it was his statement, "as far as possible, provision of various types of education should be accessible to all, whatever their social or financial circumstances", that most people considered gave rise to the greatest change in secondary education at that time, including the 11+ examination and everything that followed.

In February there were heavy bombing raids on London and in Italy the Allies began a second (unsuccessful) assault on Monte Cassino.

In March Geoffrey and Archibald Sinclair flew from Hendon to Worksop and visited Welbeck Abbey, both in Nottinghamshire, they returned the next day to Perton, near Wightwick.

Four days after a letter from a friend at the Air Ministry ended:

I am so sorry for your temporary upset and do beg of you to take things a bit easier and look after yourself. I had a long talk with the Doctor who is quite satisfied that in a very short time you will be back to full working vigour.

Astley Hall,
Stourport on Severn
4th April 1944
My dear Mander,
I am so sorry to see you have to keep quiet by order. So this is a line of best wishes for a speedy return to vigour.
Yours very sincerely,
Baldwin of Bewdley.

HANSARD
26 April
UNITED NATIONS (FLAG)
Mr Mander asked the Secretary of State for Foreign Affairs if he will consider the advisability of consulting with the other members of the

United Nations with the view to the adoption of a flag, emblem or other symbol to be used, in addition to national emblems, as a visual expression of Allied unity both during the war and in the build-up of the new world peace organisation decided on at the Moscow conference.

Geoffrey was supported by another MP, Vernon Bartlett, but the reply by Anthony Eden was noncommittal.

Mr Mander: In view of the unsatisfactory nature of the reply, I beg to give notice that I will raise this matter on the Adjournment.

A BACK-BENCHER LOOKS BACK

This comes from Geoffrey's reported meeting with General Anders, the Polish Commander-in-Chief during the lunch given by the Polish Government at the Dorchester Hotel.

The General told us of the difficulty he had found in getting the Soviet authorities to make use of the new Polish army which was most anxious to get into action as soon as possible. Nothing much happened and finally the Polish accepted a proposal that they should fight with the Western Allies in Italy where they took part in the advance and found themselves called upon to fight in the struggle for Cassino. The operation set was a most difficult one but General Anders made a moving appeal to his troops, pointing out that they had been accused of staying in Russia and not wanting to fight, that now was their opportunity to show what the Polish army could do, and that it was prepared to undertake and succeed in an impossible task.

After a third abortive attack on the German defences between Monte Cassino and the coast in March, at last, in May, the Allies broke through and on 18th May, the Polish troops captured Monte Cassino.

The capture of Cassino is, of course, one of the great epics of the war. The Polish army, with everything against it, achieved the impossible, as indeed, one would expect from the soldiers of this most gallant ally. To hear all this from General Anders himself, was indeed a moving event.

The Allies entered Rome on 5th June. On 6th June 1944 (D-Day) a massive invasion force landed in northern France.

One type of Motion is the opportunity to raise a debate, for half an hour, on the adjournment at the end of business each day. I had an embarrassing experience over this in June, 1944, on what turned out to be D-Day.

I had tried for some time to interest various people in the proposal that there should be a United Nations flag and found it very difficult to raise any interest in the Foreign Office. Since then, of course, such a flag is flown regularly in every one of the eighty members of the United Nations. I decided to raise the matter on the adjournment and went down to the House with a carefully prepared speech expecting that as usual on such occasions, there would be perhaps half a dozen members present and a few Whips. Instead of which, to my consternation, I found a packed and excited House. The explanation was not a sudden enthusiasm for the flag but the fact that it was D-Day and that the Prime Minister was expected towards the end of my half hour, to make an appearance to say how things were going in connection with the Normandy landings. In the circumstances, it will be well understood that the House was in hilarious mood and not in the least interested in a question as to whether the United Nations should have a flag or not. However, I had to go through with my speech for some twenty minutes in order to get it recorded in Hansard and reported in those sections of the press that were interested. It was a most trying experience; the House was thoroughly good tempered but I was continuously interrupted with facetious comments and would-be-comic interruptions.

When Geoffrey suggested that a song might be adopted by the United Nations too, a Scottish MP called out "What about 'Scots Wha Hae"? And later another MP asked him to sing.

However, I struggled on to the end and there was sufficient time left for Mr George Hall (Viscount Hall) to reply on behalf of the Government, not that I expected much from this. He was just getting underway when Mr Churchill entered the chamber whereupon Mr Hall immediately subsided and his reply, for what it was worth, is unknown to history. Mr Churchill then gave his report on the great events that were taking place across the Channel.

HANSARD

LANDINGS IN FRANCE

The Prime Minister (Mr Churchill): I have been at the centres where the latest information is received, and I can state to the House that this operation is proceeding in a thoroughly satisfactory manner Many dangers and difficulties which at this time last night appeared extremely formidable are behind us. The passage of the sea has been made with far less loss than we apprehended. The resistance of the batteries has been greatly weakened by the bombing of the Air Force. The landing of the troops on a broad front, both British and American Allied troops along the whole front, have been effective, and our troops have penetrated, in some cases, several miles inland. The outstanding feature has been the landings of the airborne troops, which were on a scale far larger than anything that has been seen so far in the world. These landings took place with extremely little loss and with great accuracy. Fighting is proceeding at various points. We have captured various bridges.. There is even fighting proceeding in the town of Caen, inland. But all this, although a very valuable first step, gives no indication of what may be the course of the battle in the next days and weeks. It is, therefore, a most serious time that we enter upon. Thank God we enter upon it with our great Allies, all in good heart and all in good friendship.

After the landings in France, the French resistance movement came into its own. It prevented a fast and orderly German retreat by harrying the enemy troops and by blowing up bridges and railway lines and generally disrupting all attempts at an effective defence against the advancing Allies. The SS troops killed hundreds of French civilians in reprisals for these attacks.

It was also in June that the first flying bomb was launched by the Germans on London. It was propelled by a noisy, primitive jet engine.

In the month ending 16 June, Hansard recorded that Geoffrey spoke in twenty eight debates; these occasions varied from his short interventions, to long and detailed speeches as in the debate on Foreign Affairs in May. There he touched on some of his chief concerns among which were the future of the United Nations, a national home for the Jews and what he called "a word on Ethiopia". Also during this session he contributed to discussions on Fish Sales, the Peak District (National Park), Polish-Russian relations, Works of Art (restitution by Germans) and the Permanent Court of International Justice.

On 29th June, Geoffrey asked a question in Parliament about Joint Production Committees. However, preceding him there was a brief, faintly bizarre discussion on Pilotless Aircraft (Post-War Use.)

HANSARD

Captain Plugge asked whether the pilotless plane is being considered in connection with post-war activities; and whether plans are being made for developing it for the purpose of dispatching mail over long distances at high speed.

The Joint Under-Secretary of State for Air (Captain Harold Balfour): The possibilities of such aircraft for commercial use, including the carriage of mail, are certainly not overlooked by my department.

Captain Plugge: In view of the knowledge we have acquired in the use of explosives, will my right Hon. and gallant Friend consult with the Postmaster-General over the result of the experiments of sending mail by rocket?

Captain Balfour: I think there is some confusion in the mind of my Hon. and gallant Friend. Flying bombs now in use by the enemy are an entirely different proposition. They are not expected to land safely at a particular destination, and they cannot be used more than once. Commercial aircraft are expected to land at their expected destinations and are expected to do so repeatedly.

After this Mr Mander asked the Minister of Production to what extent joint production committees or works councils are now functioning in industry; whether the results achieved are regarded as satisfactory; and if it is proposed to retain them as a permanent feature of our industrial organisation.

He was told that the committees, established solely in the engineering and allied industries, had proved to be a valuable feature in industrial collaboration between managements and workpeople. Retaining them after the war will probably be considered by the organisations concerned. As the answers he received were imprecise, Geoffrey gave notice that he would raise the question again on the Adjournment.

HANSARD

7th July

WAR PENSIONS

Mr Mander: The responsibility for looking after those who have fought and suffered in the service of the State goes back into antiquity. I noticed some words the other day which I think are worth quoting. This is what Sokon says about Pisistratus in Plutarch's "Lives": "He also made other laws himself, one of which provides that those who are maimed in war shall be maintained at the public charge." That was thousands of years ago. Therefore we should interpret that responsibility in the modern sense, and do our utmost to make those who have borne the burden of war, happy citizens of a grateful country.

On 19th August the liberation of Paris began with the French resistance groups launching an armed uprising; this was followed by the entry of the Free French forces on 25th August and their acceptance of the German surrender.

On 8th September a more advanced (and silent) flying bomb - the V2 - was dropped on London for the first time.

On 10th November Geoffrey spoke in a debate on the Social Insurance Bill.

HANSARD

Mr Mander: There was some discussion the other day in the House about the reputed parentage of this Measure. We have come now, however, to the christening stage; we have to give the scheme a name. That is very important because a child is often greatly handicapped in after life by an ill-chosen name, and, while the House may not be the parent, we are certainly the guardians of the child for the time being, and therefore we have to look carefully at its name. "Social insurance" is quite inadequate, and I hope that when we come to the Committee stage, we shall persuade the Government to adopt some term which more properly describes what the Minister is going to do. Perhaps the best phrase would be "social security".

VISITS TO FAMOUS PEOPLE AND PLACES.

This one took place on 21st November 1944 when Geoffrey called on "Miss Holiday at Greenleas, Chalfont St. Giles, Bucks."

> Miss Winifred Holiday was a well known musician and the daughter of Henry Holiday the artist and designer. She is now 79 and a delightful old lady with a clear and alert mind. She had personal recollections of such people as de Morgan, William Morris, Burne-Jones, Ruskin, Violet Hunt and others. She had a particular interest in Paderewski in view of her musical associations. She showed me a number of paintings by her father, also two pieces of stained glass by him and a large piece of sculpture, the figure of a sleeping woman. There is a good painting of her father by Philip Burne-Jones [son of Edward Burne-Jones]. Kempe she did not favour much as he had cut out her father for the stained glass at Southwark Cathedral. There was some Morris 'Rabbit' cretonne on some chairs. Altogether a delightful visit.

The next day he paid a visit to the former home of Watts-Dunton and Swinburne: No. 2, The Pines, Putney.

> By arrangement I met the present owner, Mr Hill at the house, which has suffered flying bomb damage. It appears that he is a metal broker in the City and his business partner is brother of Pritt, KC, MP. He was exceedingly kind in showing me everything from the cellars to the roof, but is a complete Philistine so far as any literary associations with the house are concerned.
>
> I told him that it was famous and that several books had been written about it, offering to give him their names, but this did not interest him. He insisted on showing me the furniture, carpets etc. which he had recently brought into the house. He promised to send me a number of cuttings from plants that were in the garden in Swinburne's day.
>
> There is now no hedge across the garden, which is quite small, and the statue has been removed, only the pedestal remaining. He also promised to send me a little door-knocker which was attached to Swinburne's door. He showed me a very small attic at the top where Swinburne was said to have done a lot of writing.

The house is now No. 11 and is described as The Pines. I walked up the hill to Putney Heath, so often used by Swinburne when he went for his morning ramble. All the houses on the same side (left hand) are typical of the worst period of Victorian architecture.

Mr Hill said that various visitors, including Americans, had been to the house during the Summer because of its associations.

After a very active few weeks in the House, Geoffrey took part, very briefly, in seven debates. The one subject close to his heart was what Mr Churchill called: "the grim, bare bones of the Polish problem." Geoffrey spoke at length on 15th December about the possible future of Poland and said: "not only does the whole fate of Poland depend on Russian good will but the whole fate of Europe and the world depends on the cordial and genuine co-operation of the three great powers. If that fails, all fails and the war will come to an end only as a preparation for another struggle later on."

10 Downing Street,
Whitehall.
December 19 1944
Sir,
I am desired by the Prime Minister to inform you that it is his intention, on the occasion of the forthcoming list of New Year Honours, to submit your name to the King with a recommendation that he may be graciously pleased to approve that the honour of Knighthood be conferred upon you in recognition of your political and public services.

Before doing so, the Prime Minister would be glad to be assured that this mark of His Majesty's favour would be agreeable to you, and I am to ask that you will be so good as to communicate with me accordingly at your earliest convenience.
Yours faithfully,
J. M. Martin

THE TIMES

1st January 1945

PUBLIC SERVICE REWARDED

The following New Year Honours have been conferred by the King.

KNIGHTS BACHELOR Mander, Geoffrey Le Mesurier, MP for Wolverhampton East since May 1929, for political and public service.

Heading this list was: "EARL Lloyd George, the Right Hon. David, OM, MP"

The local Wolverhampton papers responded to the news by printing a list covering most of Geoffrey's public service record:

He was formerly a member of Wolverhampton Town Council and Staffordshire County Council, and he has served as High Sheriff of Staffordshire, and as District Scout Commissioner for Wolverhampton. Sir Geoffrey Mander is chairman of the well known firm of Mander Bros. Ltd, Wolverhampton, a justice of the peace for Wolverhampton and Staffordshire and a member of the council of the Industrial Welfare Society.

JANUARY 1945

The Trustees of the National Portrait Gallery have the honour to inform Sir G. Le M. Mander that they wish to include his photograph in the National Record of Distinguished Persons and hope that he will find it convenient to give a special sitting for this purpose at an early date.

Below a pencil note by Geoffrey: "Oct 3 1945, taken 3.30"

In January the Russians entered Auschwitz. Later it was estimated that during Hitler's twelve years in power around six million Jews were killed.

11th January 1945

Dear Geoffrey,

I have looked up your family pedigree, and I see there are three or four generations needed to bring it up to date. This will cost something like seven or eight guineas, but I cannot tell until I know the number of people to record. If you will let me know that you wish to do this I will go into it in further detail and will write again.

Yours sincerely,

Algar Howard

In 1872 Geoffrey's grandfather, Samuel Mander, had spent time investigating his family tree. The rector of the Warwickshire parish of Lapworth found a number of Manders (spelt Maunder) in the parish register going back to 1675. The vicar of Aston Cantlow, Henley-in-Arden also found 17th century Maunders. He had to beg for payment for his searches because as he pointed out "I have a family of seventeen children and the income of the living of Aston Cantlow barely exceeds £80."

Geoffrey asked Algar Howard to go forward with investigating his pedigree.

HANSARD

16th January 1945

WAGES COUNCILS BILL

Introducing this bill Ernest Bevin said:

> It is a declaration by Parliament that the conception of what was known as sweated industry is past. The Bill also proposes to provide additional powers for establishing the Councils where voluntary machinery is inadequate or reasonable standards of remuneration are not being maintained.

Geoffrey spoke about the need for a national minimum wage and for the Bill to cover welfare matters - like the provision of canteens - and appeals against victimisation and dismissals.

Geoffrey and Rosalie's daughter was born on 16th January in Wolverhampton, at the Queen Victoria Nursing Home. Geoffrey sent a telegram from London on the 17th:

> Heartiest congratulations best love timing perfect looking forward seeing you both tomorrow.

That day the first of several clauses in the Representation of the People Bill began to be considered in Committee.

Since the Reform Acts of 1832 and 1867, several Representation of the People Acts had been passed extending the franchise to more adult males and granting it, eventually, to women.

However, in 1945, plural voting was still allowed. This meant that in addition to all householders having the vote and also those whose rent was £10 or more a year, extra votes could be cast by people who happened to be graduates of certain universities, those who owned property in places other than their home constituencies, those who were business rate payers and by Members of Parliament. This anomaly was discussed at length.

Geoffrey was particularly concerned about soldiers still serving overseas; he said:

> What message are we proposing to send them as a result of this vote tonight? Are we going to say to these men: "You are serving in all the battlefields of the world, but when it comes to exercising the franchise the vast majority of you, not all, will have one vote while certain people [including Geoffrey himself] who have the good fortune to possess a business qualification and a certain measure of wealth or have had the great advantage of a university education, will not be on a par with you. They will have two votes." I cannot feel happy about that message being sent to those who are now in the Services.

The discussion continued on 23rd January when Geoffrey argued that experiments in Proportional Representation could be carried out by local authorities "Surely it is the very essence of British development, by trial and error, to try a thing and see whether it is an improvement on something which has gone before. If it is not an improvement, then we can go back."

Despite the hours spent in discussion, plural voting continued to be allowed until it was prohibited when the Representation of the People Act 1948 was passed.

Lady Mander's family originally came from Cornwall and when the birth of the new baby was announced, the search for a Cornish name was mentioned in the papers.

Carnglaze

Liskeard. Cornwall.

22nd Jan 1945

Dear Sir Geoffrey,

According to the "Western Independent" you are searching for a characteristic Cornish name for your little daughter.

May I take the liberty of submitting two or three which although rare have been given to infants locally.

Lowenna, meaning 'joy,' Karenza = "love' and Mellen, from St. Mellion. Loveday and Jennifer are perhaps more common. Then there is the old name Ysolde.

Please pardon my intrusion in a personal matter but as a patriotic Cornishman I should not like you to miss anything that you might consider appropriate.

Yours faithfully,

W. Arthur Pascoe.

The new baby was christened Anthea Loveday Veronica. Sir Archibald Sinclair was her god-father.

Between 4th and 11th February the leaders of the Soviet Union, the United States and Great Britain met at Yalta in the Crimea to discuss plans for the future of Germany and eastern Europe after the war. Although they reached an agreement to allow eventually free elections in Poland, Czechoslovakia, Hungary, Romania and Bulgaria, after the war ended Stalin failed to honour this agreement and these countries all came under Communist rule.

A massive bombing raid was launched on Dresden on the night of 13th February. Over 130,000 people died and the city, sometimes referred to as:"Florence on the Elbe," was destroyed.

After the House considered several amendments to the Wages Councils Bill, it was read for the third time.

HANSARD

6 February

Sir G. Mander: The only people who will be disappointed at the passage of this Bill will be the bad employers for whom nobody will have any sympathy. It will tend to make them, compulsorily, into good employers. I am sure that my right Hon. Friend realises that there are certain gaps in the Bill which might have been filled in a manner which I cannot elaborate at this stage, such as, for instance, a national minimum wage. He has, nevertheless, taken a big step forward, and I hope that some day he will fill the few gaps that do remain.

At the end of the debate, the Joint Parliamentary Secretary to the Minister of Labour, Malcolm McCorquodale, in concluding, at one point, said:

I thank the Hon. member for Wolverhampton (Sir G. Mander) for his kind words of welcome. The Hon. Member did his best to bring in some new ideas; they were out of order, but I congratulate him on his ingenuity in getting an advertisement for them.

The Bill was read for the Third time and passed.

21 Kew Gardens Rd,

Kew, Richmond.

Surrey

14 Feb 1945

My dear Mander,

Dr Gordon Hake was a contemporary of Rossetti's and died ages ago - Rossetti died, as you know, in 1882 and I doubt if anyone who remembers him is now living. But his niece, Mrs Angeli, knows a good deal about him. She is a very nice woman and has a book on the stocks, or finished by now, which is of the nature of a vindication.

Marillier [a director of Morris and Co] wrote a very useful book on Rossetti, with much aid from Fairfax Murray and he lived for some years at Kelmscott House, Hammersmith. But he never met Morris and of course he never met Rossetti. I have not heard from him since the Morris firm was wound up and I do not find his name in my Telephone Directory of May 1942. He used to belong to the Bath Club and you might learn about him there.

The number of those who can claim to have known Morris is now very small. Chief among them are of course the Mackails, now living in a hotel at Chipping Campden.

Burne-Jones' daughter Margaret married William Morris' biographer, J.M. Mackail.

Not far from there is Miss Lewis, daughter of Sir George Lewis, the well known solicitor. She has many letters written to her by Burne-Jones when she was a child - probably also letters to her charming mother. Her address is Wychwood, Broadway, Worcestershire.

Very many thanks about the PM's forthcoming statement. I shall rejoice to listen to it if you can get me in. He has been doing a very good job of work.

Yours always,

Sydney Cockerell

Mrs Angeli was the daughter of Rossetti's youngest brother and Ford Madox Brown's daughter. The close friendship that grew between Helen Angeli, Geoffrey and Rosalie Mander resulted in paintings and drawings being lent and displayed at Wightwick; her daughter and grandchildren inherited her generous nature and many of their family pictures now in the house were donated by them.

FROM AN UNIDENTIFIED NEWSPAPER:

Active Back benchers No-44

SIR G. MANDER

Rosa Dartle always wanted to know. Dickens revelled in her and little thought that her interrogative descendant would someday sit in the House of Commons. Sir Geoffrey Mander (he was in the last honours list) sits on the solitary Liberal bench in Parliament. When listening to a debate he often leans back and puts his feet up on the bench in front until the Tories opposite can only see his shoes. But sooner or later the feet come down and the smiling face reappears. Geoffrey Mander wants to know something, "Does the Minister really mean-?" "Will the Hon. gentleman explain-?"

Until he became PPS to Sir Archibald Sinclair in 1942 he asked so many questions that he came almost to look like an interrogation point.

He was born sixty three years ago but like nearly all Liberals he is slim and does not look his age. Harrow suckled his boyish mind and Cambridge gave him solid food. He is in the comfortable position of being chairman of a sound family business in Wolverhampton, so that his home, his business, his constituency are all in one. He confesses in Who's Who that one of his hobbies is rambling. Would that all MPs were equally frank.

HANSARD

22 February 1945

WAR-TIME NURSERIES

Mr Mander asked the Minister of Health if he will make arrangements for war-time nurseries to remain in existence until the Ministry of Education or other interested parties shall have had an opportunity of taking over their work in part or in whole and until the position can be reviewed by his Department in the light of post-war needs.

The negative reply to this question ended: "I have no authority to provide nurseries at the cost of the Exchequer for other than war purposes."

On 1st March a debate to approve the Yalta Conference (then known as the Crimea Conference) took place in Parliament. "That this House approves the declaration of joint policy agreed to by the three great Powers at the Crimea Conference and, in particular, welcomes their determination to maintain unity of action not only in achieving the final defeat of the common enemy but, thereafter, in peace as in war."

The agreement between Russia, Great Britain and the USA was vehemently questioned by the MP for Cambridge University, Mr Pickthorn, who felt that the Soviet Union could not be trusted. He gave a long and impassioned speech, expressing doubts about the possibility of any form of democratic representation being established in some countries in the future, in particular in Poland and Yugoslavia, where free elections were not allowed.

HANSARD

Mr Pickthorn: Unless we are confident of our power and authority to make sure there is something like the free expression of public opinion in the countries for which we assert that democracy is our policy, then we are getting ourselves wholly in the wrong. I am profoundly convinced that unless not only we want there to be the real expression of public opinion in these countries, but also are sure we can see that that happens, this plebiscitary policy we are entering upon will be a bogus policy and will be the least realist and the least idealist of all policies and the one which will make most certain quarrels with our Allies.

Sir Geoffrey Mander: We ought not to allow emotional sympathy for ideal solutions of particular problems to blind us to the overriding consideration that the three Great Powers are the people on whom we must rely for peace in the world for a considerable time to come. I believe that these three, so different in their history, constitutions and methods, are at one in sincerely desiring peace and the onward and upward march of mankind.

I would like to say a few words about the new world organisation, which is much more important than some of the matters we have been discussing. The new organisation will go by the name of the United Nations. Some have criticised that on the ground that it might be a constant reminder to Germany, when she comes to join it, that she was defeated in the war. I do not think that is a strong argument against it, for it will be a good thing if Germany can be constantly reminded that she was defeated on a military basis in the war. I am sure that my right Hon. Friend the Foreign Secretary was so right last night when he referred to the certain resurgence of German propaganda. We need to be very much on our guard against the whining German. By all means let us try to make him into a civilised German, but he will be a whining German to begin with. Let us look out for him.

When the three great statesmen were at Yalta, no doubt the mountains looked very high - the physical mountains, and the political mountains too. One cannot scale the crests of success at one stage. The important thing is to get our feet firmly planted on the right path. I believe at Yalta we commenced that task.

The next day Geoffrey took part in the deliberations on Finance Corporations, when the main consideration was to determine the way in which capital would be made available for large scale reorganisation and development after the war.

HANSARD
7 March
Sir Geoffrey Mander asked the Parliamentary Secretary to the Ministry of War Transport if he will consider the advisability of introducing legislation to make permanent the war-time regulations for public control of the railways.

Mr Noel-Baker: The railways will remain under Government control for at least one year after the cessation of hostilities, and probably longer. There will, therefore, be ample time for the consideration of the important questions of the future.

Sir G. Mander: Will my Hon. Friend take care that this great public service is not handed back to private enterprise?

A letter of 7th March 1945 is from Stanley Baldwin. He found an article written by Geoffrey very interesting and wrote "publish it as it is."

He read a book he was returning to Geoffrey with much interest, but (apparently with much more enthusiasm) it was "devoured" by his wife.

Old Battersea House. SW11

March 13

Dear Sir Geoffrey,

The Collection here has been greatly increased since you saw it, and in the future will be a very large one, as so many bequests are being made to it. It will pass into the keeping of the National Trust. Recently Lady Lovelace left me a beautiful picture by my sister, Lady Bathurst has presented another, we have been given a sculptured group by Bernini, and a cabinet designed by William Morris and painted by De Morgan.

We moved all the collection twice, but had eventually to bring it back as the pictures were suffering from darkness and damp in storage. Then came the V1s and V2s, and, even before this last onslaught, 19,000 houses were smashed in Battersea. We were blasted four times but escaped with only thirty windows shattered (twice over) and the loss of two De Morgan plates!

At present we have to keep the pottery down in the crypt, or under stout oak tables when above ground. So the house is shut up and looks dismal at present, and for five years I have had no servants as mine were called up, and it has been a hard struggle, while we have been in constant danger, day and night! Only three mornings ago when I went down I found the kitchen ceiling on the breakfast table, the result of a rocket hard by in the night.

I long to get straight again, but at present I dare not unpack breakable things while the bombing continues, and the dirt from the vibrations they cause is difficult to cope with. Sometimes I feel we shall never be clean and normal in my life-time!

I am much amused at your reference to Miss Lobb. I shall never forget my first vision of her, when we motored over to Kelmscott one Sunday and found May Morris away, so we were received by Miss L. She was wearing knickerbockers, a dirty Norfolk jacket, worsted stockings with down-at-heel slippers, and had coal black nails. She said her chief occupation [was] looking after the bulls - of which there seemed an unpleasant number. Yet she was most agreeable and a charming hostess. But what a strange contrast to May Morris and her surroundings - bar the bulls!

I hope some day, if ever we are presentable again, you and Lady Mander may be able to come to see us, for when you came everything here was in its infancy, and not being endowed with much of this world's goods, we have had to "go slow" and do things by degrees. I am so sorry we have never been able to avail ourselves of your tempting invitation to see your beautiful house, but we go away little now, and perhaps it would only fill us with painful envy!

Yours sincerely,

Wilhelmina Stirling

P.S. If you ever hear of anyone who has one of my sister's pictures I am most anxious to buy any available. I wonder where Winifred Holliday is living now? I have lost sight of her and am sorry.

The Collection is owned now by the De Morgan Foundation. It has been housed at the De Morgan Centre, 38 West Hill, Wandsworth, London, since 2000 and it is open to the public.

HANSARD

20 March

NATIONAL PARKS

Sir Geoffrey Mander: I wish to call attention to the question of national parks. The principle of national parks is generally accepted by the people of this country. The question, first is, What do I mean precisely by a national park? I would say that it should consist of regions of the finest landscape in the country, which are to be preserved in all their natural beauty. There is no suggestion that farming and the ordinary pursuits of the countryside should not be continued inside these parks. You get a very good analogy of that in the houses that come under the National Trust. They are houses to which people have access so they can see beautiful and interesting things under the normal condition of life.

I want to appeal to the Government to seize this opportunity. They want to be popular I am sure. They could not do a more popular and less expensive thing than to let the country know that they are determined to go forward at once with setting up the necessary machinery to preserve this splendid part of our heritage.

During March the Allies crossed the Rhine and Winston Churchill told the troops "One good strong heave all together will end the war in Europe."

On March 24th, Eisenhower announced "We have them whipped."

On 29th March, Geoffrey asked the Minister of Town and Country Planning when the Government was going to publish the report on National Parks - apparently it had been ready since the autumn of 1944. He was concerned as well about the proposed reservoir to be erected in the Manifold Valley by Leicester Corporation and how it might affect the landscape.

> College of Arms, London. EC4.
> 6th April 1945
> Dear Geoffrey,
> Thank you for your letter and cheque.
> The Arms you mention belong to a very ancient Cornish family and we
> have a pedigree of that family down to about fifty years ago.
> It is essential that I know the names of your wife's father and grandfather
> and if possible her great grandfather. I can then tell you the position of
> affairs.
> Yours ever,
> Algar Howard.

On 12th April the death of the American president, Franklin Roosevelt, was announced. He was succeeded by Harry S. Truman.

On the same day Geoffrey asked again when the report on National Parks was likely to be published. He was told that it was likely to be some time in May.

SWINBURNE'S WALK

On April 21st 1945 Rosalie, John and I went by train from Waterloo to Putney Station to do the walk that Swinburne made almost daily for fifty years while living with Watts-Dunton at No. 2 The Pines. This is not far from the station on the left at the bottom of Putney Hill. We saw some ferns growing in the front garden similar to the ones sent to us and now growing in the Kelmscott Bed.

At the top of the hill is "The Green Man" wrongly thought by Mrs Joseph *[William Holman Hunt's daughter]* to be Swinburne's destination.

We walked across Putney Heath and Wimbledon Common about two miles to the "Rose and Crown" in Wimbledon High Street. This is where S. had his daily glass of beer.

Further up High Street we visited Miss Frost's stationer's shop where he was a frequent visitor. The hawthorns were in full bloom and S. was particularly lyrical in admiring them. Many details about all this were given in "The Home Life of Swinburne" by Clara Watts-Dunton. Two pieces of hawthorn were brought back and planted in the hope that they will survive.

The Poets' Gardens at Wightwick Manor were created in 1937. They were divided into areas devoted to specific poets including Shelley, Tennyson and Morris [the Kelmscott garden] using seeds, cuttings and plants from their gardens. Over the years the collection of plants grew to include shrubs from Dickens' garden, and plants from Old Place, the home of Charles Kempe who designed stained glass for Wightwick in 1887 and 1893.

Also on April 21st Geoffrey presented a radio talk at 7.45pm on "The Week in Westminster"

The eventful day this week was certainly Tuesday when many things happened; one of them quite unexpected, but then that is typical of Parliamentary life.

Everyone was waiting for the tribute to be paid by the Prime Minister, on behalf of the whole House, to the memory of his and our great friend President Roosevelt. This he did in moving and matchless words, ending on this note: "For us it remains only to say that in Franklin Roosevelt there died the greatest American friend we have ever known, and the greatest champion of freedom who has ever brought help and comfort from the new world to the old." The House was full, the galleries were packed, amongst those present, as they say, being Princess Juliana of the Netherlands and the Ambassadors of our principal Allies.

Before, however, the House was able to approach this memorable interlude, there arose a controversy when two new Members came to be introduced. There was no trouble about the Member for the Scottish Universities - that distinguished Scotsman, Sir John Boyd-Orr. There was, however, with the newly elected Scottish Nationalist Member for Motherwell. As you must all have read in the papers, it has long been customary for Members, when introduced after a by-election, to have two other Members as sponsors belonging to their own party. There was a Motion passed in 1688 laying down that this must be done. The object of it - quite a practical one no doubt at that time - was, that by this means the identity of the new Member was established. For a long time, however, it has been more an act of comradeship and courtesy than anything else. But there are no other members of Dr. McIntyre's party and he wasn't willing to accept anyone else's help so he advanced up the floor alone. The Speaker had to tell him to withdraw behind the bar and this he did. On Wednesday however he changed his mind - he took his seat in the ordinary way accompanied by two Scottish Labour Members. [On Tuesday] In spite of the fact that the Prime Minister was waiting and the galleries were full, the House insisted on discussing the real issue. This was the right of a citizen freely elected by a constituency to take his seat in the House of Commons. It was felt that this should be done at the earliest possible moment, but also that there should be no unnecessary breach of old and familiar customs. On a division the latter view prevailed.

Incidentally, some of these customs have curious origins. For instance, when Members are passing out of the division lobbies after voting, they bow or take off their hats. I believe the object of this was to prevent Members continuing the habit - of course a very long time ago - that had grown up of sending in their men servants to vote for them, and by taking off their hats - and Members nearly all wore them in those days - they could be identified.

There was an interesting little debate in the Lords on Wednesday raised by Lord Mottistone, who wanted to know whether the Government proposed to adhere to the Parliamentary custom, by which the House of Lords attended thanksgiving services in state in Westminster Abbey. He was assured by Lord Listowel that there was no intention of altering the custom. It's interesting to note that while for centuries both Houses had recourse to the Abbey, in 1621, in a moment of Puritan zeal on a question of ritual, the Commons migrated to St. Margaret's, Westminster, which they have ever since regarded as their church. Memorial services for Members, for instance, are held there. On happier occasions, however, Members can make use of the Crypt of the House of Commons for the purpose of being married or having their children christened, and it's available for any Christian denomination. The Crypt has known many changes; it was first of all, in 1292, the Chapel of St. Mary-Under-Croft; it has been at times the Speaker's dining room; a coal cellar; and Cromwell is said to have stabled his horses there.

There was a debate on the San Francisco Conference, opened by Mr Attlee who commented on the basic principles of collective security. Geoffrey also reported on the Committee stage of the bill dealing with the future of land that had been requisitioned during the war, and then, at the end of the week, the Army and Air Force Annual Bill included a discussion on facilities to be granted to those in the Services in connection with the General Election and the use of troops in industrial disputes.

So passed another week in the great pageant of British Parliamentary history. Its most lasting work will have been, I think, to have given assurance to those who are going out as delegates to San Francisco that they have behind them the backing of the whole nation in trying to build up a new World organisation which will banish from men's minds the fear of war for ever.

3,000 delegates from fifty nations gathered together for the San Francisco Conference in April 1945, with the object of establishing both the United Nations Organisation and the International Court of Justice. For two months the delegates developed and added to the proposals first promoted at the Dumbarton Oaks

Conference in Washington in 1944 and at Yalta earlier in 1945. In June the charter was approved and signed by the delegates, and then after approval by the parliaments of all its members, the United Nations Organisation came into existence on October 24th 1945.

On 28th April, in Italy, Benito Mussolini was executed by partisans after a very brief trial. Two days later, Hitler and Eva Braun committed suicide in the German Chancellery.

Newspaper cutting from THE GUARDIAN
May 2, 1945.
HITLER DIES IN THE CHANCELLERY
Hitler has died in Berlin. This was announced on the German radio last night by Admiral Doenitz, who has been appointed his successor. The news was given to the German people in the following terms:
'From the Fuhrer's headquarters it is announced that our Fuhrer, Adolf Hitler, this afternoon at his command post fell for Germany. The end of this, his struggle, and of his unswerving straight path of life, is marked by his heroic death'.

HANSARD
8 May 1945
GERMANY (UNCONDITIONAL SURRENDER)
The Prime Minister (Mr Churchill). Mr Speaker, I have just had the duty of making an official statement to the nation and the British Empire and Commonwealth, and I thought it might perhaps be convenient to the House if I repeated it.
He then announced that all German land, sea and air forces had signed an act of unconditional surrender and outlined the procedures involving ratification and confirmation of the treaty.
Hostilities will end officially at one minute after midnight tonight, Tuesday 8th May, but in the interests of saving lives the "Cease Fire" began yesterday to be sounded along all fronts. The Germans are still in places resisting Russian troops. It is not surprising that on such long fronts and in the existing disorder of the enemy the orders of the German High

Command should not in every case have been obeyed. This does not, in our opinion, constitute any reason for withholding from the nation the facts communicated to us by General Eisenhower of the unconditional surrender already signed at Rheims nor should it prevent us from celebrating today and tomorrow - Wednesday - as Victory-in-Europe-Days. The German war, Mr Speaker, is therefore at an end.

He went on to express gratitude to "our splendid Allies" and to "this House of Commons, which has proved itself the strongest foundation for waging war that has ever been seen in the whole of our long history."

Whereupon Mr Speaker and the Members proceeded to the Church of St. Margaret, Westminster, and attended a Service of Thanksgiving to Almighty God.

THE DAILY MIRROR

May 8th 1945

GERMANY SURRENDERS

The Germans broadcast to the world that they had accepted unconditional surrender and that the war in Europe was over after five years, eight months and four days.

The surrender [on 7th May] took place at the little red school house which is General Eisenhower's HQ, according to an Agency message from Rheims.

In the surrender terms there is understood to be a clause insisting on the formal handing over of the German Fleet to the United Nations. British, Russian and American warships will take part in the ceremony. Special steps have been taken to ensure that there is no repetition of the 1918 incident when the German fleet scuttled itself.

The difficulties of implementing "special steps" in a chaotic situation was illustrated by a small paragraph in The Daily Mirror:

HUNS SURRENDER TO "CAPT. BLIGH"

Most of the twenty-three ships which have surrendered at Ancona, the Italian Adriatic port, are prizes of twenty-six-year-old 'Captain Bligh'.

With a force of three motor torpedo boats, Lieutenant-Commander T.J. Bligh, senior officer of the 57th M.T.B. Flotilla, encountered a convoy of about forty German vessels fleeing from Trieste to Pola. When he demanded their surrender many of the Germans preferred to blow up their ships or run them aground.

All night Bligh kept watch outside the small Adriatic port to which the surviving Germans had fled and by morning they had surrendered.

From The Daily Mirror again:

IT GOES ON IN ROOM 109

There was no V-Night in Room 109 - no peace, no holiday, no paper hats. There were only the wild sounds of rejoicing floating through the half-bricked windows from Whitehall to tell the great news to its four occupants.

For Room 109 at the War Office is the operational nerve-centre of the war that is not yet won - the war of the million men in South-East Asia Command.

As gladness thrilled through London and workers all over the nation stopped after five and a half years in thanksgiving and joy, the little pins moved slowly forward on the secret map in Room 109. There was still war in Room 109.

I watched fascinated, as the major swiftly organised the constant flow of secret intelligence. He moved a pin in Burma. Less than an hour before, while London laughed, some British troops had moved in the jungle - forward.

Business continued as usual in the House of Commons the day after the celebrations.

HANSARD

9 May 1945

Sir Geoffrey Mander asked the Minister of Works if he is aware that there are brick kilns in the neighbourhood of Willenhall, Staffordshire, where no production is taking place; and whether, in view of the urgent need of bricks for housing, he will take steps to bring these into operation forthwith.

Mr Sandys: Closed brickworks will be progressively re-opened as the building programme expands

When Geoffrey offered to give the Minister names of the Willenhall brickworks so they might be given high priority, Mr Sandys said that he was sure Geoffrey would not wish preferential treatment to be given to those firms.

The next question also came from Geoffrey when he asked about prefabricated houses, including Swedish and American ones, and how many had actually been erected. The answer was about 1,800 British ones.

Late that afternoon, he took part in the debate on the Local Government (Boundary Commission) Bill. He talked about the re-organisation of local government bodies, in particular those in South Staffordshire and hoped that the Boundary Commission would come to some decision soon.

On Tuesday 15th May Geoffrey asked what assistance would be given to returning service men in order to help them set up in business; this was followed by a number of concerned queries from other MPs. Amendments to the Income Tax Bill were discussed in Committee later in the day and Geoffrey drew attention to an anomaly in tax concessions made to comparable businesses.

Two days later, again in Committee, Geoffrey took part in a discussion on the Family Allowances Bill. He was especially in favour of a proposal to extend benefits to countries both within and outside the British Empire.

On 23rd May the wartime coalition government was dissolved. Churchill headed a temporary Conservative government until a general election could be held.

After the Whitsun holiday, the House of Commons met again on Tuesday 29th May.
HANSARD
Sir Geoffrey Mander asked the Prime Minister whether it is proposed to introduce legislation before the General Election to implement the recommendations of the Speaker's Conference with regard to the limitation of election expenses and other matters.
The Prime Minister: No, Sir.
This led to a number of questions from other MPs who were unhappy with his answer.

The next question, also about the coming General Election, prompted a heated discussion about holiday weeks in Lancashire, Scotland and many other industrial areas which all fell during election period, when thousands of people would be away from home and unable to vote. A number of suggestions included provision for holiday makers to vote on holiday, to vote during the following week or to postpone the election until the Autumn. None of these ideas was accepted.

Geoffrey spoke in a debate on coal charges - he described a visit to Hilton Main colliery - and during the next few days he took part in discussions on Syria and Lebanon, Joint Production Committees, Holidays with Pay, Housing for ex-servicemen, the possible reduction in the duty on tea and tobacco for pensioners, and whether the names of all repatriated prisoners of war had been entered on the electoral register. He also expressed concern about the length of time temporary housing erected in public open spaces would remain there.

During a debate on Civil Aviation, Geoffrey said, "I feel that ultimate control of any civil aviation scheme ought to be vested in the State, working through a public utility company, however much freedom of experiment within they care to give."

On 15th June, after the King's address to both Houses of Parliament had been read by the Lord Chancellor [Viscount Simon] he announced, "We do, in His Majesty's Name and in obedience to His Majesty's Commands, prorogue this Parliament to Tuesday, the third day of July, one thousand nine hundred and forty five."

> Chelwood Gate,
> Haywards Heath.
> 19 June '45
> Dear Mander,
> I wish I could come and speak for you at Wolverhampton but at my age one has to give up that kind of thing. I am very sorry because I hope you will get in and I should like to help. To us, the question of how peace can be best served is greater than anything else at this election. I know how much you have done for that cause and it will be a serious national loss if you are not a member of the new House to carry on your good work.
> With all good wishes,
> Yours very sincerely,
> Cecil [Lord Cecil]
> Please use this letter in any way you think best!!

The General Election was held on 5th July 1945. The results were not announced until 26th July so that postal votes from the forces abroad could be included

Thurso Castle,
Thurso.
15th July 1945
Dear Geoffrey,

I have only just heard from Percy that you have been ill during the Election. This is frightfully bad luck, and I do hope that it was nothing serious. Personal popularity is a brittle reed for most people at Election times, but yours was so great and so well-deserved that I hope it has pulled you through, in spite of your incapacity to take your usual part in the campaign.

I have had a tough fight here against two very active candidates and, of course, the fortnight which I allowed myself is much too short a time in which to cover this huge constituency. Nevertheless, I am hopeful of being returned.

Please let me take this opportunity of thanking you again for the splendid work which you did at the Air Ministry. You held everybody's confidence and affection, both on the Service and the Civil sides and this, with your popularity in the House of Commons, made you a firm and valuable link between Parliament and the Department. To me your companionship, your wise counsel and your staunch support were inestimably precious, and I shall always look back with pride and pleasure to the time when we made war in common against our enemies, both at home and abroad.

Please remember us affectionately to Rosalie: I am afraid she must have had a very hard time during your illness. Marigold was magnificent here. She held the fort for a fortnight before I arrived and organised the whole campaign.

I am planning to be in London when the results are declared on the 26th July, and I shall hope to see you as soon as possible afterwards. Let me know when you will be coming up.

Yours ever,
Archie [Sinclair]

The envelope containing this letter from his brother Lionel, posted in Los Angeles, was addressed to "Sir Geoffrey Mander KB MP?".

July 15th '45

Dear Geoffrey,

Just a line to let you know that I had a letter from Theo [his son] this week telling me he had learnt to fly and he wanted me to write to you to know if you could give him any advice about acquiring a second hand machine from the government. He says he's heard that they are already disposing of some models to civilians. He is advised that the Taylorcraft "Austen" is a likely plane for such as he. I told him to write to you direct and I should be very glad and obliged if you could advise him in this respect. Your experience at the Air Ministry will presumably help.

I notice from the Times that your opponent was Garthwaite. His brother Tony is out here, after a tough war, in the Consulate - an old Harrovian and an able young fellow.

I presume that as you had no split in the Liberal vote your majority will be substantial.

Yours affectionately,

Lionel

P.S. My heart still beats something. I'm taking this new hormone treatment to strengthen the muscles.

The election results were announced on 26th July. Only twelve Liberals were elected and Geoffrey lost his seat after sixteen years in Parliament.

Report from The Manchester Guardian, 27th July, 1945.

ATTLEE COMES TO POWER.

So Mr Churchill has not been able to save the Tory party from defeat!

It has fallen as low as that. One of the half dozen greatest leaders in war that we have produced, while at the summit of his achievement and prestige, could not induce the British people to give the Tories another lease of power.

Most people at the beginning of the election assumed that multitudes would cast a vote for the Tories simply in order to keep Mr Churchill at the helm. Such an exercise of independent judgement has rarely been witnessed in a democracy, and it has been reached in the teeth of one of the most fierce and unscrupulous campaigns ever waged by the Tory party and its press. The Tory party is not merely condemned for its past; it is rejected because it has no message for the times.

The swing is probably a much vaguer movement, than some Labour left wingers would like to think. It could be interpreted as a vote for bold action on reconstruction, demobilisation, housing, town planning and fuel, coupled with a willingness to accept state action where it can be shown to be indispensable to a successful attack on these problems.

45 Yatscombe,
Boars Hill,Oxford.
27th July 1945
My dear Mander,
Well, our ship was caught in a typhoon, and the best seamanship could not save it. You will be terribly missed in the House, not only by Liberals, but by all who value courage in the support of good causes.
Yours ever,
M.
[Gilbert Murray]

FROM THE BISHOP OF LICHFIELD.
I cannot tell you how sorry I am at your being "out" in this election; I never dreamt that your constituency could be so misguided! It is all the more sad, partly because of their long Liberal tradition, and partly because you - if I may say so - are the sort of person which the House of Commons can ill afford to miss. I do hope you may get back again before very long. Love to the family.

77 Great Russell Street,
WC1
6th August 1945
My dear Sir Geoffrey,
I have waited a few days before writing to express my very deep regret that you have not been returned to Parliament. You will be sadly missed there - and I am not thinking only of ourselves - but I feel sure that it will prove to be no more than a temporary interruption, and that you will

soon be back. But for the time being it is a great loss to us and our cause, though I hope you will still continue to give us the benefit of your advice and support.

Please accept my heartfelt thanks for all your understanding help in the past - may it long continue! - and looking forward to seeing you soon, I remain,

With kindest regards, very sincerely yours,

C. Weizmann

There had been signs during the election campaign that Geoffrey might lose his seat. Some voters had come up to him to shake his hand and to thank him for his work on their behalf - but then told him they would have to vote for Labour: he may have expected the final result but he was, nevertheless, desperately upset.

FROM JOHN'S AUTOBIOGRAPHY

Though my father was defeated in June *[sic]* 1945, the overwhelming victory of the Left gave him deep pleasure. Many of the men now in the House had been his friends, and they (not the Chamberlainites) now formed the government. In his heart, he was a stricken man: but he took comfort from this victory of so many of the ideas he had struggled for.

EPILOGUE

It must have frustrated Geoffrey to watch from the sidelines in 1945 as the new, innovative Labour Government implemented many of the proposals he had advocated, and occasionally introduced, during his years in the House of Commons.

His knowledge, and support, of Poland and Czechoslovakia and their leaders, and his many friendships with Russian and Jewish politicians, might have been usefully employed even in opposition, particularly during the early Cold War years. His successful three years as PPS to Archibald Sinclair demonstrated that he was very capable and energetic and before the election he would have been justified in feeling that the chance to achieve so much more lay tantalisingly within his grasp. As The Eastern Daily Press had commented, "a Parliamentary Under-Secretaryship has always been regarded as a stepping stone to higher things." It must have been a tremendous blow to lose that exciting vision of possibilities yet to come.

All his life Geoffrey's sympathies had been with the Left so when, in 1948, he joined the Labour Party it was a logical step for him to take. Eventually he was elected as Labour member of Staffordshire County Council for Brierley Hill.

> House of Commons,
> 10th June 1948
> My dear Geoffrey,
> Thank you very much for your letter. It was good of you to give me advance news of your decision.
> All I will say is - better that way than the other.
> Yours ever,
> Megan.

Megan Lloyd George (1902-1966) was the daughter of David Lloyd George. She entered Parliament, like Geoffrey in 1929 as a Liberal and later she too joined the Labour party.

In the mid 1950s when Geoffrey started to research and write his political autobiography, "A Back-Bencher Looks Back", he was helped in his research by C.

Royle, MP for Salford West, who received this letter from the Statistical Division of the House of Commons.

23rd January 1957

PARLIAMENTARY ACTIVITY OF GEOFFREY LE MESURIER MANDER, MP FOR WOLVERHAMPTON EAST, 1929-1945.

Dear Mr Royle,

We have received your request for (a) the number of Questions asked (b) the number of speeches in Debate made, by the above former Member in each year of the period 1929 to 1945.

I am very sorry to say that we do not feel it proper to answer it, as it would involve a disproportionate expenditure of time and would impinge too severely on our obligations to other Members and on our other Library duties.

To give you some idea of the difficulties involved: Mr Mander was clearly by no means an inactive Member, for during his very first session here (1929/30) references under his name occupy twenty columns of the Hansard Sessional Index. Just to be certain that 1929/30 was not an abnormally active period for Mr Mander, I turned up two other sessions, the one (1937/38) towards the middle of his career, the other (1944/45) at the very end. The results were as follows:

SESSION: 1937/38.

Columns of Index = 12+. Number of separate volumes: 14.

Number of references to be consulted: 650-700.

SESSION: 1944/45.

Columns of index = 2. Number of separate volumes: 6

Number of references to be consulted: 125.

You will observe that even 1944/45 (a comparatively light session among the sixteen to be covered) would involve the consultation of six different volumes and the tracing of one hundred and twenty five separate references.

For these reasons we do not feel justified in undertaking your enquiry in its present form. Perhaps, however, the figures I have given will be of some use for your purpose?

Yours sincerely,

E.C. Thompson.

After it was rejected for publication, Geoffrey abandoned work on his political autobiography However his life after Parliament was still full of interest as he carried on attending to those additional concerns he had always addressed during his parliamentary career. He retained his position as Chairman of Mander Brothers and served on a number of committees, one of which was the Executive Committee of the United Nations Association. He was also Chairman of the Staffordshire branch of the Campaign to Protect Rural England. He received a number of requests to speak at political rallies, and was asked to serve as Chairman or committee member by a number of organisations such as the local Historical Society and the local branch of the National Trust.

Air Ministry,
Whitehall, SW1.
11 October 1951
My dear Geoffrey,
I do not know whether you have any free dates, and whether you will care
to speak for me in Rowley Regis. If so, I should be very happy to have you
on my platform.
Perhaps you would let me know?
Yours sincerely,
Arthur Henderson.

He was the third son of Labour MP Arthur Henderson who died in 1935. He served with his father in Parliament and was listed in Hansard as - Henderson, Mr A., Jnr. He was re-elected in 1929 as Labour MP for Kingswinford. Although the Labour Party lost the General Election in 1951 Arthur Henderson won the seat of Rowley Regis and Tipton and held it until he retired in 1966 when he was made Baron Rowley.

This letter was sent to Wightwick in July 1960:
Dear Sir Geoffrey,
It has been felt for some time, that the formation of a Civic Society in
the Wolverhampton District was desirable, in order to keep a watch
on the development of the area. I am sure you will agree that there are
often cases of bad development or the demolition of old and historical
buildings, which might have been prevented had the public been fully

informed and able to express its opinion through a local organisation.

In consequence of this, a Wolverhampton Civic Society is now in process of formation and it is hoped that it will prove of great worth to the district.

I hope you will consent to allow your name to appear as one of our Vice Presidents, in which case I shall be glad to hear from you, as soon as possible, in order that I may inform the Committee.

Wightwick Manor was a source of constant interest for Geoffrey. As well as showing visitors round the house on open days he also continued to add to the collection in the house. He and Lady Mander attended auctions where they were able to buy paintings and furniture. James Lees-Milne, working for the National Trust, was a great help. These quotations come from the 1949 section of his book of memoirs, "Midway on the Waves":

To the Tate Gallery with Sir Geoffrey Mander to choose Pre-Raphaelite paintings for Wightwick.

Having taken much trouble in consulting several experts I told Sir Ralph Millais it was not worth more than £200. He, very trusting, agreed to sell it to the National Trust for that sum. So I have purchased it for Wightwick Manor. Hope to God we haven't swindled the poor man.

The painting he bought was "Effie Ruskin: the Foxglove" by John Millais (1853). It hangs in the Upper Hall at Wightwick

A letter from Nikolaus Pevsner, written in November 1951, evidently refers to a list, drawn up by Walter Tower, of stained glass windows designed by his cousin Charles Kempe.

I did not realise that you wanted a copy of the whole of Mr Tower's list. This, I can assure you, would be quite a formidable task. Mrs Michaelson has extracted for me seventeen counties and then we gave up because in looking at the windows I found the later windows are not really worth regarding singly. So for the remaining counties she will only make notes of early work.

Geoffrey continued to track down Kempe domestic glass and he received this letter in 1960:

The glass filled the large west window of the drawing room at the Wood

House. I took the glass out because it entirely hid a magnificent view of twelve miles and because it made the room quite extraordinarily dark. When we left the Wood House [in Epping, Essex] it was carefully put away in the small garage. As far as I know, the glass is still in the garage and has not been disposed of.

Presumably Geoffrey did not go to Essex as no more Kempe glass was installed at Wightwick after the 1930s.

He bought Morris wallpaper, fabrics, glass and carpets for the house and continued to add appropriate plants to the Poets' (and Writers') Gardens.

A LETTER FROM THE POET EDMUND BLUNDEN

Dear Sir Geoffrey,

If I can get over to Bracknell and once more find the way clear into Shelley's old garden (1813) - the house is now a furniture store and a shame to see it so misused, but it at least stands - I will certainly bring away something which might grow in your garden.

C. Dickens might not quite like a Shelley selection near him! but I suppose the two are to be kept in order at last!

In 1962 Geoffrey was offered some family photographs of the sculptor Thomas Woolner, one of the original members of the Pre-Raphaelite group. A photograph of Woolner, in his studio, is displayed upstairs at Wightwick and may be one of the pictures to which the letter writer was referring.

Judging by the number of letters arriving at Wightwick, Geoffrey's correspondence was as prolific as ever. Letters came from C.P. Snow, Isaac Foot - "I congratulate you on your birthday yesterday. At 78 you are only a stripling!" and from Frank Pakenham:

Hurst Green,

Sussex.

August 7th 1953

My dear Geoffrey,

I cannot tell you how pleased I am that you should like my book. As I hope you know - but there is no harm in saying it again - Elizabeth and I not only value greatly the friendship of Rosalie and yourself but have the highest respect for your standards, whether in politics, literature or morals. I always feel that the process by which you came to the Labour Party was deeply impressive and although I know you were not looking for recognition I cannot help hoping that one day it will be more fully accorded.

I know there are many others who share my hope.

Yours

Frank.

Showborough House,

Twyning,

Nr. Tewkesbury.

7th April 1960

My dear Mander,

I am so glad you like reading about the Macdonald sisters. I hoped and thought you would, because it was easy for me to see when I visited you in your house where some, at least, of your interests lay. It is not a book for the many, nor I suppose for the present generation; only for a handful of the likes of us. I read last year, I think, words by the art critic of (again I think) The Times about an exhibition of pictures - words like - Ah yes, I have them here: 27/3/57 "If such a person as the Pre-Raphaelite enthusiast still exists." Well, our lot were a bit post Pre-Raphaelite, but I dare say they'd be included in the writer's liberal contempt (I don't mean Liberal, politically). He goes on to speak of "this muddle-headed, rapt, but often vulgar movement".

Anyway, now that I've put those sisters on record as accurately as I possibly can, I am satisfied that a little gap has been more or less filled, or bridged, or plugged, or whatever gaps have to have done to annihilate them.

Thank you again so much for writing and Lady Mander too.

Yours sincerely,

Baldwin of Bewdley

Arthur Baldwin, 1904-1976, was the second son of Geoffrey's friend Stanley Baldwin, and succeeded to the title in 1958 on the death of his brother Oliver, 2nd Baron Bewdley. His grandmother and great aunts were the Macdonald sisters.

The archives at Wightwick Manor are an invaluable source of information, particularly those papers relating to Geoffrey's life. Their abundance is largely due to the advice he received from Dr. Crichton-Miller of the Tavistock Clinic. Geoffrey's daughter Anthea wrote a little about this in 1990:

> He told my father to write everything down to structure and make sense of his life. So in the family archives there are lists - of walks, visitor numbers, tennis games, high jump records, fish caught, birds and wild flowers seen and Xmas 'boxes' for staff long since gone. And on the walls are quotations that he treasured and wanted to share.

Geoffrey continued to write his reports on visits to interesting people and places,. Many had Pre-Raphaelite connections but this is one of the few visits to someone with political associations:

> TO EDWARD R. PEASE - JUNE 13TH 1951 AT LIMPSFIELD.
> He is 94 and very deaf, otherwise quite well; can read without glasses.
> He is the only living founder of the Labour Party and was secretary for many years of the Fabian Society and wrote its history.
> He knew William Morris and used to attend meetings and occasionally spoke at Kelmscott House [in Hammersmith]. Says Morris was a poor speaker. Morris used to have parties for the Boat Race at K.H. and these he attended.

Geoffrey called on his friend, Sidney Cockerell, at 21 Kew Gardens Road on 22nd May 1957.

> He has been in bed for two or three years owing to a heart block but is reasonably well. Many friends come to see him. He is about ninety one. He spoke of his Pre-Raphaelite recollections; thought the last "Life of Morris" was too political and mentioned his three weeks tour with Ruskin in France. He was very pleased with Ronald Fuller and his poetry for schools. He dined at The Pines, Putney, several times. Swinburne was very entertaining in his conversation but could not hear a word that was said to him.
> He did not think much of Miss Lobb. He said it was true that May Morris was in love with Bernard Shaw but at that time Shaw was a penniless writer and matrimony was out of the question.
> It appears he stayed at Compton Hall - a mile from Wightwick - several

times with Mr Lawrence Hodson who was the Manager of Butlers' Brewery. He [Hodson] appears to have lost the job through failure to make profits but he was an enthusiast for all that Morris stood for and there are still remains of the decoration at the house, now used as a nurses' home. Morris was there too.

Compton Hall is now Compton Hospice; it is appreciated and well supported locally. Morris' wallpaper "Compton" was designed for Lawrence Hodson's house, he also commissioned three tapestries from the firm. They are now on show in Birmingham Museum and Art Gallery.

In 1950 the sale of the Red House at Bexley Heath was announced. The house, built and furnished in 1859 for William Morris, incorporated many of his ideas about architecture and design; he described it as, "a small Palace of Art of my own". A newspaper report stated that this will, "make many people anxious that it shall find an owner to care for it properly, for no house built during the past hundred years has had so profound an architectural influence."

In April 1951 Geoffrey visited Red House for the second time. He was one of the people anxious about the future of the house and there are replies to his many letters about it at Wightwick; eventually in 1952, when the house was sold to two architects, a friendly letter from the estate agent ended:

> I should like to take this opportunity of thanking you very much for your helpful endeavours in the past and assure you that there is at least one more person better acquainted with the life and works of William Morris than at this time last year."

****

In 1946, in his published diary "Caves of Ice" James Lees-Milne had written about Geoffrey - "he is a very decent, good, thoughtful man."

He is still remembered with affection in Wolverhampton, often by visitors to Wightwick and a number of their stories support James Lees-Milne's observation.

A visitor's grandfather, who was a painter and decorator, arrived at Wightwick, wearing a bowler hat and dressed in his good suit. Geoffrey met him and, leaving his hat, they set off to tour the house inspecting what decorating had to be done. When they returned to the kitchen they discovered that Geoffrey's dog had chewed the bowler hat, ruining it. The painter was bundled into Geoffrey's car and driven into Wolverhampton to Dunn's, the outfitters, where Geoffrey bought him a replacement.

As he grew older, he had a chauffeur who drove him every morning to the Works in Wolverhampton. The journey took him along the bus route and when Geoffrey recognised an employee waiting for the bus he would stop and give him a lift. Apparently, some days on arrival, quite a large group would emerge from the car.

Illness overtook him in December 1961 but he made a surprising recovery after an operation and was able to attend the eightieth birthday celebrations planned for him by Mander Brothers.

> House of Commons,
> London
> 16th April 1962
> My dear Geoffrey,
> Many thanks for your letter of the 10th April. It was most kind of you to offer to entertain Dora and myself during our visit to the West Midlands in July. Our plans are not quite complete. Could I possibly let you know about this a little later on.
> Of course I quite understand that you will not be able to come to the Wolverhampton meeting and do hope that you are now well on the way to recovering from your operation.
> Yours ever,
> Hugh Gaitskell

Gaitskell was leader of the Labour party from 1955 until his death in 1963.

Geoffrey wrote to his cousin Philip Mander in July arranging to resign as Chairman of Mander Brothers:

> I have been Chairman of the company since 1929 when your grandfather died and I have greatly enjoyed this activity and my association with the directors. I shall be delighted to co-operate with you in getting out a statement in writing for the [Wolverhampton] Express and Star. Many thanks for your kind remarks about my 33 years of chairmanship.

Geoffrey remained as President and Philip took over as Chairman

From the late summer of 1962 he became too weak to leave his room; he died peacefully, at Wightwick, on Sunday 9th September.

From an account of Geoffrey's life written in 1962.

He was a member of the Modern Churchman's Union: he also subscribed to the Society for Psychical Research and attended their meetings: he played chess, particularly by correspondence, and he was fond of reading, keeping up with contemporary political memoirs and going back for refreshment of the spirit to his favourite Browning. For exercise he enjoyed walking along the canal from Wightwick or, for longer outings, planning routes following the course of a river or inspecting some part of the countryside threatened with destruction. When there were children on these walks he would take the lead in collecting wild flowers or starting games of word-making. He played lawn tennis throughout the year on his court at Wightwick - the last game was on the 5th November 1961 when he was three months short of eighty years of age.

He was buried in the family grave in Pattingham churchyard and a memorial service was held later in St. Peter's, Wolverhampton.

His friend Frank Pakenham wrote his obituary in The Times:

There was never a more selfless politician than Geoffrey Mander. Perhaps he should not be thought of as a politician at all, for all his love of the House of Commons and the political life. He was supremely a man of causes. Abyssinia, Czechoslovakia, anti-Fascism, Collective Security - he preached them all indefatigably and inflexibly, though with unfailing good humour and what he preached he practised. His horror at the whole policy of appeasement culminating in Munich led him to harry the Government with an endless stream of questions in the House of Commons, to the irritation of his opponents and the admiration of his friends. His staunchness and energy in the struggle for peace never flagged. It is the greatest of pities that he was without a seat in either House during the post-war years. But whether in his own Midlands or in national and international politics he continued to find ways of rendering service that counted.

APPENDICES

Miles Mander

Miles Mander.

Geoffrey's brother Lionel began his career as an actor, writer and director in the 1920s and adopted the stage name Miles Mander.

In March 1929, The Green Can printed a film review.
"A Remarkable Triumph for British Films. The Screen Version of Henry Arthur Jones' famous Play "The Physician". Miles Mander in the role of Walter Amphiel gives a striking study of a dipsomaniac, and incidentally establishes himself as the leading dramatic actor on the British screen. Mr Mander is now in Berlin to play the lead in a film of pre-war Russia entitled "Nijni Noveorod" directed by the well-known Danish director Svend Gade."

In 1933 he appeared as Wriothesley in "The Private Life of Henry VIII " produced by Alexander Korda and starring Charles Laughton, Robert Donat and Merle Oberon. Time Out Film Guide describes "The Private Life of Henry VIII" as "probably the most commercially successful British film ever made"

In 1934 Faber published a book by Miles Mander. With the title "To my Son - in Confidence", it was addressed to Theo, his only child by his second wife Kathleen French.

Miles contested the Putney constituency in London for Labour, unsuccessfully, in the 1935 General Election.

In 1938, he, appeared in three films - in a version of "Kidnapped", as Disraeli in "Suez" starring Tyrone Power, and in "The Mad Miss Manton" starring Barbara Stanwyck. From 1938 to 1941 he had a radio programme, in America, in which he answered questions and provided information about the British Empire, politics and history. In 1940 he made more than seven films, in one of which, "The Primrose Path," he appeared as Ginger Rogers' father.

"Being Churchill's favourite film may not be much of a recommendation, but it's easy to see why he welcomed this wartime offering [1941] from the English community in Hollywood."
From the 2001 Time Out review of "That Hamilton Woman" (aka "Lady Hamilton"), starring Vivien Leigh, Laurence Olivier and Gladys Cooper with Miles Mander as Lord Keith.

During 1942 he performed in fourteen films. He was uncredited in four and in two of those he provided voices only: that of Winston Churchill in "Captains of the Clouds" and of a German agent in "Mrs Miniver".

In 1943 he appeared in more than six films but often he was uncredited He played Colonel Wallace in "First Comes Courage" and another soldier, Colonel Fitzhume, in "Five Graves to Cairo" directed by Billy Wilder.

During 1944 he again had a number of uncredited film roles although some of the characters he played did have names: Sir Frederick Fleet in "The Return of the Vampire" and Major Loring in "The White Cliffs of Dover". He had more significant roles in two Sherlock Holmes films with Basil Rathbone and Nigel Bruce "The Scarlet Claw" and "The Pearl of Death" and he played Mr Grayle in one of the best films of 1944, "Farewell My Lovely" adapted from Raymond Chandler's novel and starring Dick Powell.

Lionel had roles in five films in 1945. He played Chief Inspector Allison in "The Brighton Strangler" and he appeared in "The Picture of Dorian Gray" with George Sanders and Angela Lansbury. It was described as "that rare thing: a Hollywoodian literary adaptation that both stays faithful and does justice to its source".
"Confidential Agent" was based on Graham Green's novel and starred Charles Boyer and Lauren Bacall. Lionel played Mr Brigstock. His other 1945 films, "Crime Doctor's Warning" and "Weekend at the Waldorf" seem to have sunk without trace.

He died of a heart attack in America in 1946.

Geoffrey's Letters

Geoffrey Mander was an energetic letter writer and corresponded with a wide range of people. This is a list of everyone who's replies to him were included in the original manuscript of this book. In most cases we lack Geoffrey's half of the correspondence, making some of the letters difficult to understand. Many of them are not in themselves particularly interesting, even when they are from interesting people. For those reasons some letters have been omitted from this final version of the book. The writers of those letters are indicated by an asterisk.

A. Herbert Gray	Congregational Minister. Helped form what became the Marriage Guidance Council.
A. Maude Royden	Pacifist, suffragist and campaigner for the ordination of women.
Alfred Back	Great uncle of Rosalie Glynn Grylls/Mander.
Alfred Hewett	Of Morris and Company.
Algar Howard	Officer of arms at the College of Arms in London.
Antony Eden	Three time Conservative Foreign Secretary and then Prime Minister, 1955-57.
Archibald Sinclair	Leader of the Liberal Party and, during WW2, Secretary of State for Air.
Archibald Wavell*	Senior Officer in the British Army and then Viceroy of India, 1943-47.
Arthur Baldwin	Second son of Stanley Baldwin.
Arthur Goodhart	Master of University College and editor of 'The Quarterly Review'.
Arthur Henderson	Chairman of the World Disarmament Conference.
Arthur Henderson Jr.	Politician and third son of Labour M.P. Arthur Henderson.
Arthur Ponsonby*	Liberal M.P.
Austen Chamberlain*	Conservative politician and older half-brother of Prime Minister Neville Chamberlain.
Beatrice Webb*	With husband Sydney Webb, early member of the Fabian Society.
Bernard Law Montgomery	1st Viscount Montgomery of Alamein.
Chaim Weizmann	The Jewish Agency for Palestine.
Charles G. Stirling*	Husband of Wilhelmina Stirling.
Charles Robert Ashbee*	Architect and designer.
Charles Trevelyan*	Liberal and then Socialist M.P. until 1931.

Chas. J. Richardson	Society of British Printing Ink Makers.
Crawford Balcarres*	Chairman of the Fine Art Commission.
Daisy Mander*	Geoffrey's cousin.
David Low	Cartoonist.
Duff Cooper	Conservative Politician.
E.C. Welldon*	Headmaster of Harrow, 1885-1898. Dean of Durham, 1919-1933.
E.C. Thompson	Statistical Division of the House of Commons.
Edmund Blunden	Poet.
Edward Sydney Woods	Bishop of Lichfield, 1937-53.
Elizabeth Mander	Geoffrey's daughter from his first marriage.
Ernest Barnes*	Bishop of Birmingham, 1924-53.
Ernest Bevin*	Labour politician.
Frank Pakenham	Lord Longford. Labour politician.
Fyodor Gusev	Soviet Ambassador, 1943-46.
G. Hewitt	Of Morris and Company.
G.J. Townsend	Lord Great Chamberlain's Office.
General Sir F.A. Pile*	During WW2, General Officer Commanding Anti-Aircraft Command.
Geo. M. Gillett*	Parliamentary Secretary, Overseas Trade Department.
Geoffrey Shakespeare*	Parliamentary Secretary in the Ministry of Health.
George H. Barnes*	President. The New Commonwealth.
Gilbert Murray	Classical scholar and President of the League of Nations from 1916.
Haile Selassie	Emperor of Ethiopia.
Harold Ford Rossetti*	Grandson of Dante Gabriel Rossetti's brother, William Michael Rossetti.
Harold Macmillan*	Conservative politician. Prime Minister, 1957-63.
Harold Nicolson*	Parliamentary Secretary at the Ministry of Information.
Henry Gladstone*	Son of Prime Minister William Gladstone.
Herbert Morrison*	Labour politician and cabinet minister.
Herbert Samuel	Liberal politician. Party leader from 1931-35.
Hugh Dalton*	Labour M.P. and Chancellor of the Exchequer(1945).
Hugh Gaitskell	Leader of the Labour party, 1955-63.
Ivan Maisky	Soviet Ambassador, 1932-43.
J. Harry Wilkes*	Political supporter of Geoffrey Mander.
J.B. Priestley*	Playwright.

Jan Masaryk*	Czechoslovak Minister.
John Augustine Kempthorne*	Bishop of Lichfield, 1913-37.
John Buchan*	Writer.
John Miller Martin	Principal Private Secretary to the Prime Minister, Winston Churchill.
John W. Cooper*	Political supporter of Geoffrey Mander.
John Whelan Dulanty	High Commissioner for Ireland.
Joseph Hunter*	Liberal party election organiser in Bromley, 1930s.
Lionel Mander	Geoffrey's brother. Acted and directed in films as Miles Mander.
Lord Beaverbrook*	Newspaper publisher.
Lord Esmé Gordon-Lennox	Great Chamberlain's Office, House of Lords.
Lord Halifax*	Foreign Secretary under Neville Chamberlain and an architect of the policy of appeasing Adolf Hitler.
Lord Meston*	President of the Liberal Party, 1936-43.
Lord Robert Cecil	One of the architects of the League of Nations.
Lt. Gen. Sergěj Ingr	Czechoslovak Minister of Defence.
May Morris	Daughter of William Morris.
Megan Lloyd George	Liberal, then Labour politician. Daughter of David Lloyd George.
Miles Malleson*	Actor and screenwriter.
Neville Chamberlain*	Conservative politician. Prime Minister 1937-40.
Nikolaus Pevsner	Art Historian. Wrongly called Nicholas in text.
Oliver Lyttleton	Minister for War Production.
Peter Neville	Nephew of Geoffrey Mander.
Philip Noel Baker	Parliamentary Secretary to the Ministry of War Transport during the war.
Philip Sassoon*	Cousin of the poet Siegfried Sassoon and a Liberal M.P.
Phyllis Biscoe*	Secretary, Common Interests Committee.
R.A. Butler*	'Rab' Butler. Conservative politician.
R.W. Moore*	Headmaster of Harrow School and son of George Moore who worked for Mander Brothers.
Ralph Verney	Acting Secretary to the Speaker of the House of Commons, 1940s.
Richard S. Smith	Assistant Curator, Walthamstow Museum.
Richard Sheppard	Aka Dick Sheppard, the 'radio parson' in the 1920s and pacifist campaigner in the 30s.

Robert of Austria*	Unclear who this was. Letter received in 1930. Robert, Archduke of Austria-Este was only fifteen then, so unlikely to be him.
Rt. Hon. J. Moore-Brabazon*	English aviation pioneer and Conservative politician.
S. Eeley	Managing Director, Grand Hotel Eastbourne.
Sir Francis Acland*	Liberal MP, 1906-39.
Sir Kingsley Wood	Secretary of State for Air and then Chancellor of the Exchequer.
Stanley Baldwin	Three time Conservative Prime Minister.
Stephen Tallents*	Empire Marketing Board, then G.P.O., then Deputy Director General of the BBC under Lord Reith.
Sydney Cockerell	Director of the Fitzwilliam Museum, Cambridge. Was William Morris's private secretary in the 1890s.
T. Golling	Hatter, Hosier and Outfitter, Shrewsbury.
T.A. Ryder	Casselton Elliott & Co. Liquidator for Morris and Co.
T.G.B. Cocks	Clerk in the House of Commons.
Thomas Cook & Son*	Travel firm.
Vera Brittain*	Journalist and author. Her daughter was Shirley Williams.
Violet Bonham Carter*	President of Liberal Party, 1945-47. Daughter of PM Herbert Asquith. Grandmother of actress Helena Bonham Carter.
Viscount Cranborn	Conservative Politician. Secretary of State for Dominion Affairs, 1940-42.
Viscount Sankey*	Formerly Sir John Sankey, Lord Chancellor from 1929 to 1935.
W. Arthur Pascoe	Advised Geoffrey Mander on traditional Cornish names for his second child with Rosalie Mander.
W. Ormsby-Gore*	Secretary of State at the Colonial Office.
W. Arthur Peacock*	Secretary-Manager of the National Trade Union Club.
W.G. Worthington	Of Elkin Mathews Limited, Booksellers.
Walter Elliot*	Minister of Agriculture, 1932-36. Secretary of State for Scotland, 1936-38. Minister of Health, 1938-40.
Wilhelmina Stirling	Sister-in-law of William De Morgan.
William Graham	Labour politician. President, Board of Trade, 1929-31.
William Wedgwood Benn*	Labour Secretary of State for India until 1931. Father of Tony Benn.
Wladyslaw Raczkiewicz	President of the Polish government-in-exile.

Photo Credits

Images of the Mander family etc. on pages 6, 8, 13, 31, 48, 83, 144 and 165 are © The National Trust and are reproduced with permission.

About the Author

Patricia Pegg was born in Berkshire and lived in the Midlands from the age of four. Following art college she taught art and art history in a number of secondary schools. She then worked as a freelance lecturer for sixteen years, specialising in 19th century design. She was a National Trust guide at Wightwick Manor in Wolverhampton for twenty years, and was married with two sons. She died in 2012.

In 1996 she wrote 'A Very Private Heritage', based on the family papers of Theodore Mander, who built Wightwick Manor in Wolverhampton. In 2009 she completed this book, about Theodore's son, Geoffrey Mander, but it had not been published at the time of her death.

Acknowledgements

Thanks are due to The Sir Geoffrey Mander Will Trust for their support in publishing this book.

Thanks also to the staff and volunteers at Wightwick Manor and Gardens.

Index

D

E

flamethrower
    164, 165
Fletcher, Reginald
    112, 192
Ford, Maddox Ford
    100, 198, 199
France
    14, 30, 68, 78, 85, 86, 103, 116, 118, 127, 129, 133, 139, 142, 145, 146, 149, 150,
    152, 179–81, 183, 185, 207, 216, 218, 220, 252, 258
Franco, General
    88, 99, 133
Fuhrer
    64, 237

G

Gaitskell, Hugh
    254
Geneva
    14, 30, 32, 72, 73, 91
Germans
    66, 69, 74, 99, 102, 116–18, 125–27, 130–33, 137–43, 146, 149, 150, 152–54, 157,
    159, 174, 175, 179, 181, 185, 195, 196, 201, 202, 206, 211, 214, 216, 218–20, 230,
    237–39, 259
Germany
    28, 30, 64, 65, 67, 69, 73, 74, 87, 88, 99, 103, 109, 112, 117, 118, 123, 129, 130,
    132, 133, 137, 138, 140, 141, 143, 149, 153, 155, 172, 175, 176, 178, 181, 182,
    185, 211, 226, 230, 237, 238
Gestapo
    143
Gibralter
    209
Gill, Mrs A.M.
    136
Gilliat-Smith, Bernard J.
    89
Glynn Grylls, Rosalie (see: Mander, Rosalie (née Glynn Grylls))
Goebbels
    130
Goering
    103
Gordon-Lennox, Esme
    30, 201
governess
    143
Gray, A. Herbert
    45, 46

273

Lightning Source UK Ltd.
Milton Keynes UK
UKHW021832130621
385448UK00003B/27

9 781916 057036